anarchist pocketbooks

THE GREAT FRENCH REVOLUTION

1789-1793

Peter Kropotkin

Introduction by Alfredo M. Bonanno

Volume I

Elephant Editions

This pocketbook edition published in 1986 by
Elephant Editions, B.M. Elephant, London WC1N3XX

Translated from the French by
N. F. Dryhurst

Cover illustration and design by Clifford Harper

Printed in Catania by
Alfa Grafica Sgroi
Via S. Maria della Catena 87 — Catania (Italy)
September 1986

CONTENTS

Chapter   Page

VOLUME I

	Introduction	7
	Preface by Kropotkin	15
I	The Two Great Currents of the Revolution	21
II	The Idea	25
III	Action	31
IV	The People before the Revolution	36
V	The Spirit of Revolt: the Riots	39
VI	The Convocation of the States-General becomes Necessary	50
VII	The Rising of the Country Districts during the Opening Months of 1789	55
VIII	Riots in Paris and its Environs	66
IX	The States-General	70
X	Preparations for the Coup d'Etat	77
XI	Paris on the Eve of the Fourteenth	87
XII	The taking of the Bastille	98
XIII	The Consequences of July 14 at Versailles	108
XIV	The Popular Risings	114
XV	The Towns	118
XVI	The Peasant Rising	129
XVII	August 4 and its Consequences	138
XVIII	The Feudal Rights remain	149
XIX	Declaration of the Rights of Man	161
XX	The Fifth and Sixth of October 1789	166
XXI	Fears of the Middle Classes – The New Municipal Organisation	178
XXII	Financial Difficulties–Sale of Church Property	188
XXIII	The fete of the Federation	194
XXIV	The "Districts" and the "Sections" of Paris	200
XXV	The Sections of Paris under the New Municipal Law	209
XXVI	Delays in the Abolition of the Feudal Rights	215
XXVII	Feudal Legislation in 1790	225
XXVIII	Arrest of the Revolution in 1790	233
XXIX	The Flight of the King–Reaction–End of the Constituent Assembly	246
XXX	The Legislative Assembly–Reaction in 1791-1792	257
XXXI	The Counter-Revolution in the South of France	267
XXXII	The Twentieth of June 1792	275
XXXIII	The Tenth of August: Its Immediate Consequences	288

INTRODUCTION

Kropotkin's work on the French Revolution is without doubt one of the fundamental interpretations of events that were to transform the destiny of humanity. Its importance lies in two premises: the design of a revolutionary development that is different and more significant than that usually suggested by bourgeois historians, and the individuation of the first symptoms of the current of thought and action which, a century later, was to take the name of anarchism.

We are able to draw a series of observations of great relevance to our political work today from these two premises. It should not be forgotten that research on events of the past, and in particular on the French Revolution, is relevant in so far as it acts as a starting point from which to explore a number of revolutionary problems belonging to the present.

From the point of view of historical investigation some aspects of Kropotkin's work can be considered to be out of date. The documentation is often incomplete, partly because he was unable to gain access to the French archives and had to work on the British Museum collection. The most recent studies by Lefebvre, Mathiez, Soboul and others have examined the archives and repaired many of the oversights of the historians of the preceding generation. But this new generation, with the exception of Guérin and a few lesser known writers, have made their interpretation according to strict Marxist observance—when they do not go so far as a Stalinist view with its unrestrained exaltation of Jacobinism.

However, this is not the most important problem. We are not proposing a reading of Kropotkin's work for documentation on the French Revolution, but because certain phenomena which were to develop in successive years and which, in many ways, are still in the course of development, are recorded in it with great accuracy.

Throughout, the interpretation is tied to popular action in the course of the revolutionary events. This action is seen as something continuous, not as something that first saw the light with the beginning of the French Revolution. There had already been symptoms of what was later to become the great tempest, in the riots and unorganised revolts. In fact it is possible to go back in time indefinitely from these revolts: in this way the whole of the history of mankind becomes the history of the struggle and rebellion against authority.

Kropotkin lays great stress on the existence of both illuminist ideas and popular action. He tries to amalgamate these two components, considered predominant, with an analysis of the economic and social conditions at the beginning of the revolution. But, apart from the presence of certain ideas among the popular masses, what strikes us most today is the existence of a democratic organisation of the base, self-managed, that worked very well until it was killed by bourgeois power.

As happened again later during the Russian Revolution, lack of collective maturity concerning objectives gave a free hand to the more prepared and more conscious minorities, following its initial strongly popular imprint. Reactionary historians have tried to underestimate the value of this attempt at direct democracy, but without success (cf. A. Cochin, *La Revolution et la libre pensée*, Paris 1924). The same has been done, for other reasons, by the Marxist historians (cf. A. Soboul, *La Rivoluzione francese*).

The state of the economy and social relations at the time the French Revolution exploded was such that the bourgeoisie were easily able to take the upper hand. They responded immediately with great class solidity when confronted with the egalitarian solicitations of the people, oppressing them to guarantee their own class freedom. The regeneratory strength of the people emerges clearly in Kropotkin's work, as well as the importance of its message to future generations, for future revolutions. Danial Guérin, who has attempted to re-evaluate Kropotkin's interpretation, (*La lutte des classes sous la Première République*, 2 volumes, Paris 2nd ed. 1968), writes that the re-enforcing of central power in 1793 had the aim of confronting the counter-revolution in appearance only; in fact there was a conscious attempt to repress the direct democracy of the *sans-culottes* (cf. op. cit. vol 2 pages 3-7). And elsewhere, in a piece of work where he attempted to identify the origins of anarchy in the French Revolution (*Jeunesse du socialisme libertaire*, Paris 1959), he writes: "Is it not strikingly obvious, for example, that the December 4 decree on the re-enforcing of central power coincides with less, rather than increasing severity towards the counter-revolutionaries? Jaurès saw well that this decree was to a great extent war machinery against the 'Hébertistes', i.e. against the popular vanguard." (cf. op. cit. page 48).

The second premiss of Kropotkin's work is the presence of fermentation that can be defined as anarchist within the French Revolution. He gives much space to the groups referred to as "anarchists" by Brissot and combatted as such, but the discourse should be gone into in the field of the history of anarchism. Kropotkin makes reference to a pamphlet by Brissot which we were able to find in the national library of Paris, which begins: "Since the beginning of the Convention I have been denouncing the presence of a disorganisatory party in France whose intent is to dissolve the republic at the very moment of its birth. The existence of this party has been denied; the incredulous in good faith must now declare themselves convinced. I shall prove today: a) that this party of anarchists has dominated and dominates almost all the deliberations of the Convention and the operations of the executive Council; and b) that this party has been and still is the sole cause of all the evils, both internal and external, that are afflicting France." (J.P. Brissot, *A ses commettans, sur la situation de la Convention Nationale, sur l'influence des Anarchistes, et les maux qu'elles a causés, sur la né-cessite d'anéanter cette influence pour sauver la Republique*, Paris, May 23, 1793).

The concern was that the "anarchists" did not want to stop the re-volution with the constitution and the death of the king, they wanted to go forward with the people—and in opposition to the Jacobins—to true equality and freedom. Brissot starts off from the principle, so dear to the Stalinists of today, that with the people supreme after the killing of the king, they can no longer want revolution as they would be making revolution against themselves. So those who support the need for its continuation are counter-revolutionaries for the same reason as they were revolutionaries yesterday.

It was Varlet who was to be the most coherent revolutionary theoretician of the time, capable of seeing the danger that opened up in the face of popular conquests: that of being instrumentalised by a mili-tary legislative and bureaucratic minority. In a series of pamphlets written under the imminence of events he illustrates the anarchist prin-ciple of the self-managed and libertarian popular revolution. The most important is that published in 1794, after Thermidor. I found two ed-itions of the same pamphlet with different titles in the Paris Biblio-teque Nationale: the first is one of the 10th vendémiaire, the second of the 15th; the first carries the title *L'explosion*, the second *Gare l'explo-sion*, with the addition of a motto that does not appear in the first edi-tion: "Better that the revolutionary government perish than a prin-ciple". The two pamphlets are identical in content. They are an anar-chist classic in the true sense of the word. We cannot speak of it here in detail but it is enough to quote this brief extract: "What a social mon-strosity, what a work of art of machiavellianism, is this revolutionary government! For every reason, *government and revolution* are incom-patible, unless people do not want to build a durable basis of insurrect-ional power against themselves, which it would be absurd to believe." (cf. op. cit. page 8).

To re-discover a vein of anarchist thought in the French Revolution today, alongside Kropotkin's reflections clarifying the argument in his time, links the process of the development of anarchism to a much wider one: that of man's struggle against power, a struggle that goes all through history marking it on the side of the losers. To reflect on this problem means, in essence, to ask oneself: what is to be done, to-day, in the face of the responsibilities that await us? It was precisely in this sense that Kropotkin defined the French Revolution "the mother of us all", and arguments and debates are still going on about this to this day. This is where we must now focus our attention.

In 1957 P. Naville wrote, "The critique of the State can all be found in the French Revolution" (cf. *De l'alienation á la jouissance*, Paris 1957 page 91). In fact, all revolutionaries have studied this grandiose event in depth. First Proudhon, with detailed analyses (*Idée générale de la Révolution au XIXme siecle*, Paris 1851). Bakunin was to return to it time and time again (cf Kaminski, *Bakounine*, Paris 1938). Rocker has described the influence of the old Jacobins on Liebknecht (cf. Rocker, *Johann Most*, Berlin, 1924, page 53). The passages of Marx and Engels on the subject are too well known to need quoting. Let us not overlook the ever-forgotten Stirner who makes an interesting distinction between Third Estate and mass in the French Revolution.

This constant interest has sparked off a debate between authoritarians and anti-authoritarians, just as Jacobins and anti-Jacobins (Hébertistes, enragés, anarchists, etc) came face to face during the course of the Revolution itself. The disagreement is not merely theoretical, it is about the very essence of the revolutionary discourse.

The origins of the authoritarianism of Marxism and Leninism can thus be traced to the Jacobin tendency in the French Revolution. The interpretation of the Revolution as a mass event, but directed in a disciplined way by a minority of professional revolutionaries; organisation of the post-revolutionary State; the creation of new power structures; all that is typical of the authoritarians who exalt the Jacobins of 1793, not realising that the interests followed were exactly those of the bourgeoisie.

These good people often fall into a curious contradiction: on the one hand they praise the efficiency of the Jacobins' revolutionary centralisation, sometimes hinting at the bad sort that befell these supporters of the popular revolution (the first to end up on the guillotine); on the other hand they consider the Jacobins' action to have been a necessary evil, a centralisation brought about to "save" the revolution.

The Marxists, for example, recognise the fact that the Jacobins were bourgeois and that their ideal was exactly that of the bourgeoisie, but they—especially Lenin—cannot avoid praising their methods because they were useful to the immediate aims of the revolution.

Now, if the Jacobins were the bourgeois revolutionaries of 1793, their methods cannot be neatly separated from their ideals. Their ideal was to eliminate any attempt at emancipation by the masses and to conquer power through a restricted elite of technicians and bureaucrats. Their methods were those of "terror". If revolutionaries of today are struggling for a proletarian revolution they certainly cannot embrace the bourgeois ideal, on this they are all agreed. But, strangely, not all of them accept the refusal of the methods that accompanied the bourgeois ideal—precisely those of "terror".

Authoritarianism, under whatever form it presents itself, always remains a strictly bourgeois phenomenon. Once they develop in an authoritarian way with recourse to the terroristic methods of the old Jacobinism, even struggles in the name of the proletariat can do no other than rebuild a new dominant class, different to the old bourgeoisie in name, but identical in substance and intent. The lessons that reach us from the Russian Revolution cannot be forgotten.

In 1921 Rudolf Rocker wrote, "To refer to the French Revolution so as to justify the tactics of the Bolsheviks in Russia means to completely ignore historical facts...Historical experience shows us precisely the contrary. In all the decisive moments of the French Revolution the true initiative of action arose directly from the people. It is in this creative activity of the masses that the whole secret of the revolution resides today. What happened in France in March 1794 is being repeated today in Russia." (cf. R. Rocker, *Der Bankrott des russissichen Staatskommunismus*, Berlin, 1921, page 28-31).

For the first time in history, the classical process of revolutionary involution prepared and brought about by authoritarianism can be seen clearly. The other great example was to be the Russian Revolution.

The Jacobins themselves were divided within their own organisation on this problem: whether to see the revolutionary capacity as springing from the base or to see it as something issuing from above. The "plebians"among the Jacobins obviously supported the popular revolution mediated by a revolutionary vanguard, but they were the first to go on the guillotine; the bourgeoisie, having the management of the Jacobin movement in their hands, managed to impose their interpretation of a revolution dominated by a power elite, and end up next on the guillotine, killed in turn by the reactionary conservatives who saw clearly how that thesis had seen its day.

The revolution is always an event that emerges from a contrast: in the absence of contrast there would be no revolution, but the harmonious, idyllic development of a perfect society which would continually reconstitute itself, differently, but always remain the same in its own perfection.

The main contrast is the economic one, a contrast which in the period of maximum development of capitalism assumes such macroscopic characteristics that lead some analysts to declare it to be the only one worth considering because it is able to condition the whole of reality. In fact the revolution, although based on the economic contrast between exploited and exploiter, is too complex to be enclosed within a dogmatic formula. During its maturation it can be interpreted with the help of history and past experience, but only up to a point: its realisation brings with it so many modifications, so many new aspects, so many explosions of creativity, that those assigned to the work do not always manage to understand it in its full importance.

That is why the study of revolutions of the past, and in particular the French Revolution, is of great importance, even although it cannot be considered a methodological study aimed at finding the best revolutionary systems in order to use them as such. This is where Lenin was mistaken when he identified himself with the Jacobin methods of "terror". Every event has its own historical dimension, presents itself in its own peculiar way, in other words, is unrepeatable. And revolutions do not escape this rule.

For their part, Marx and Engels remained undecided between the one interpretation and the other concerning the meaning and value of the French Revolution. Their concept of "dictatorship of the proletariat" sometimes referred to the events of 1793, and at others was considered an adaptation, a modern analytical find to redirect the proletariat to the modernity of the class conflict. But the very presence of the word "dictatorship" clearly indicates the persistence of bourgeois and Jacobin traditions within the new Marxist interpretation. In fact, the concept of dictatorship is something estranged from the masses in their spontaneous movement of revendication and struggle, and from the creative advances of a new social organisation. Dictatorship by whom? And over what? Certainly not by the mass and not over themselves! That would not make sense. So Rocker says, "The idea of the "soviet" is a precise expression of what we mean by social revolution; it corresponds to the constructive part of socialism. The idea of dictatorship of the proletariat is of purely bourgeois origin, and has nothing to do with socialism. The two notions can be artificially brought together, but the result will always be a caricature of the original idea of the Soviets, and will always prejudice socialism". (*Freie Arbeiterstimme*, New York, 15 May 1920).

The idea of "dictatorship" implies the presence of a person (dictator) or a specific organisation (party), which can enforce it in the name of other persons (the mass). In fact, and particularly in the Leninist elaboration which is far more clear on this point, the dictatorship of the proletariat becomes a dictatorship not exercised by the proletariat—which would happen in the contradiction mentioned above—but a dictatorship by the party in the name of the proletariat.

One sees clearly here how the Jacobin and bourgeois idea of revolutionary organisation that must take power and manage it reappears. But power comes to be assumed, not over the old bosses, but also over the proletariat themselves and their spontaneous organisations of struggle, whenever the latter try to propose their autonomous and independent management. In this way the mass (the proletariat themselves) and the bosses, are considered counter-revolutionary alike and indiscriminately taken to the guillotine (rightly considered a toy compared to today's tanks); this is the way they intervene in Hungary, Czechoslovakia and Poland.

Dictatorship in the name of the proletariat can become a dictatorship over the proletariat at any moment whatsoever. This is how concentration and forced labour camps are opened. It is the way socialism is transformed into a tragic farce.

But the reading of Kropotkin's volume can illuminate us concerning the other possibility opened up by the same French Revolution, that of the construction of real socialism, starting from the base in a self-managed way. If the modern authoritarian Marxists are derived in direct line from the Jacobins, it is from their opponents that today's anti-authoritarians are descended. The *sans-culottes* discovered direct democracy spontaneously, having as a basis their clubs and area groups, something absolutely different to everything that had been theorised and reaslised before. The concept of spontaneity and creativity was born, even with all the limitations that made the easy victory of the authoritarian bourgeoisie possible.

This is why we say the Great Revolution was not only the cradle of bourgeois parliamentarian democracy, but was also the cradle of proletarian direct democracy, even though the times and the level of cohesion and consciousness of the workers were not mature enough for those seeds to be fully brought to fruition.

The authoritarians have always put forward the concept of "need" to justify the destruction of the libertarianism of the base during the revolution. Even the Stalinist scourge has been justified by the "need" for communism in one country. It is an alibi that does not hold. The arrival of the bourgeois technicians, and the new-style bureaucracy's taking over the key points of revolutionary dominion have always been considered the two main points of the success of the 1793 revolution. In fact this was done in order to kill the internal dynamism of the revolution, to deny any creative possibility to popular initiative and lay the foundation for the future centralised State.

The truth is that in all the decisive moments of the French Revolution it was always popular initiative that created the conditions necessary for victory, then, in the end, bourgeois oppression with its structures and techniques, with its "needs" and its bureaucracy, took over, killing any spontaneity and creativity and rebuilding the State.

Catania, April 21 1975

ALFREDO M. BONANNO

PREFACE

THE more one studies the French Revolution the clearer it is to see how incomplete is the history of that great epoch, how many gaps in it remain to be filled, how many points demand elucidation.

How could it be otherwise ? The Great Revolution, that set all Europe astir, that overthrew everything, and began the task of universal reconstruction in the course of a few years, was like the working of cosmic forces dissolving and re-creating a world. And if in the writings of the historians who deal with that period, and especially of Michelet, we admire the immense work they have accomplished in disentangling and co-ordinating the innumerable facts of the various parallel movements that made up the Revolution, we realise at the same time the vastness of the work which still remains to be done.

The investigations made during the past thirty years by the school of historical research represented by M. Aulard and the Société de la Révolution française, have certainly furnished most valuable material. They have shed a flood of light upon the acts of the Revolution, on its political aspects, and on the struggles for supremacy that took place between the various parties. But the study of the economic side of the Revolution is still before us, and this study, as M. Aulard rightly says, demands an entire lifetime. Yet without this study the history of the period remains incomplete and in many points wholly incomprehensible. In fact, a long series of totally new problems presents itself to the historian as soon as he turns his attention to the economic side of the revolutionary upheaval.

It was with the intention of throwing some light upon these economic problems that I began in 1886 to make separate studies of the earliest revolutionary stirrings among the peasants ; the peasant risings in 1789 ; the struggles for and against the feudal laws ; the real causes of the movement of May 31, and so on. Unfortunately I was not able to make any researches in the National Archives of France, and my studies have, therefore, been confined to the collections of printed matter in the British Museum, which are, however, in themselves exceedingly rich.

Believing that it would not be easy for the reader to appreciate the bearing of separate studies of this kind without a general view of the whole development of the Revolution understood in the light of these studies, I soon found it necessary to write a more or less consecutive account of the chief events of the Revolution. In this account I have not dwelt upon the dramatic side of the episodes of these disturbed years, which have been so often described, but I have made it my chief object to utilise modern research so as to reveal the intimate connection and interdependence of the various events which combined to produce the climax of the eighteenth century's epic.

This method of studying separately the various parts of the work accomplished by the Revolution has necessarily its own drawbacks : it sometimes entails repetition. I have preferred, however, to take the risk of reproach for this fault in the hope of impressing more clearly upon the reader's mind the mighty currents of thought and action that came into conflict during the French Revolution—currents so intimately blended with the very essence of human nature that they must inevitably reappear in the historic events of the future.

All who know the history of the Revolution will understand how difficult it is to avoid errors in facts when one tries to trace the development of its impassioned struggles. I shall, therefore, be extremely grateful to those who will be good enough to point out any mistakes I may have made. And I wish to express here my sincerest gratitude to my friends, James Guillaume and Ernest Nys, who have had the kindness to read my manuscript and to help me in this work with their knowledge and their criticisms.

PETER KROPOTKIN

THE GREAT FRENCH
REVOLUTION

CHAPTER I

THE TWO GREAT CURRENTS OF THE REVOLUTION

Main causes of Great Revolution—Previous risings—Union of middle classes and people necessary—Importance of part played by people

Two great currents prepared and made the Great French Revolution. One of them, the current of ideas, concerning the political reorganisation of States, came from the middle classes ; the other, the current of action, came from the people, both peasants and workers in towns, who wanted to obtain immediate and definite improvements in their economic condition. And when these two currents met and joined in the endeavour to realise an aim which for some time was common to both, when they had helped each other for a certain time, the result was the Revolution.

The eighteenth-century philosophers had long been sapping the foundations of the law-and-order societies of that period, wherein political power, as well as an immense share of the wealth, belonged to the aristocracy and the clergy, whilst the mass of the people were nothing but beasts of burden to the ruling classes. By proclaiming the sovereignty of reason ; by preaching trust in human nature—corrupted, they declared, by the institutions that had reduced man to servitude, but, nevertheless, certain to regain all its qualities when it had reconquered liberty—they had opened up new vistas to mankind. By proclaiming equality among men, without distinction of birth ; by demanding from every citizen, whether king or peasant, obedience to the law, supposed to express the will of the nation when it has been made by the representatives

of the people; finally, by demanding freedom of contract
between free men, and the abolition of feudal taxes and services—by putting forward all these claims, linked together
with the system and method characteristic of French thought,
the philosophers had undoubtedly prepared, at least in men's
minds, the downfall of the old *régime*.

This alone, however, would not have sufficed to cause the
outbreak of the Revolution. There was still the stage of passing from theory to action, from the conception of an ideal to
putting it into practice. And the most important point in the
study of the history of that period is to bring into relief the
circumstances that made it possible for the French nation at a
given moment to enter on the realisation of the ideal—to
attempt this passage from theory to action.

On the other hand, long before 1789, France had already
entered upon an insurrectionary period. The accession of
Louis XVI. to the throne in 1774 was the signal for a whole
series of hunger riots. These lasted up to 1783; and then
came a period of comparative quiet. But after 1786, and still
more after 1788, the peasant insurrections broke out again with
renewed vigour. Famine had been the chief source of the
earlier disturbances, and the lack of bread always remained one
of the principal causes of the risings. But it was chiefly
disinclination on the part of the peasants to pay the feudal
taxes which now spurred them to revolt. The outbreaks
went on increasing in number up to 1789, and in that year
they became general in the east, north-east and south-east of
France.

In this way the disaggregation of the body social came about.
A jacquerie is not, however, a revolution, even when it takes
such terrible forms as did the rising of the Russian peasants in
1773 under the banner of Pougatchoff. A revolution is
infinitely more than a series of insurrections in town and
country. It is more than a simple struggle between parties,
however sanguinary; more than mere street-fighting, and
much more than a mere change of government, such as was
made in France in 1830 and 1848. A revolution is a swift
overthrow, in a few years, of institutions which have taken

centuries to root in the soil, and seem so fixed and immovable that even the most ardent reformers hardly dare to attack them in their writings. It is the fall, the crumbling away in a brief period, of all that up to that time composed the essence of social, religious, political and economic life in a nation. It means the subversion of acquired ideas and of accepted notions concerning each of the complex institutions and relations of the human herd.

In short, it is the birth of completely new ideas concerning the manifold links in citizenship—conceptions which soon become realities, and then begin to spread among the neighbouring nations, convulsing the world and giving to the succeeding age its watchword, its problems, its science, its lines of economic, political and moral development.

To arrive at a result of this importance, and for a movement to assume the proportions of a revolution, as happened in England between 1648 and 1688, and in France between 1789 and 1793, it is not enough that a movement of ideas, no matter how profound it may be, should manifest itself among the educated classes ; it is not enough that disturbances, however many or great, should take place in the very heart of the people. The revolutionary action coming from the people must coincide with a movement of revolutionary thought coming from the educated classes. There must be a union of the two.

That is why the French Revolution, like the English Revolution of the preceding century, happened at the moment when the middle classes, having drunk deep at the sources of current philosophy, became conscious of their rights, and conceived a new scheme of political organisation. Strong in their knowledge and eager for the task, they felt themselves quite capable of seizing the government by snatching it from a palace aristocracy which, by its incapacity, frivolity and debauchery, was bringing the kingdom to utter ruin. But the middle and educated classes could not have done anything alone, if, consequent on a complete chain of circumstances, the mass of the peasants had not also been stirred, and, by a series of constant insurrections lasting for four years, given to the dissatisfied among the middle classes the possibility of combating both King and Court, of upsetting old institutions and changing the political constitution of the kingdom.

The history of this double movement remains still to be written.   The history of the great French Revolution has been told and re-told many times, from the point of view of as many different parties; but up to the present the historians have confined themselves to the political history, the history of the triumph of the middle classes over the Court party and the defenders of the institutions of the old monarchy.

Thus we know very well the principles which dominated the Revolution and were translated into its legislative work.   We have been enraptured by the great thoughts it flung to the world, thoughts which civilised countries tried to put into practice during the nineteenth century.   The Parliamentary history of the Revolution, its wars, its policy and its diplomacy, has been studied and set forth in all its details.   But the *popular* history of the Revolution remains still to be told.   The part played by the *people* of the country places and towns in the Revolution has never been studied and narrated in its entirety. Of the two currents which made the Revolution, the current of *thought* is known; but the other, the current of *popular action*, has not even been sketched.

It is for us, the descendants of those called by their contemporaries the " anarchists," to study the popular current, and to try to reconstruct at least its main features.

CHAPTER II

THE IDEA

Modern States—Influence of English and American Revolutions on French Revolution—Condition and aims of middle classes—Centralisation of authority—Attitude towards peasants—Influence of eighteenth-century philosophy

To understand fully the idea which inspired the middle classes in 1789 we must consider it in the light of its results—the modern States.

The structure of the law-and-order States which we see in Europe at present was only outlined at the end of the eighteenth century. The system of the centralised authority, now in full working order, had not then attained either the perfection or uniformity it possesses to-day. That formidable mechanism, by which an order sent from a certain capital puts in motion all the men of a nation, ready for war, and sends them out to carry devastation through countries, and mourning into families; those territories, overspread with a network of officials whose personality is completely effaced by their bureaucratic apprenticeship, and who obey mechanically the orders emanating from a central will; that passive obedience of citizens to the law; that worship of law, of Parliament, of judges and their assistants, which we see about us to-day; that mass of hierarchically organised and·disciplined functionaries; that system of schools, maintained or directed by the State, where worship of power and passive obedience are taught; that industrial system, which crushes under its wheels the worker whom the State delivers over to its tender mercies; that commerce, which accumulates incredible riches in the hands of those who monopolise the land, the mines, the ways of communication and the riches of *Nature*, upon which

the State is nourished ; and finally, that science, which libe-
rates thought and immensely increases the productive powers
of men, but which at the same time aims at subjecting them
to the authority of the strongest and to the State—all this
was non-existent before the Revolution.

However, long before the Revolution had by its mutterings
given warning of its approach, the French middle classes—the
Third Estate—had already developed a conception of the
political edifice which should be erected on the ruins of feudal
royalty.   It is highly probable that the English Revolution had
helped the French middle class towards a comprehension of the
part they would be called on to play in the government of
society.   And it is certain that the revolution in America
stimulated the energies of the middle-class revolutionaries.
Thanks to Hobbes, Hume, Montesquieu, Rousseau, Voltaire,
Mably, d'Argenson and others, ever since the beginning of the
eighteenth century the study of Politics and the constitution
of organised societies based on elective representation had
become popular, and to this Turgot and Adam Smith had just
added the study of economic questions and the place of property
in the political constitution of a State.

That is why, long before the Revolution broke out, the idea
of a State, centralised and well-ordered, governed by the classes
holding property in lands or in factories, or by members of the
learned professions, was already forecast and described in a
great number of books and pamphlets from which the men of
action during the Revolution afterwards drew their inspiration
and their logical force.

Thus it came to pass that the French middle classes in 1789,
at the moment of entering upon the revolutionary period, knew
quite well what they wanted.   They were certainly not republicans—are they republicans even to-day ?   But they no
longer wanted the King to have arbitrary powers, they refused
to be ruled by the princes or by the Court, and they did not
recognise the right of the nobility to seize on all the best places
in the Government, though they were only capable of plunder-
ing the State as they had plundered their vast properties without adding anything to their value.   The middle classes were

perhaps republican in sentiment, and desired republican simplicity of manners, as in the growing republic of America ; but they desired, above all things, government by the propertied classes.

They inclined to free thought without being Atheists, but they by no means disliked the Catholic form of religion. What they detested most was the Church, with its hierarchy and its bishops, who made common cause with the princes, and its priests who had become the obedient tools of the nobility.

The middle classes of 1789 understood that the moment had arrived in France, as it had arrived one hundred and forty years before in England, when the Third Estate was to seize the power falling from the hands of royalty, and they knew what they meant to do with it.

Their ideal was to give France a constitution modelled upon the English constitution, and to reduce the King to the part of a mere enregistering scribe, with sometimes the power of a casting-vote, but chiefly to act as the symbol of national unity. As to the real authority, that was to be vested in a Parliament, in which an educated middle class, which would represent the active and thinking part of the nation, should predominate.

At the same time, their ideal was to abolish all the local powers which at that time constituted so many autonomous units in the State. They meant to concentrate all governmental power in the hands of a central executive authority, strictly controlled by the Parliament, but also strictly obeyed in the State, and combining every department—taxes, law courts, police, army, schools, civic control, general direction of commerce and industry—everything. By the side of this political concentration, they intended to proclaim complete freedom in commercial transactions, and at the same time to give free rein to industrial enterprise for the exploitation of all sorts of natural wealth, as well as of the workers, who henceforth would be delivered up defenceless to any one who might employ them.

All this was to be kept under the strict control of the State, which would favour the enrichment of the individual and the accumulation of large fortunes—two conditions to which great importance was necessarily attached by the middle classes, seeing that the States General itself had been convoked to ward off the financial ruin of the State.

On economic matters, the men of action belonging to the Third Estate held ideas no less precise. The French middle classes had studied Turgot and Adam Smith, the creators of political economy. They knew that the theories of those writers had already been applied in England, and they envied their middle-class neighbours across the Channel their powerful economic organisation, just as they envied them their political power. They dreamed of an appropriation of the land by the middle classes, both upper and lower, and of the revenue they would draw from the soil, which had hitherto lain unproductive in the hands of the nobility and the clergy. In this they were supported by the lower middle class settled in the country, who had become a power in the villages, even before the Revolution increased their number. They foresaw the rapid development of trade and the production of merchandise on a large scale by the help of machinery ; they looked forward to a foreign trade with distant lands, and the exportation of manufactured goods across the seas to markets that would be opened in the East, to huge enterprises and colossal fortunes.

But before all this could be realised they knew the ties that bound the peasant to his village must be broken. It was necessary that he should be free to leave his hut, and even that he should be forced to leave it, so that he might be impelled towards the towns in search of work. Then, in changing masters, he would bring gold to trade, instead of paying to the landlords all sorts of rents, tithes and taxes, which certainly pressed very heavily upon him, but which after all were not very profitable for the masters. And finally, the finances of the State had to be put in order ; taxation would be simplified, and, at the same time, a bigger revenue obtained.

In short, what they wanted was what economists have called freedom of industry and commerce, but which really meant the relieving of industry from the harassing and repressive supervision of the State, and the giving to it full liberty to exploit the worker, who was still to be deprived of his freedom. There

were to be no guilds, no trade societies; neither trade wardens
nor master craftsmen; nothing which might in any way check
the exploitation of the wage-earner. There was no longer to
be any State supervision which might hamper the manufacturer. There were to be no duties on home industries, no
prohibitive laws. For all the transactions of the employers,
there was to be complete freedom, and for the workers a strict
prohibition against combinations of any sort. *Laisser faire* for
the one; complete denial of the right to combine for the others.

Such was the two-fold scheme devised by the middle classes.
Therefore when the time came for its realisation, the middle
classes, strengthened by their knowledge, the clearness of their
views and their business habits, without hesitating over their
scheme as a whole or at any detail of it, set to work to make
it become law. And this they did with a consistent and intelligent energy quite impossible to the masses of the people,
because by them no ideal had been planned and elaborated
which could have been opposed to the scheme of the gentlemen
of the Third Estate.

It would certainly be unjust to say that the middle classes
were actuated only by purely selfish motives. If that had been
the case they would never have succeeded in their task. In
great changes a certain amount of idealism is always necessary
to success.

The best representatives of the Third Estate had, indeed,
drunk from that sublime fount, the eighteenth-century philosophy, which was the source of all the great ideas that have
arisen since. The eminently scientific spirit of this philosophy;
its profoundly moral character, moral even when it mocked at
conventional morality; its trust in the intelligence, strength and
greatness of the free man when he lives among his equals; its
hatred of despotic institutions—were all accepted by the revolutionists of that time. Whence would they have drawn otherwise the powers of conviction and the devotion of which they
gave such proofs in the struggle? It must also be owned that
even among those who worked hardest to realise the programme
of enriching the middle classes, there were some who seriously
believed that the enrichment of the individual would be the

best means of enriching the nation as a whole. Had not the best economists, with Adam Smith at their head, persuasively preached this view ?

But however lofty were the abstract ideas of liberty, equality and free progress that inspired the sincere men among the middle classes of 1789–1793, it is by their practical programme, by the application of their theories, that we must judge them. Into what deeds shall the abstract idea be translated in actual life ?   By that alone can we find its true measure.

If, then, it is only fair to admit that the middle classes of 1789 were inspired by ideas of liberty, equality (before the law), and political and religious freedom, we must also admit that these ideas, as soon as they took shape, began to develop exactly on the two lines we have just sketched ; liberty to utilise the riches of Nature for personal aggrandicement, as well as liberty to exploit human labour without any safeguard for the victims of such exploitation, and political power organised so as to assure freedom of exploitation to the middle classes. And we shall see presently what terrible struggles were evolved in 1793 when one of the revolutionary parties wished to go further than this programme.

CHAPTER III

ACTION

The people—Revolution and Socialism—Equal rights of all to land—" Communism "—Situation not clearly understood by people—Hatred of poor towards aristocracy and clergy—Hatred of feudalism—People's readiness to take up arms

But what of the people ?   What was their idea ?

The people, too, had felt to a certain extent the influence of the current philosophy. By a thousand indirect channels the great principles of liberty and enfranchisement had filtered down to the villages and the suburbs of the large towns. Respect for royalty and aristocracy was passing away. Ideas of equality were penetrating to the very lowest ranks. Gleams of revolt flashed through many minds. The hope of an approaching change throbbed in the hearts of the humblest. " Something was to be done by some great folk for such poor ones " ; she did not know who, nor how ; " but God send us better," said an old woman, in 1789, to Arthur Young,* who travelled through France on the eve of the Revolution. That " something " was bound to bring an alleviation of the people's misery.

The question whether the movement which preceded the Revolution, and the Revolution itself, contained any element of Socialism has been recently discussed. The word " Socialism " was certainly not in either, because it dates only from the middle of the nineteenth century. The idea of the State as Capitalist, to which the Social-Democratic fraction of the great Socialist party is now trying to reduce Socialism, was certainly not so much in evidence as it is to-day, because the founders of Social-Democratic " Collectivism," Vidal and Pecqueur, did not

* Arthur Young, *Travels in France*, p. 167 (London, 1892).

write until the period between 1840 and 1849. But it is impossible to read the works of the pre-Revolutionary writers without being struck by the fact that they are imbued with ideas which are the very essence of modern Socialism.

Two fundamental ideas—the equal rights of all citizens to the land, and what we know to-day under the name of communism—found devoted adherents among the more popular writers of that time, Mably, d'Argenson, and others of less importance. Manufacturing production on a large scale was in its infancy, so that land was at that time the main form of capital and the chief instrument for exploiting human labour, while the factory was hardly developed at all. It was natural, therefore, that the thoughts of the philosophers, and later on the thoughts of the revolutionists, should turn towards *communal possession of the land*. Did not Mably, who much more than Rousseau inspired the men of the Revolution, declare about 1768, in his *Doutes sur l'ordre naturel et essentiel des sociétés*, that there should be equal rights to the land for all, and communist possession of it ? The rights of the nation to all landed property, and to all natural wealth—forests, rivers, waterfalls, &c.—was not this the dominant idea of the pre-Revolutionary writers, as well as of the left wing of the revolutionary masses during the period of upheaval ?

Unfortunately, these communistic aspirations were not formulated clearly and concretely in the minds of those who desired the people's happiness. While among the educated middle classes the ideas of emancipation had taken the form of a complete programme for political and economic organisation, these ideas were presented to the people only in the form of vague aspirations. Often they were mere negations. Those who addressed the people did not try to embody the concrete form in which their *desiderata* could be realised. It is even probable that they avoided being precise. Consciously or not, they seemed to say : " What good is there in speaking to the people of the way in which they will be organised later on ? It would only chill their revolutionary ardour. All they want is the strength to attack and to march to the assault of the old institutions. Later on we shall see what can be done for them."

Are there not many Socialists and Anarchists who act still in the same way ? In their hurry to push on to the day of revolt they treat as soporific theorising every attempt to throw some light on what ought to be the aim of the Revolution.

It must be said, also, that the ignorance of the writers—city men and bookmen for the most part—counted for much in this. Thus, in the whole of that gathering of learned or experienced business men who composed the National Assembly—lawyers, journalists, tradesmen, and so forth—there were only two or three legal members who had studied the feudal laws, and we know there were among them but very few representatives of the peasants who were familiar by personal experience with the needs of village life.

For these reasons the ideas of the masses were expressed chiefly by simple negations. " Let us burn the registers in which the feudal dues are recorded ! Down with the tithes ! Down with ' Madame Veto ' ! Hang the aristocrats ! " But to whom was the freed land to go ? Who were to be the heirs of the guillotined nobles ? Who was to grasp the political power when it should fall from the hands of " Monsieur Veto," the power which became in the hands of the middle classes a much more formidable weapon than it had been under the old *régime ?*

This want of clearness in the mind of the people as to what they should hope from the Revolution left its imprint on the whole movement. While the middle classes were marching with firm and decided steps towards the establishment of their political power in a State which they were trying to mould, according to their preconceived ideas, the people were hesitating. In the towns, especially, they did not seem to know how to turn to their own advantage the power they had conquered. And later, when ideas concerning agrarian laws and the equalising of incomes began to take definite form, they ran foul of a mass of property prejudices, with which even those sincerely devoted to the cause of the people were imbued.

A similar conflict was evoked by the conceptions of the political organisation of the State. We see it chiefly in the antagonism which arose between the governmental prejudices of the democrats of that time and the ideas that dawned in the hearts of the people as to political decentralisation, and the prominent place which the people wished their municipalities to take both in the division of the large towns and in the village assemblies. This was the starting-point of the whole series of fierce contests which broke out in the Convention. Thence, too, arose the indefiniteness of the results obtained by the Revolution for the great mass of the people in all directions, except in the recovery of part of the land from the lords, lay and clerical, and the freeing of all land from the feudal taxes it formerly had to pay.

But if the people's ideas were confused on constructive lines, they were, on the other hand, extremely clear on certain points in their negations.

First of all, the hatred felt by the poor for the whole of the idle, lazy, perverted aristocracy who ruled them, while black misery reigned in the villages and in the dark lanes of the great towns. Next, hatred towards the clergy, who by sympathy belonged more to the aristocracy than to the people who fed them. Then, hatred of all the institutions under the old *régime*, which made poverty still harder to bear because they denied the rights of humanity to the poor. Hatred for the feudal system and its exactions, which kept the labourer in a state of servitude to the landowners long after personal serfdom had ceased to exist. Lastly, the despair of the peasant who in those years of scarcity saw land lying uncultivated in the hands of the lord, or serving merely as a pleasure-ground for the nobility while famine pressed hard on the villages.

It was all this hatred, coming to a head after long years as the selfishness of the rich became more and more apparent in the course of the eighteenth century. And it was this *need of land* —this *land hunger*, the cry of the starving in revolt against the lord who refused them access to it—that awoke the spirit of revolt ever since 1788. And it was the same hatred, and the same need, mingled with the hope of success, which stimulated the incessant revolts of the peasants in the years 1789–1793, revolts which enabled the middle classes to overthrow the old *régime* and to organise its own power under the new one, that of representative government.

Without those risings, without that disorganisation of authority in the provinces which resulted in never-ceasing *jacqueries*, without that promptitude of the people of Paris and other towns in taking up arms, and in marching against the strongholds of royalty whenever an appeal to the people was made by the revolutionaries, the middle classes would certainly not have accomplished anything. But it is to this true fount and origin of the Revolution—the people's readiness to take up arms— that the historians of the Revolution have not yet done justice —the justice owed to it by the history of civilisation.

CHAPTER IV

THE PEOPLE BEFORE THE REVOLUTION

Condition of people previous to 1789—Wanton luxury of
aristocrats—Poverty of majority of peasants—Rise and
importance of well-to-do peasant class

It would be waste of time to describe here at any length the
condition of the peasants in the country and of the poorer
classes in the towns on the eve of 1789.

All the historians who have written about the great French
Revolution have devoted eloquent pages to this subject. The
people groaned under the burden of taxes levied by the State,
rents and contributions paid to the lord, tithes collected by
the clergy, as well as under the forced labour exacted by all
three. Entire populations were reduced to beggary and wan-
dered on the roads to the number of five, ten or twenty
thousand men, women and children in every province; in
1777, one million one hundred thousand persons were officially
declared to be beggars. In the villages famine had become
chronic; its intervals were short, and it decimated entire
provinces. Peasants were flocking in hundreds and thousands
from their own neighbourhood, in the hope, soon undeceived,
of finding better conditions elsewhere. At the same time, the
number of the poor in the towns increased every year, and
it was quite usual for food to run short. As the municipalities
could not replenish the markets, bread riots, always followed
by massacres, became a persistent feature in the everyday life
of the kingdom.

On the other hand might be seen the superfine aristocrat
of the eighteenth century squandering immense fortunes—
hundreds of thousands and millions of francs a year—in unbridled and absurd luxury. To-day a Taine can go into

raptures over the life they led because he knows it only from a distance, a hundred years away, and through books ; but, in reality, they hid under their dancing-master manners roisterous dissipations and the crudest sensuality ; they were without interest, without thought, without even the simplest human feeling. Consequently, boredom was always tapping at the doors of the rich, boredom at the Court of Versailles, boredom in their châteaux ; and they tried in vain to evade it by the most futile and the most childish means. We also know what they were worth, these aristocrats, when the Revolution broke out ; how they left " their " King, and " their " Queen to defend themselves, and hastened to emigrate, calling for a foreign invasion to protect their estates and privileges against the revolted people. Their worth and their " nobility " of character can be estimated by the colonies of *émigrés*, which they established at Coblentz, Brussels and Miíau.

Those extremes of luxury and misery with which life abounded in the eighteenth century have been admirably depicted by every historian of the Great Revolution. But one feature remains to be added, the importance of which stands out especially when we study the condition of the peasants at this moment in Russia on the eve of the great Russian Revolution.

The misery of the great mass of French peasants was undoubtedly frightful. It had increased by leaps and bounds, ever since the reign of Louis XIV., as the expenditure of the State increased and the luxury of the great lords became more exquisite in the extravagancies revealed for us in certain memoirs of that time. What helped to make the exactions of the nobility unendurable was that a great number of them, when ruined, hiding their poverty under a show of luxury, resorted in desperation to the extortion of even the least of those rents and payments in kind, which only custom had established. They treated the peasants, through the intermediary of their stewards, with the rigour of mere brokers. Impoverishment turned the nobility, in their relations with their ex-serfs, into middle-class money-grubbers, incapable, however, of finding any other source of revenue than the exploitation of ancient privileges, relics of the feudal age.

This is why we find in certain documents, during the fifteen years of Louis XVI.'s reign which preceded the Revolution, indisputable traces of a recrudescence of seigneurial exactions.

But though the historians are right in depicting the condition of the peasants in very dark colours, it would be a mistake to impeach the veracity of those who, like Tocqueville, mention *some amelioration* in the conditions of the country during those very years preceding the Revolution. The fact is, that a double phenomenon became apparent in the villages at that time : the impoverishment of the great mass of the peasants and the bettering of the condition of a few among them. This may be seen to-day in Russia since the abolition of serfdom.

The great mass of the peasants grew poorer. Year after year their livelihood became more and more precarious : the least drought resulted in scarcity and famine. But a new class of peasant, a little better off and with ambitions, was forming at the same time, especially in districts where aristocratic estates were disintegrating rapidly. The village middle classes, the well-to-do peasants, came into being, and as the Revolution drew near these furnished the first speakers against feudal rights, and demanded their abolition. It was this class which, during the four or five years the Revolution lasted, most firmly insisted that these feudal rights should be abolished without compensation, and that the estates of the royalist nobles should be confiscated and sold in small parcels. It was this class, too, which was most bitter, in 1793, against *les ci-devants*, the dispossessed nobles, the ex-landlords.

For the time being, at the approach of the Revolution, it was through the peasant who had become of some importance in his village that hope filled men's hearts and inspired the spirit of revolt.

Traces of this awakening are evident, for since the accession of Louis XVI., in 1774, revolts were continually on the increase. It may be said, therefore, that if despair and misery impelled the people to riot, it was the hope of obtaining some relief that incited them to revolt.

Like every other revolution, that of 1789 was inspired by the hope of attaining certain important results.

CHAPTER V

THE SPIRIT OF REVOLT: THE RIOTS

Reforms at beginning of reign of Louis XVI.—Turgot—
Question of National Representation—Character of Louis
XVI.—Revolution in America—Riots on accession of Louis
—Their consequences—Large towns revolt in turn—" Par-
liaments " and " Plenary Courts "—Paris parliament refuses
to grant money to Court—Action of King—Insurrections in
Brittany—Grenoble—Queen's letter to Count de Mercy—
Gradual awakening of revolutionary spirit—Louis compelled
to convoke Assembly of Notables and States-General

As is usual in every new reign, that of Louis XVI. began with
some reforms. Two months after his accession Louis XVI.
summoned Turgot to the ministry, and a month later he
appointed him Controller-General of Finance. He even
supported him at first against the violent opposition that
Turgot, as an economist, a parsimonious middle-class man
and an enemy of the effete aristocracy, was bound to meet
with from the Court party.

Free trade in corn was proclaimed in September 1774,*
and statute labour was abolished in 1776, as well as the old
corporations and guilds in the towns, which were no longer of
any use except to keep up a kind of industrial aristocracy, and
by these measures hopes of reform were awakened among the
people. The poor rejoiced to see the breaking down of the
toll-gates, which had been put up all over France, and prevented the free circulation of corn, salt and other objects of
prime necessity. For them it meant the first breach in the
odious privileges of the landowners ; while the peasants who

* Before that the farmer could not sell his corn for three months
after the harvest, the lord of the manor alone being entitled to do that.
It was one of the feudal privileges, which enabled the lord to sell it at
a high price.

were better off rejoiced to see the joint liability of the tax-payers abolished.* Finally, in the August of 1779, mortmain and personal servitude were suppressed upon the King's private estates, and the following year it was decided to abolish torture, which was used in the most atrocious forms established by the Ordinance of 1670.† "Representative Government," such as was established by the English after their revolution, and was advocated in the writings of the contemporary philosophers, also began to be spoken of. With this end in view, Turgot had even prepared a scheme of provincial assemblies, to be followed later on by representative government for all France in which the propertied classes would have been called upon to constitute a parliament. Louis XVI. shrank from this proposal, and dismissed Turgot; but from that moment all educated France began to talk of a Constitution and national representation.‡ However, it was no longer possible to elude the question of national representation, and when Necker became minister in July 1777, it came up again for discussion. Necker, who understood very well the wishes of his master, and tried to bring his autocratic ideas

---

* This has been abolished in Russia also.

† Statute of August 24, 1780. Breaking on the wheel existed still in 1785. The parliaments, in spite of the Voltaireanism of the period, and the general refinement in the conception of life, enthusiastically defended the use of torture, which was abolished definitely only by the National Assembly. It is interesting to find (E. Seligman, *La justice en France pendant la Révolution*, p. 97) that Brissot, Marat and Robespierre by their writings contributed to the agitation for the reform of the penal code.

‡ The arguments upon which Louis XVI. took his stand are of the highest interest. I sum them up here according to E. Samichon's *Les réformes sous Louis XVI.: assemblées provinciales et parlements*. The King found Turgot's schemes dangerous, and wrote: "Though coming from a man who has good ideas, his constitution would overthrow the existing State." And again, further on: "The system of a rent-paying electorate would tend to make malcontents of the non-propertied classes, and if these were allowed to assemble they would form a hot-bed of disorder. . . . The transition from the abolished system to the system M. Turgot now proposes ought to be considered: we see well enough what is, but only in our thoughts do we see what does not yet exist, *and we must not make dangerous experiments if we do not see where they will end*." *Vide* also, in Samichon's Appendix A, the very interesting list of the chief laws under Louis XVI. between 1774 and 1789.

into some accord with the requirements of finance, attempted to manœuvre by proposing the introduction of provincial assemblies only and relegating the possibility of a national representation to the distant future. But he, too, was met by a formal refusal on the part of the King. " Would it not be a happy contingency," wrote the crafty financier, " that your Majesty, having become an intermediary between your estates and your people, your authority should only appear to mark the limits between severity and justice ? " To which Louis replied : " *It is of the essence of my authority not to be an intermediary, but to be at the head.*" It is well to remember these words in view of the sentimentalities concerning Louis XVI. which have been propagated by historians belonging to the party of reaction. Far from being the careless, inoffensive, good-natured person, interested only in hunting, that they wished to represent him, Louis XVI. for fifteen years, until 1789, managed to resist the necessity, felt and declared, for new political forms to take the place of royal despotism and the abominations of the old *régime*.

The weapon used by Louis XVI., in preference to all others was deceit. Only fear made him yield, and, using always the same weapons, deceit and hypocrisy, he resisted not only up to 1789, but even up to the last moment, to the very foot of the scaffold. At any rate, in 1778, at a time when it was already evident to all minds of more or less perspicacity, as it was to Turgot and Necker, that the absolute power of the King had had its day, and that the hour had come for replacing it by some kind of national representation, Louis XVI. could never be brought to make any but the feeblest concessions. He convened the provincial assemblies of the provinces of Berri and Haute-Guienne (1778 and 1779). But in face of the opposition shown by the privileged classes, the plan of extending these assemblies to the other provinces was abandoned, and Necker was dismissed in 1781.

The revolution in America had, meanwhile, helped also to awaken minds, and to inspire them with a breath of liberty and republican democracy. On July 4, 1776, the English colonies in North America had proclaimed their independence, and the new United States were recognised by France in 1778, which led to a war with England that lasted until 1783. All historians mention the effect which this war had on men's minds. There is, in fact, no doubt that the revolt of the English colonies and the constitution of the United States exercised a far-reaching influence in France, and helped powerfully in arousing the revolutionary spirit. We know, too, that the Declaration of Rights, drawn up by the young American States influenced the French Revolutionists profoundly, and was taken by them as a model for their declaration. It might be said also that the war in America, during which France had to build an entire fleet to oppose England's, completed the financial ruin of the old *régime* and hastened its downfall. But it is nevertheless certain that this war was also the beginning of those terrible wars which England soon waged against France, and the coalitions which she organised against the Republic. As soon as England recovered from her defeats and felt that France was weakened by internal struggles, she used every means, open and secret, to bring about the wars which we shall see waged relentlessly from 1793 till 1815.

All these causes of the Great Revolution must be clearly indicated, for like every event of primordial importance, it was the result of many causes, converging at a given moment, and creating the men who in their turn contributed to strengthen the effect of those causes. But it must be understood that in spite of the events which prepared the Revolution, and in spite of all the intelligence and ambitions of the middle classes, those ever-prudent people would have gone on a long time waiting for a change if the people had not hastened matters. The popular revolts, growing and increasing in number and assuming proportions quite unforeseen, were the new elements which gave the middle class the power of attack they themselves did not possess.

The people had patiently endured misery and oppression under Louis XV., but as soon as that King died, in 1774, they began to revolt, knowing well that, with a change of masters at the palace, there comes an inevitable slackening of authority. A continuous series of riots broke out between 1775 and 1777.

These were the riots of hunger that had been repressed until then only by force. The harvest of 1774 had been bad, and bread was scarce. Accordingly rioting broke out in April 1775. At Dijon the people took possession of the houses of the monopolists, destroyed their furniture and smashed up their flour-mills. It was on this occasion that the governor of the town—one of the superfine gentlemen of whom Taine has written with so much complacence—said to the people those fatal words which were to be so often repeated during the Revolution : " The grass has sprouted, go to the fields and browse on it." Auxerre, Amiens, Lille, followed Dijon. A few days later the " robbers," for so the majority of historians designate the famished rioters, having assembled at Pontoise, Passy and Saint-Germain with the intention of pillaging the granaries, turned their steps towards Versailles. Louis XVI. wanted to go out on the balcony of the palace to speak to them, to tell them that he would reduce the price of bread ; but Turgot, like a true economist, opposed this. The reduction in the price of bread was not made. The " robbers," in the meantime, entered Paris and plundered the bakeries, distributing whatever food they could seize among the crowd ; but they were dispersed by the troops, and two of the rioters were hanged at the Place de la Grève, and as they were being hanged they cried out that they were dying for the people. Since that time the legend began to circulate in France about " robbers " overrunning the country—a legend which had such an important effect in 1789, as it furnished the middle classes in the towns with a pretext for arming themselves. And from that time also began the placards insulting the King and his ministers which were pasted up at Versailles, containing threats to execute the King the day after his coronation, and even to exterminate the whole of the royal family if bread remained at the same price. Forged governmental edicts, too, began to be circulated through the country. One of them asserted that the State Council had reduced the price of wheat to twelve livres (francs) the measure.

These riots were of course suppressed, but they had far-reaching consequences. Strife was let loose among the various parties. It rained pamphlets. Some of these accused the minister, while others spoke of a plot of the princes against the King, or made fun of the royal authority. In short, with men's minds already in a state of ferment, the popular outbreaks were the sparks which ignited the powder. Concessions to the people, never dreamed of before, were openly discussed; public works were set on foot; taxes on milling were abolished, and this measure led the people of Rouen to declare that *all* manorial dues had been abolished, so that they rose in July to protest against ever paying them again. The malcontents evidently lost no time and profited by the occasion to extend the popular risings.

We have not the necessary documents for giving a full account of the popular insurrections during the reign of Louis XVI.—the historians did not trouble about them; the archives have not been examined, and it is only by accident that we learn that in such-and-such a place there were "disorders." Thus, there were riots of a somewhat serious nature in Paris, after the abolition of the trade-guilds in 1776—and all over France, in the course of the same year—as a result of the false reports respecting the abolition of all obligations in the matter of statute labour and dues claimed by the landowners. But, according to the printed documents, it would appear also that there was a decrease in the rioting in the years 1777 to 1783, the American war having perhaps something to do with this.

However, in 1782 and 1783, the riots recommenced, and from that time went on increasing until the Revolution. Poitiers revolted in 1782; in 1786 it was Vizille's turn; from 1783 to 1789 rioting broke out in the Cevennes, the Vivarais and the Gévaudan. The malcontents, who were nicknamed *mascarats*, wanting to punish the "practitioners" who sowed dissension among the peasants to incite them to go to law, broke into the law courts and into the houses of the notaries and attorneys and burned all the deeds and contracts. Three of the leaders were hanged, others were sent to penal servitude, but the disorders broke out afresh, as soon as the closing of the *parlements* (Courts of justice) furnished them with a new pretext.* In 1786 it was Lyons that revolted.† The silk-weavers went on strike ; they were promised an increase of wages, but troops were called out, whereupon there was a fight and three of the leaders were hanged. From that moment, up to the Revolution, Lyons became a hotbed of revolt, and in 1789 it was the rioters of 1786 who were chosen as electors.

Sometimes these risings had a religious character ; sometimes they were to resist military enlistment—every levy of soldiers led to a riot, says Turgot ; or it might be the salt tax against which the people rebelled, or the exactions of the tithes. But revolts went on without intermission, and it was in the east, south-east and north-east—future hotbeds of the Revolution—that these revolts broke out in the greatest number. They went on steadily growing in importance, and at last, in 1788, after the dissolution of the Courts of Justice, which were called *parlements* and were replaced by " Plenary Courts," insurrections broke out in every part of France.

It is evident that for the mass of the people there was not much to choose between a *parlement* and a " Plenary Court." If the *parlements* had refused sometimes to register edicts made by the King and his minister, they had on the other hand displayed no solicitude for the people. But the *parlements* had shown opposition to the Court, that was enough ; and when emissaries of the middle classes sought popular support for rioting, they were given it willingly, because it was a way of demonstrating against the Court and the rich.

In the June of 1787 the Paris *parlement* had made itself very popular by refusing a grant of money to the Court. The law of the country was that the edicts of the King should be registered by the *parlement*, and the Paris *parlement* unhesitatingly registered certain edicts concerning the corn trade, the convocation of provincial assemblies and statute labour. But it refused to register the edict which was to establish fresh taxes—a new " territorial subvention," and a new stamp duty. Upon this the King convoked what was called a " Bed of

* C. de Vic and J. de Vaissete, *Histoire générale du Languedoc*, continued by du Mège, 10 vols., 1840–1846.
† Chassin, *Génie de la Révolution*.

Justice," and compelled his edicts to be registered. The *parlement* protested, and so won the sympathy of the middle classes and the people. There were crowds round the Courts at every sitting; clerks, curious idlers and common men collected there to applaud the members. To stop this, the King banished the *parlement* to Troyes, and then riotous demonstrations began in Paris. The popular hatred was then being directed against the princes chiefly, especially against the Duke d'Artois and the Queen, who was nicknamed "Madame Déficit."

The Exchequer Court of Paris (*Cour des Aides*), supported by the popular outburst, as well as by the provincial *parlements* and the Court of Justice, protested against this act of royal power, and, as the agitation was growing, the King was compelled to recall the exiled *parlement*. This was done on September 9, and evoked fresh demonstrations in Paris, during which the minister Calonne was burnt in effigy.

These disturbances were chiefly confined to the lower middle classes. But in other localities they assumed a more popular character.

In 1788 insurrections broke out in Brittany. When the military Commander of Rennes and the Governor of the province went to the Breton *parlement* to announce the edict by which that body was abolished, the whole town turned out immediately. The crowd insulted and hustled the two functionaries. The people in their hearts hated the Governor, Bertrand de Moleville, and the middle classes profited by this to spread a rumour that the edict was all owing to the Governor. "He is a monster that deserves to be strangled," said one of the leaflets distributed among the crowd. When he came out of the palace, therefore, they pelted him with stones, and after several attempts some one threw a cord with a slip-knot over him. Fighting was about to begin—the young men in the crowd breaking through the ranks of the soldiers—when an officer threw down his sword and fraternised with the people.

By degrees troubles of the same kind broke out in several other towns in Brittany, and the peasants rose in their turn when grain was being shipped at Quimper, Saint-Brieuc,

Morlaix, Pont-l'Abbé, Lamballe and other places. It is interesting to note the active part taken in these disorders by the students at Rennes, who from that time fraternised with the rioters.* In Dauphiné, especially at Grenoble, the insurrection assumed a still more serious character. As soon as the military commander, Clermont-Tonnerre, had promulgated the edict which dissolved the *parlement* the people of Grenoble rose. The tocsin was rung, and the alarm spreading quickly to the neighbouring villages, the peasants hastened in crowds to the town. There was a sanguinary affray and many were killed. The commander's guard was helpless and his palace was sacked. Clermont-Tonnerre, with an axe held over his head, had to revoke the royal edict.

It was the people, and chiefly the women, who acted on this occasion. As to the members of the *parlement*, the people had a good deal of trouble to find them. They hid themselves, and wrote to Paris that the people had risen against their will, and when the people laid hands on them they were kept prisoners—their presence giving an air of legality to the insurrection. The women mounted guard over these arrested members, unwilling to trust them even to the men, lest they should be allowed to escape.

The middle classes of Grenoble were in a state of terror. During the night they organised a militia of citizens that took possession of the town gates as well as of some military posts, which they yielded to the troops soon after. Cannon were trained on the rebels, while the *parlement* took advantage of the darkness to disappear. From June 9 to 14 reaction triumphed, but on the 14th news came that there had been a rising at Besançon and that the Swiss soldiers had refused to fire on the people. Upon this the people's spirit revived, and it was proposed to convoke the Estates of the province. But fresh reinforcements of troops having been sent from Paris the disturbance subsided by degrees. The agitation, however, kept up chiefly by the women, lasted some time longer.†

* Du Châtellier, *Histoire de la Révolution dans les départements de l'ancienne Bretagne*, 6 vols., 1836 ; vol. ii. pp. 60-70, 161, &c.

† Vic and Vaissete, vol. x. p. 637.

Besides these two risings mentioned by the majority of the historians, many others broke out at the same time in Provence, Languedoc, Rousillon, Béarn, Flanders, Franche-Comté and Burgundy. Even where no serious riots occurred advantage was taken of the prevailing excitement to keep up the discontent and to make demonstrations.

At Paris, after the dismissal of the Archbishop of Sens, there were numerous demonstrations. The Pont Neuf was guarded by troops, and several conflicts occurred between them and the people, of whom the leaders were, as Bertrand de Moleville remarks,* " those who later on took part in all the popular movements of the Revolution." Marie-Antoinette's letter to the Count de Mercy should also be read in this connection. It is dated August 24, 1788, and in it she tells him of her fears, and announces the retirement of the Archbishop of Sens and the steps she had taken to recall Necker ; the effect produced on the Court by those riotous crowds can therefore be understood. The Queen foresaw that this recall of Necker would lessen the King's authority ; she feared " that they may be compelled to nominate a prime minister," but " the moment is pressing. It is very essential that Necker should accept." †

Three weeks later, September 14, 1788, when the retirement of Lamoignon became known, the riotings were renewed. The mob rushed to set fire to the houses of the two ministers, Lamoignon and Brienne, as well as to that of Dubois. The troops were called out, and in the Rue Mélée and the Rue de Grenelle there was a horrible slaughter of poor folk who could not defend themselves. Dubois fled from Paris. " The people themselves would execute justice," said Les deux amis de la liberté. Later still, in October 1788, when the parlement

* Vic and Vaissete, p. 136.

† J. Feuillet de Conches, Lettres de Louis XVI., Marie-Antoinette et Madame Elisabeth (Paris, 1864), vol. i. pp. 214-216 ; " The Abbé has written to you this evening, sir, and has notified my wish to you," wrote the Queen. " I think more than ever that the moment is pressing, and that it is very essential that he (Necker) should accept. The King fully agrees with me, and has just brought me a paper with his own hand containing his ideas, of which I send you a copy." The next day she wrote again ; " We must no longer hesitate. If he can get to work to-morrow all the better. It is most urgent. I fear that we may be compelled to nominate a prime minister."

that had been banished to Troyes was recalled, " the clerks and the populace " illuminated the Place Dauphine for several evenings in succession. They demanded money from the passers-by to expend on fireworks, and forced gentlemen to alight from their carriages to salute the statue of Henri Quatre. Figures representing Calonne, Breteuil and the Duchess de Polignac were burned. It was also proposed to burn the Queen in effigy. These riotous assemblies gradually spread to other quarters, and troops were sent to disperse them. Blood was shed and many were killed and wounded in the Place de la Grève. Those who were arrested, however, were tried by the *parlement* judges, who let them off with light penalties.

In this way the revolutionary spirit awoke and developed in the van of the Great Revolution.* The initiative came from the middle classes certainly—chiefly from the lower middle classes—but, generally speaking, the middle classes took care not to compromise themselves, and the number of them who opposed the Court, more or less openly, before the convoking of the States-General was very limited. If there had been only their few attempts at resistance France might have waited many years for the overthrow of royal despotism. Fortunately a thousand circumstances impelled the masses to revolt. And in spite of the fact that after every outbreak there were summary hangings, wholesale arrests and even torture for those arrested, the people did revolt, pressed on one side by their desperate misery, and spurred on the other by those vague hopes of which the old woman spoke to Arthur Young. They rose in numbers against the governors of provinces, tax-collectors, salt-tax agents and even against the troops, and by so doing completely disorganised the governmental machine.

From 1788 the peasant risings became so general that it was impossible to provide for the expenses of the State, and Louis XVI., after having refused for fourteen years to convoke the representatives of the nation, lest his kingly authority should suffer, at last found himself compelled to convoke, first the two Assemblies of Notables, and finally the States-General.

* For fuller information, *see* Félix Roquain, *L'esprit révolutionnaire avant la Révolution.*

CHAPTER VI

THE CONVOCATION OF THE STATES-GENERAL BECOMES NECESSARY

Irresponsibility of old *régime*—Miserable condition of peasants —Discontent of middle classes—They encourage riots among the people—Change in political system of France—Necker —Financial crisis—Assembly of Notables convoked—Louis convokes States-General—Increased representation granted to Third Estate

To any one who knew the condition of France it was clear that the irresponsible *régime* of the Court could not last. The misery in the country districts went on increasing year by year, and it became more and more difficult to levy the taxes and at the same time compel the peasants to pay rent to the landlords and perform *the innumerable statute labours* exacted by the provincial government. The taxes alone devoured half and often two-thirds of what the peasants could earn in the course of the year. Beggary and rioting were becoming normal conditions of country life. Moreover, it was not only the peasants who protested and revolted. The middle classes, too, were loudly expressing their discontent. They profited certainly by the impoverishment of the peasants to enrol them in their factories, and they took advantage of the administrative demoralisation and the financial disorders of the moment to seize on all kinds of monopolies, and to enrich themselves by loans to the State.

But this did not satisfy the middle classes. For a while they managed to adapt themselves to royal despotism and Court government. A moment came, however, when they began to fear for their monopolies, for the money they had invested in loans to the State, for the landed property they had acquired, for the factories they had established, and afterwards to encourage the people in their riots in order that they might break down the government of the Court and establish their own political power. This evolution can be plainly traced during the first thirteen or fourteen years of Louis XVI.'s reign, from 1774 to 1788.

An important change in the entire political system of France was visibly taking place. But Louis XVI. and his Court resisted that change, and they opposed it so long that when the King at last decided to yield, it was just when those modest reforms that would have been so welcome at the beginning of his reign had already been found insufficient by the nation. Whereas, in 1775, a *régime* of autocracy mingled with national representation would have satisfied the middle classes, twelve or thirteen years later, in 1787 and 1788, the King was confronted by a public opinion which would no longer hearken to compromise, but demanded representative government with all the limitation of royal power which it involved.

We have seen how Louis XVI. rejected Turgot's very modest proposals. The mere thought of limiting the royal power was repugnant to him. Therefore Turgot's reforms—abolition of statute labour, abolition of trade-wardens and a timid attempt to make the two privileged classes—the nobility and clergy—pay some of the taxes, had no substantial results. Everything is interdependent in a State, and everything under the old *régime* fell in ruins together.

Necker, who followed closely on Turgot, was more a financier than a statesman. He had the financier's narrow mind which sees things only in their petty aspects. His proper element was financial transactions—raising loans. To read his *Pouvoir exécutif* is to understand how his mind, accustomed only to reason about *theories* of government, instead of clearing itself in the shock of human passions and *desiderata* that find expression in a society at a given moment, was incapable of comprehending the vast problem, political, economic, religious and social, that was thrust upon France in 1789.*

* *Du pouvoir exécutif dans les grands états*, 2 vols., 1792. The idea of this book is, that if France was passing through a revolutionary

Necker, moreover, never dared to use to Louis XVI. the clear, exact, severe and bold language which the occasion required. He spoke to him very timidly about representative government, and he limited his reforms to what could neither solve the difficulties nor satisfy any one, while they made every one feel the necessity of a fundamental change.

The provincial assemblies, eighteen of which Necker added to those already instituted by Turgot, leading in turn to the establishment of district and parish councils, were evidently brought to discuss the most difficult questions and to lay bare the hideous corruption of the unlimited power of royalty. And these discussions, which could not but spread all over the country down to the villages, no doubt helped powerfully in the fall of the old *régime*. In this way the provincial assemblies, which in 1776 might have acted as lightning conductors and lessened the force of the storm, were helping towards the insurrection of 1788. Likewise the famous *Compte rendu*, the report upon the state of the provinces, that Necker published in 1781, a few months before quitting office, was a heavy blow to royal autocracy. As always happens on such occasions, he helped to shake down the system which was already tottering to its fall, but he was powerless to prevent the fall from becoming a revolution : probably he did not even perceive that it was impending.

The financial crash came after Necker's first dismissal, in the years 1781 to 1787. The finances were in such a miserable condition that the debts of the State, the provinces, the State

crisis in 1792, it was the fault of her National Assembly for having neglected to arm the King with a strong executive power. " Everything would have gone its course more or less perfectly if only care had been taken to establish in our midst a tutelary authority," says Necker, in the preface to this work ; and he enlarges in these two volumes on the boundless rights with which the royal power should be invested. It is true that in his book, *Sur la législation et le commerce des grains*, published in 1776, he had developed, by way of protesting against a system of free trade in corn, supported by Turgot, some ideas showing sympathy with the poor, in advocating that the State should intervene to fix the price of wheat for their benefit, but that was the limit of his " State-Socialism." The essential thing, in his opinion, was a strong Government, a throne respected and surrounded with that object by high functionaries and a powerful executive.

departments and even of the King's household were accumulating in an alarming fashion.   At any moment the bankruptcy of the State might have been declared, a bankruptcy which the middle classes, now interested in the State finances as creditors, did not want at any price.   With all this, the mass of the people were already so impoverished that they could no longer pay the taxes—they did not pay, and revolted ; while the clergy and the nobility refused to make any sacrifice in the interests of the State.   Under such conditions the risings in the villages necessarily brought the country nearer to the Revolution.   And it was in the midst of these difficulties that the minister Calonne convoked an Assembly of the Notables at Versailles for February 22, 1787.

To convoke this Assembly of Notables was to do exactly what ought not to have been done at that moment : it was exactly the half-measure which on one side made the National Assembly inevitable, and on the other hand inspired distrust of the Court and hatred of the two privileged orders, the nobility and the clergy.   Through that Assembly it was learned that the national debt had mounted up to sixteen hundred and forty-six millions—an appalling sum at that time—and that the annual deficit was increasing by one hundred and forty millions annually.   And this in a country ruined as France was !   It came to be known—every one talked of it ; and after every one had talked about it, the Notables, drawn from the upper classes and practically a ministerial assembly, separated on May 25 without having done or decided anything. During their deliberations Calonne was replaced by Loménie de Brienne, Archbishop of Sens.   But the new minister, by his intrigues and his attempted severity, only succeeded in stirring up the *parlements*, in provoking widely spread riots when he wished to disband them, and in exciting public opinion still more against the Court.   When he was dismissed on August 25, 1788, there was general rejoicing all over France. But as he had proved clearly the impossibility of despotic government there was nothing for the Court but to submit. On August 8, 1788, Louis XVI. was at last obliged to convoke the States-General, and to fix the opening for May 1, 1789.

Even in this the Court and Necker, who was recalled to the ministry in 1788, managed so as to displease every one. It was the general opinion in France that in the States-General, in which the three classes would be separately represented, the Third Estate ought to have twice as many members as the two others, and that the voting should be by individuals. But Louis XVI. and Necker were opposed to this, and even convoked a second Assembly of Notables on November 6, 1788, which would, they were sure, reject the doubling of numbers in the Third Estate and the individual vote. This was exactly what happened ; but in spite of that, public opinion had been so predisposed in favour of the Third Estate by the provincial Assemblies that Necker and the Court were obliged to give in. The Third Estate was granted a double representation—that is to say, out of a thousand deputies the Third would have as many as the clergy and nobility combined. In short, the Court and Necker did everything they possibly could to turn public opinion against them, without gaining any advantage for themselves. The Court's opposition to the convocation of a national representative Assembly was in vain. The States-General met at Versailles on May 5, 1789.

CHAPTER VII

THE RISING OF THE COUNTRY DISTRICTS DURING THE OPENING MONTHS OF 1789

Heroism of middle classes at beginning of Revolution over-rated—Abolition of serfdom—Statute labour and other im-positions upon peasants—Failure of crops in 1789—Riots follow—Nature of riots—" Vive la Liberté ! "—Riots at Agde—Concessions granted to people—Effect of riots on elections—Agitation in rural districts—Importance of peasant insur-rection

NOTHING could be more erroneous than to imagine or describe France as a nation of heroes on the eve of 1789, and Quinet was perfectly right in destroying this legend, which some historians had tried to propagate. It is evident that if we were to collect into a few pages the occasional instances, very rare after all, of open resistance to the old *régime* on the part of the middle classes—such as d'Espréménil's opposition—we could compose a tolerably impressive picture. But what is particularly apparent in making a survey of the conditions of the time is the absence of serious protests, of assertions of the individual, the servility of the middle classes. " Nobody makes himself known," says Quinet, very justly. There is no oppor-tunity even to know oneself.* And he asks : " What were they doing—Barnave, Thouret, Sieyès, Vergniaud, Guadet, Roland, Danton, Robespierre, and all the others, who were so soon to become the heroes of the Revolution ? "

Dumbness, silence, prevailed in the provinces and in the towns. The central power had to summon men to vote, and invite them to say aloud what they had been saying in whispers, before the Third Estate issued their famous *cahiers*. And

* Quinet, *La Révolution*, ed. 1869, vol. i. p. 15.

even then ! If in some of the *cahiers* we find daring words of revolt, what submissiveness and timidity appear in most of them, what moderation in their demands ! For, after the right to carry arms, and some legal guarantees against arbitrary arrests, it was chiefly a little more liberty in municipal affairs that was asked for in the *cahiers* of the Third Estate.* It was later on, when the deputies of the Third saw themselves supported by the people of Paris, and when the mutterings of the peasant insurrection began to be heard, that they grew bolder in their attitude towards the Court.

Fortunately, the people began to revolt everywhere, after the disturbances provoked by the *parlements* during the summer and autumn of 1788, and the tide of revolt, gathering force, swept onward to the rising of the villages in July and August of 1789.

It has already been said that the condition of the peasants and workers in the towns was such that a single bad harvest sufficed to bring about an alarming increase in the price of bread in the towns and sheer famine in the villages. The peasants were no longer serfs, serfdom having long been abolished in France, at least on private estates. After Louis XVI. had abolished it within the royal domains in 1779, there remained in 1788 only about 80,000 persons held by mortmain in the Jura, at most about 1,500,000 in the whole of France, perhaps even less than a million ; even those subject to mortmain were not serfs in the strict meaning of the term. As to the majority of the French peasants, they had long ceased to be serfs. But they went on paying in money, and in working for their personal liberty with statute labour as well as with

* With regard to the demands which afterwards excited the fury of the landowners, it is well to note these : The tax on bread and meat to be fixed according to the average prices, demanded by Lyons, Troyes, Paris and Châlons ; that " wages should be regulated periodically according to the daily needs," demanded by Rennes ; that work should be guaranteed to all able-bodied poor, demanded by several towns. As to the Royalist-Constitutionalists, who were numerous, it can be seen by the proposals of the " *Cahier général*," analysed by Chassin (*Les élections et les cahiers de Paris en 1789*, vol. iii., 1889, p. 185), that they wished to limit the deliberations of the States-General to questions of finance and of retrenchments in the household expenditures of the King and the princes.

work of other kinds. These dues were extremely heavy and
variable, but they were not arbitrary, and they were considered
as representing payments for the right of holding land, whether
collectively by the community or privately as farm-land. And
each parcel of land or farm had its dues, as varied as they were
numerous, carefully recorded in the feudal registers, the
terriers.

Besides, the right of manorial justice had been retained, and
over large districts the lord was still judge, or else he nominated
the judges ; and in virtue of this ancient prerogative he retained all kinds of personal rights over his ex-serfs.* When
an old woman bequeathed to her daughter one or two trees
and a few old clothes—for example, " my black quilted petti-
coat," a bequest such as I have seen—" the noble and generous
lord or the noble and generous lady of the castle levied so
much on the bequest. The peasant paid also for the right of
marriage, of baptism, of burial ; he paid likewise on everything
he bought or sold, and the very right of selling his crops or his
wine was restricted. He could not sell before the lord had
sold his own. Lastly, there were all manner of tolls (*banalités*)
—for the use of the mill, of the wine-press, the public bakehouse,
the washing-places, on certain roads or particular fords—all
maintained since the days of serfdom, as well as contributions
of nuts, mushrooms, linen, thread, formerly considered as gifts
for festive occasions."

As to statute labour, it took an infinite variety of forms :
work in the fields of the lord, work in his parks and his gardens,
work to satisfy all sorts of whims. In some villages there was
even an obligation to beat the pond during the night in order
that the frogs should not prevent his lordship from sleeping.

---

* In an excellent pamphlet, *Les fléaux de l'agriculture, ouvrage pour
servir à l'appui des cahiers des doléances des campagnes,* by D. . . .
(April 10, 1789), we find this statement of causes preventing the development of agriculture : The enormous taxes, the tithes, joint and individual, " solites " and " insolites," and these always increasing ;
the large quantities of game preserved through abuse of privileges and
sport ; and the vexation and abuse of the seigneurial law courts. It
is here shown that " it was by means of the attachment of manorial
law courts to the fief that the landlords had made themselves despots
and held the inhabitants of the country districts in the chains of
slavery " (p. 95).

Personally the man was free, but all this network of dues and exactions, which had been woven bit by bit through the craft of the lords and their stewards in the centuries of serfdom—all this network still clung round the peasant.

More than that, the State was there with its taxes, its fines, its twentieths, its statute labours ever increasing, too, and the State, as well as the steward of my lord, was always ready to exercise ingenuity in devising some new pretext for introducing some new form of taxation.

It is true that, since Turgot's reforms, the peasants had ceased paying certain feudal taxes, and some provincial governors had even refused to resort to force to levy certain dues, which they considered to be injurious exactions. But the principal feudal dues attaching to the land were exacted in full, and they became all the heavier as the State and provincial taxes, to which they were added, continually increased. There is, therefore, not a word of exaggeration in the gloomy pictures of life in the villages drawn by every historian of the Revolution. But neither is there any exaggeration in saying that in each village there were some peasants who had created for themselves a certain amount of prosperity, and that these were the men who especially wished to shake off all feudal obligations, and to win individual liberty. The two types depicted by Erckmann and Chatrian in their *Histoire d'un paysan*—the middle-class man of the village, and the peasant crushed beneath the burden of his poverty—are true to life. Both of them existed. The former gave political strength to the Third Estate; while the bands of insurgents that, since the winter of 1788–1789 had begun to force the nobles to relinquish the feudal dues inscribed in the *terriers*, were recruited from among the starving poor in the villages, who had only mud cabins to live in, and a few chestnuts or the gleanings of the fields for food.

The same remark applies also to the towns, to which the feudal rights extended, as well as to the villages. The poorer classes in the towns were just as much crushed beneath feudal taxes as the peasants. The right of seigneurial justice remained to its full extent in many a growing city, and the hovels of the artisans and mechanics paid the same dues, in cases of sales or inheritance, as the huts of the peasants. Several towns had even to pay a perpetual tribute as redemption from their former feudal subjection. Besides this, the majority of the towns paid the *don gratuit*—the voluntary gift—to the King, just to maintain a shadow of municipal independence, and the burden of these taxes pressed hardest on the poor. If we add to all this the heavy royal taxes, the provincial contributions, the fines, the salt tax and the rest, as well as the caprices of the functionaries, the heavy expenses incurred in the law courts, and the impossibility of a mere commoner's obtaining justice against a noble, even if he were a rich member of the middle classes, and if we take into consideration the many forms of oppression, insult and humiliation to which the lower classes were subject, we shall be able to form some idea of the condition of the poor on the eve of 1789.

It was, however, these poorer classes who, by revolting in the towns and villages, gave the representatives of the Third Estate in the States-General courage to oppose the King and to declare the Assembly a constituent body.

Drought had caused a failure of the crops in 1788, and the winter was very severe. Before that there had certainly been winters as severe, and crops quite as bad, and even riots among the people. Every year there was scarcity in some part of France, and often it affected a fourth or a third part of the kingdom. But this time hopes had been awakened by preceding events—the provincial assemblies, the Convocation of Notables, the disturbances connected with the *parlements* in the towns, which spread, as we have seen, at least in Brittany, to the villages also. And these insurrections in 1789 soon became alarming both in extent and character.

I learn through Professor Karéeff, who has studied the effect of the Great Revolution upon the French peasants, that in the National Archives there is a huge bundle of documents bearing on the risings of the peasants which preceded the taking of the Bastille.* For my own part, never having been able to study

* It is now known that Taine, who pretended that he had studied the reports of the Governors of the provinces concerning these insurrections, had only glanced through twenty-six referring to 1770, as M. Aulard has shown (*Taine : historien de la Révolution française*, Paris, 1907).

the archives in France, but having consulted many provincial histories of that period,* I had already, in former works, arrived at the conclusion † that a great number of riots had broken out in the villages after January 1789, and even after December 1788. In certain provinces the situation was terrible on account of the scarcity, and everywhere a spirit of revolt, until then but little known, was taking possession of the people. In the spring, the insurrection became more and more frequent in Poitou, Brittany, Touraine, Orléanais, Normandy, Ile de France, Picardy, Champagne, Alsace, Burgundy, Nivernais, Auvergne, Languedoc and Provence.

Nearly all these riots were of the same character. The peasants, armed with knives, scythes, cudgels, flocked in a body to the town, and compelled the labourers and farmers who had brought the corn to the market to sell it at a certain " honest " price, such as three livres the bushel ; or else they went to the corn merchants, took out the wheat and " divided it among themselves at a reduced price," promising to pay for it after the next harvest. In other places they forced the landowner to forego his dues upon flour for a couple of months, or they compelled the municipality to tax bread, and sometimes " to increase by four sous the daily wage." Where famine was severest, as at Thiers, the town workers went to collect wheat in the country districts. Often they broke open the granaries belonging to religious communities and merchant monopolists, or even those belonging to private persons, and provided the bakers with flour. Moreover, from this time, too, dated the formation of bands composed of peasants, wood-cutters, sometimes even of contrabandists, who went from village to village seizing the corn. By degrees they began also to burn the land registers and to force the landlords to abdicate their feudal rights—these were the same bands which gave the middle classes the pretext for arming their militias in 1789.

---

* *La Jura*, by Sommier ; *Le Languedoc*, by Vic and Vaissete ; *Castres*, by Combes ; *La Bretagne*, by du Châtellier ; *La Franche-Comté*, by Clerc ; *L'Auvergne*, by Dulaure ; *Le Berry*, by Regnal ; *Le Limousin*, by Leymarie ; *L'Alsace*, by Strobel ; &c.

† *La Grande Révolution* (pamphlet), Paris, 1893 ; " The Great French Revolution and its Lesson," anniversary article in *The Nineteenth Century*, June 1889 ; articles on the Revolution in *La Révolte*.

Ever since January there was heard, too, in these riots the cry of " Vive la Liberté ! " and from that time, and still more markedly after the month of March, we find the peasants here and there refusing to pay the tithes and feudal dues, or, indeed, even the taxes. Outside the three provinces, Brittany, Alsace and Dauphiné, which are cited by Taine, traces are to be found of similar movements nearly all over the eastern part of France.

In the south, at Agde, after the riots of April 19, 20 and 21, " the people foolishly persuaded themselves that they were everything," wrote the mayor and the consuls, " and they may do everything according to the pretended will of the King concerning the equality of rank." The people threatened to sack the town if the price of all provisions was not lowered, and the provincial dues on wine, fish and meat suppressed ; further-more—and here we see already the *communalist* good sense of the masses of the people in France—" they wished to nominate consuls, some of whom would be drawn from their own class," and these demands were acceded to the insurgents. Three days after the people demanded that the duty on milling should be reduced by one-half, and this also was granted.*

This insurrection was the counterpart of a hundred others. To obtain bread was the prime cause of the movement, but soon there were also demands in the direction where economic conditions and political organisation meet, the direction in which popular agitation always goes forward with the greatest confidence and obtains some immediate results.

In Provence, at least in March and April of 1789, more than forty large villages and towns, among them Aix, Marseilles and Toulon, abolished the tax on flour, and here and there the mob pillaged the houses of officials whose duty was to levy the taxes on flour, hides, butcher's meat, &c. The prices of pro-visions were reduced and a maximum established for all provisions, and when the gentlemen of the upper middle classes protested, the mob replied by stoning them, or else a trench was dug before their eyes which might serve for their grave. Sometimes even a coffin was brought out the better to impress the refractory

* Taine, vol. ii. 22, 23.

who apparently hastened to comply. All this took place in April 1789, without the shedding of a drop of blood. It is " a kind of war declared on proprietors and property," say the reports from the governors and municipalities. " The people still declare that they will pay nothing, neither taxes, nor dues, nor debts."*

Before that, since April, the peasants began to plunder the great country houses and to compel the nobility to renounce their rights. At Peinier, they forced the lord " to sign a document by which he renounced his seigneurial rights of every kind." †   At Riez they wanted the bishop to burn the records. At Hyères and elsewhere they burned the old papers concerning the feudal rents and taxes. In short, in Provence, from the month of April, we can already see the beginning of the great rising of the peasants which forced the nobility and clergy to make their first concessions on August 4, 1789.

It is easy to discern the influence that these riots and this excitement exercised upon the elections for the National Assembly. Chassin, in his *Génie de la Révolution*, says that in some localities the nobility exercised a great influence on the elections, and that in these localities the peasant electors dared not make any complaints. Elsewhere, especially at Rennes, the nobles took advantage even of the sitting of the States-General of Brittany at the end of December 1788, and in January 1789, to try to stir up the starving people against the middle classes. But what could these last convulsive efforts of the nobles do against the pouplar tide, which rose steadily ? The people saw more than half the land lying idle in the hands of the nobility and clergy, and they understood better than if statisticians had demonstrated it to them, that so long as the peasants did not take possession of the land to cultivate it famine would be always present among them.

The very need to live made the peasant rise against the monopolisers of the soil. During the winter of 1788–1789, says Chassin, no day passed in the Jura without convoys of wheat being plundered.‡   The military authorities could think of

* Letters in the National Archives, 1453, cited by Taine, vol. ii. p. 24.   † Letter in the Archives.   ‡ Chassin, p. 162.

nothing but " Suppression of the riots " ; but the tribunals refused to sentence or even to judge the famished rioters. Similar riots broke out everywhere, north, south, east and west, says Chassin.*

The elections brought with them a renewal of life and of hope in the villages. The lordly influence was great everywhere, but now in every village there was to be found some middle-class man, a doctor or lawyer, who had read his Voltaire, or Sieyès, or the famous pamphlet—*Qu'est-ce que le tiers état ?* Everything was changing wherever there was a weaver or a mason who could read and write, were it only the printed letters. The peasants were eager to put " their grievances " on paper. It is true that these grievances were confined for the greater part to things of secondary importance ; but throughout we see cropping up, as in the insurrection of the German peasantry in 1523, the demand that the lords should prove their *right* to the feudal exactions.† When the peasants sent in their *cahiers*, they waited patiently for the result. But the tardiness of the States-General and the National Assembly exasperated them, and as soon as that terrible winter of 1788–1789 came to an end, as soon as the sun shone again, and brought with it hope of a coming harvest, the riots broke out afresh, especially after the spring work in the fields was over.

The intellectual middle classes evidently took advantage of the elections to propagate revolutionary ideas. "A Constitutional Club " was formed, and its numerous branches spread themselves even into the smallest towns. The apathy which had struck Arthur Young in the eastern towns no doubt existed ; but in some of the other provinces the middle classes extracted all the profit they desired from the electoral agitation. We can even see how the events which took place in June at Versailles in the National Assembly were prepared severla months before in the provinces. Thus the union of the Three Estates and the vote by head had been agreed to in Dauphiné since the month of August 1788 by the States of the province, under pressure of the local insurrections.

* Chassin, p. 163.
† Doniol, *La Révolution française et la féodalité.*

It must not be thought, however, that the middle-class people who took a prominent part in the elections were in the least degree revolutionary. They were moderates, " peaceful rebels," as Chassin says. As regards revolutionary measures, it was usually the people who spoke of them, since secret societies were found among the peasants, and unknown persons began to go about appealing to the people to pay taxes no longer, but to make the nobles pay them. Or else emissaries went about declaring that the nobles had already agreed to pay the taxes, but that this was only a cunning trick on their part. " The people of Geneva were emancipated in a day. . . . Tremble, ye nobles ! " There were also pamphlets addressed to the peasants and secretly distributed, such as *L'Avis aux habitants des campagnes*, distributed at Chartres. In short, as Chassin says, and no one has more carefully studied this aspect of the Revolution : " Such was the agitation in the rural districts that even if the people of Paris had been vanquished on July 4, it was no longer possible to restore the condition in which the country had been previous to January 1789." To do that, it would have been necessary to conquer each village separately. After the month of March the feudal taxes were no longer paid by any one.*

The importance of this profound agitation in the country districts can be easily understood. Although the educated middle classes did undoubtedly profit by the conflicts with the Court and the *parlements* to arouse political ferment, and although they worked hard to disseminate discontent, it is nevertheless certain that the peasant insurrection, winning over the towns also, made the real basis of the Revolution, and gave the deputies of the Third Estate the determination, presently to be expressed by them at Versailles, to reform the entire system of the government in France, and to initiate a complete revolution in the distribution of wealth.

Without the peasant insurrection, which began in winter and went on, ever growing, until 1793, the overthrow of royal despotism would never have been effected so completely, nor would it have been accompanied by so enormous a change,

* Chassin, p. 167 *et seq.*

political, economic and social.   France might, indeed, have had a sham parliament, even as Prussia had in 1848 ; but this innovation would not have assumed the character of a revolution : it would have remained superficial, as it did in the German States after 1848.

CHAPTER VIII

RIOTS IN PARIS AND ITS ENVIRONS

Activity in Paris—" Réveillon Affair "—First conflict between
people of Paris and rich—" English gold "—Paris becomes
centre of Revolution

UNDER such conditions it is easy to imagine that Paris could
not remain quiet. Famine had set its grip upon the rural
districts in the neighbourhood of the great city, as elsewhere.
Provisions were as scarce in Paris as in the other large towns,
and those who came in search of work could do nothing more
than simply increase the multitude of the poor, especially in
prospect of the great events which every one felt were on the
way.

Towards the end of winter—in March and April—some
hunger-riots and pillagings of corn are mentioned in the
reports of the Governors of the provinces at Orléans, Cosnes,
Rambouillet, Jouy, Pont-Sainte-Maxence, Bray-sur-Seine, Sens,
Nangis, Viroflay, Montlhéry, &c. In other places within the
region, in the forests around Paris, the peasants, as early as
March, were exterminating all the rabbits and hares ; even the
woods belonging to the Abbey of Saint-Denis were cut down
and carried away in the full view and knowledge of every one.

Paris was devouring revolutionary pamphlets, of which ten,
twelve, or twenty were published every day, and passed rapidly
from the hands of those who could afford to buy them into
those of the poorest. People were excitedly discussing the
pamphlet by Sieyès, *Qu'est-ce que le tiers ?* Rabaud de Saint-
Etienne's *Considérations sur les intérêts du tiers état,* which was
tinctured with Socialism, *Les droits des états-généraux,* by
d'Entraigues, and a hundred other less famous, but often more

mordant. All Paris was becoming excited against the Court and the nobles, and soon the middle-class revolutionaries went to the poorest suburbs and into the taverns on the outskirts to recruit the hands and the pikes that they needed to strike at royalty. Meanwhile, on April 28, the insurrection, known later as "The Réveillon Affair" broke out, an affair which seemed like one of the forerunners of the great days of the Revolution.

On April 27, the Electoral Assemblies met in Paris, and it seems that during the preparation of the *cahiers* in the Faubourg Saint-Antoine there was a disagreement between the middle classes and the working-men. The workers stated their grievances and the middle-class men replied with insults. Réveillon, a paper-manufacturer and stainer, formerly a workman himself, now by skilful exploitation come to be the employer of three hundred operatives, made himself especially prominent by the brutality of his remarks. They have been repeated many times since. "The working man can live on black bread and lentils : wheat is not for the likes of him," &c.

Is there any truth in the connection which was made later on by the rich people, after the inquiry into "The Réveillon Affair," between the insurrection itself, and this fact mentioned by the toll-keepers, who declared that an immense multitude of suspicious-looking poor people clothed in rags had entered Paris just at that time ? On this point there can only be conjectures, vain conjectures after all. Given the prevalent state of mind, with revolt simmering in the neighbourhood of Paris, was not Réveillon's attitude towards the workers quite enough in itself to explain what happened the following day ?

On April 27, the people, infuriated by the opposition of the rich manufacturer and his brutal speeches, carried his effigy to the Place de la Grève for sentence and execution. At the Place Royale a rumour spread that the Third Estate had just condemned Réveillon to death. But evening came, and the crowds dispersed, spreading terror among the rich by their cries, which resounded in the streets all through the night. Finally, on the morning of the 28th, the crowds went to Réveillon's factory and compelled the workers to stop work ; they then attacked the warehouse and plundered it. The troops arrived, and the people forthwith defied them by throwing stones, slates and furniture from the windows and the roof. On this the troops opened fire and for several hours the people defended themselves with great fury. The result was that twelve soldiers were killed and eighty wounded; and on the people's side there were two hundred killed and three hundred wounded. The workers took possession of their comrades' dead bodies and carried them through the streets of the suburbs. Several days after a riotous mob of five or six hundred men gathered at Villejuif, and tried to break open the doors of the Bicêtre prison.

Here, then, was the first conflict between the people of Paris and the rich, a conflict which produced a deep impression. It was the first sight of the people driven to desperation, a sight which exercised a powerful influence on the elections by keeping away the reactionaries.

Needless to say that the gentlemen of the middle classes tried to prove that this outbreak was arranged beforehand by the enemies of France. Why should the good people of Paris have risen against a manufacturer? "It was English money that incited them to revolt," said some; "the gold of the aristocrats," said the middle-class revolutionaries. No one was willing to admit that the people revolted simply because they suffered, and had endured enough of the arrogance of the rich, who added insults to their sufferings! * From that time we see the growth of the legend which later on was to be used to reduce the Revolution to its parliamentary work, and to represent all the popular insurrections during the four years of the Revolution as *accidents*—the work of brigands or of agents paid either by Pitt or by the party of reaction. Still later the historians revived the legend: "Since the Court was able to use this riot as a pretext for rejecting the overtures of the States-General, therefore it must have been only the work of reactionaries." How often have we not heard the same methods of reasoning used in our own time!

* Droz (*Histoire du règne de Louis XVI.*), a reactionary historian, has remarked aptly that the money found on some of the slain men may well have been the proceeds of plunder.

In reality the days from April 24 to 28 were merely fore-runners of the days of July 11 to July 14. A revolutionary spirit began to manifest itself among the people of Paris from that time onwards. Close by the Palais Royal, the revolutionary focus of the middle classes, were the faubourgs, the centres of the popular risings. Henceforth Paris became the focus of the Revolution, and the States-General, which were about to assemble at Versailles, came to rely upon Paris for the support they needed in pressing their demands and in their struggles against the Court.

CHAPTER IX

THE STATES-GENERAL

Opening of States-General—King's distrust—People not represented—" Third Estate "—Establishment of National Assembly—Oath in Tennis Court—King annuls resolutions of Assembly—Speech of Mirabeau—People threaten force

ON May 4, 1789, the twelve hundred deputies of the States-General assembled at Versailles, repaired to the church of Saint Louis to hear Mass in connection with the opening ceremony, and the next day the King opened the session in the presence of a crowd of spectators. And already from this opening meeting the tragic inevitability of the Revolution began to unfold itself.

The King felt nothing but distrust towards the representatives of the nation whom he had convoked. He had at last resigned himself to convoking them, but he complained before the deputies themselves of " the restlessness of spirit," the general ferment throughout the country, as if such restlessness was in itself factitious, and not caused by the actual condition of France ; as if that assemblage had been a useless and capricious violation of kingly rights.

France, too long held back from reform, had at last come to feel the necessity of a complete revision of *all* her institutions— and the King only mentioned a few trifling reforms in finance, for which a little economy in expenditure would have sufficed. He demanded " the agreement of the Orders " at a time when the provincial assemblies had already proved to men's minds that the existence of separate Orders was superannuated—a dead weight, a survival of the past. At a time, too, when everything, as in Russia to-day, needed reconstruction, the King expressed his fear above all things of " innovation " ! Thus, in the

King's speech, the life-and-death struggle about to begin between royal autocracy and representative power was already foreshadowed.

As to the nation's representatives, they themselves in their divisions were already displaying signs of the deep cleavage which was to manifest itself throughout the Revolution between those who would cling to their privileges and those who would strive to demolish them.

The national representation, in fact, even then showed its chief defect. *The people were not represented at all, the peasants were absent.* It was the middle classes who took it upon themselves to speak for the people in general ; and with regard to the peasantry, in the whole of this assembly, made up of lawyers, notaries, attorneys, there were perhaps five or six who knew anything about the real position, much less the legal position of the immense mass of the peasants. All of them, being townsmen, were well able to defend the townsman ; but as to the peasant, they did not even know what he required, or what would be injurious to him.

Civil war already exists within these precincts, where the King, surrounded by nobles, speaks as master to the Third Estate, and reminds them of his " benefits." The Keeper of the Seals, Barentain, disclosing the real intention of the King, dwells upon the part to which the States-General should confine themselves. They are to consider the taxes which they will be asked to vote, they are to discuss the reform of civil and criminal law, they are to vote on a law concerning the Press, to check the liberties which it had recently arrogated to itself, and that will be all. There were to be no dangerous reforms : " All just demands have been granted ; the King has not been stopped by indiscreet murmurs ; he has indulgently deigned to ignore them ; *he has pardoned even the expression of those false and extravagant matters under cover of which it was intended to substitute harmful chimeras for the unalterable principles of the monarchy.* Gentlemen, you will reject with indignation these dangerous innovations."

All the struggles of the four succeeding years lay in these words, and Necker, who followed the King and the Keeper of the Seals, in his speech lasting three hours, added nothing to advance either the great question of representative government, which absorbed the middle classes, or that of the land and the feudal exactions, which interested the peasants. The adroit Comptroller of Finance knew how to make a three-hours' speech without compromising himself either with the Court or the people. The King, faithful to the views he had already expressed to Turgot, did not understand the seriousness of the moment, and left to the Queen and princes the task of intriguing to prevent the concessions which were demanded of him.

But neither did Necker comprehend that it was a question of surmounting not merely a financial crisis, but a political and social crisis of the utmost seriousness, and that under these circumstances a policy of manœuvring between the Court and the Third Estate was bound to be fatal. For if it was not already too late to prevent a Revolution, it was at least necessary to make some attempt at an honest, straightforward policy of concessions in the matter of government; the time had come to bring forward, in their most important aspects, the great land problems on which the misery or well-being of a whole nation depended.

And as to the representatives themselves, neither the two privileged orders, nor yet " the Third," grasped the full extent of the problem which was confronting France. The nobilit dreamed of regaining their ascendency over the Crown ; the clergy thought only of maintaining their privileges ; and the Third Estate, although it knew quite well what steps to take for the conquest of power in favour of the middle classes, did not perceive that there was yet another problem, infinitely more important to solve—that of giving back the land to the peasant, in order that, possessing a land freed from heavy feudal exactions, he might double and treble the production of the soil, and so put an end to the incessant periods of scarcity which were undermining the strength of the French nation.

Could there be any way out of these conditions but by conflict and struggle ? The revolt of the people : the rising of the peasants, the Jacquerie, the insurrection of the workers in the towns, and of the poor in general—in a word, the Revolution, with all its struggles, its hatreds, its terrible conflicts and its revenges, were they not all inevitable?

For five weeks the "deputies of 'the Third'" tried by parleying to induce the deputies of the other two Orders to sit together, while the Royalist committees on their side worked to maintain the separation. The negotiations led to nothing. But as the days went by the people of Paris assumed a more and more menacing attitude. In Paris, the Palais Royal, turned into an open-air club to which every one was admitted, voiced the general exasperation. It rained pamphlets for which the people scrambled. "Every hour produces something new," says Arthur Young. "Thirteen came out to-day, sixteen yesterday and ninety-two last week. . . . Nineteen-twentieths of these productions are in favour of liberty. . . . The ferment at Paris is beyond conception." * The orators who harangued openly in the streets, standing on a chair in front of a *café*, already spoke of seizing upon the palaces and châteaux of the noble landlords. One heard already, like the rumbling of a coming storm, threatenings of the coming Terror, while at Versailles the people collected at the doors of the Assembly to insult the aristocrats.

The deputies of the "Third" felt that they were being supported. By degrees they grew bolder, and on June 17, upon a motion of Sieyès, they declared themselves at last a "National Assembly." In this way the first step towards the abolition of the privileged classes was taken, and the people of Paris greeted this first step with thunderous acclamations. Thus encouraged, the Assembly voted that the established taxes, being illegal, should be levied only provisionally, and only for as long as the Assembly sat. The people should not be any longer bound to pay them when once the Assembly should be dissolved. A "Committee of Subsistence" was appointed to combat the famine, and capitalists were reassured by the Assembly's consolidation of the National Debt—an act of the greatest prudence at that moment, since the National repre-sentation had to maintain itself at any cost, and to disarm a

* Arthur Young, *Travels in France*, pp. 153, 176 (London, 1892).

power, the power of the money-lender, who would be dangerous if he took sides with the Court.

But this meant revolt against the Royal authority. Accordingly the princes, d'Artois, Condé and Conti, together with the Keeper of the Seals, began to plan a *coup d'état*. On a given day the King was to go in great state to the Assembly. There he would annul all the resolutions of the Assembly, he would decree the separation of the Orders, and would himself fix the few reforms, which should be passed by the Three Orders sitting separately. And what did Necker, that perfect representative of the middle classes of the period, oppose to this stroke of authority, to the *coup d'état* prepared by the Court ? Compromise ! He, too, wanted a display of authority, a Royal Session, and in this session the King was to grant the capitative vote without distinction between the Three Orders in the matter of taxes ; but for everything concerning the privileges of the nobility and clergy separate sittings of the Orders were to be maintained. Now, it is evident that this measure was still less possible to realise than that of the princes. A *coup d'état* is not risked for a half-measure, which, moreover, could not be maintained for more than a fortnight. How could taxation have been reformed without impinging on the privileges of the two superior Orders ?

It was on June 20, therefore, that the deputies of " the Third," emboldened by the more and more threatening attitude of the people in Paris, and even at Versailles, decided to resist the plans for dismissing the Assembly, and for that purpose to bind themselves together by solemn oath. Seeing their Assembly Hall closed on account of the preparations that were being made for the Royal Session, they went in procession to a kind of private hall, the hall of the Tennis Court in the Rue Saint-François. A crowd lmarched with the procession through the streets of Versailes, headed by Bailly. Some volunteer soldiers offered their services to mount guard for them. The enthusiasm of the crowds which surrounded them on all sides upheld the deputies.

Arrived at the hall of the Tennis Court, excited and touched by a fine emotion, they all but one took a solemn oath not to separate before they had given France a Constitution.

No doubt these were but words ; there was even something theatrical in this oath ; but that matters little. There are moments when words are required to make hearts vibrate. And the oath taken in the hall of the Tennis Court made the hearts of revolutionary youth vibrate throughout the length and breadth of France. Woe to the Assemblies that are incapable of such an attitude and such words.

Besides, this act of courage on the part of the Assembly bore immediate fruit. Two days later the Third Estate, being obliged to sit in the church of Saint Louis, found the clergy coming to take part in their deliberations.

The great blow of the Royal Session was struck the following day, June 23, but its effect was already weakened by the oath in the Tennis Court and the sitting in the church of Saint Louis. The King appeared before the deputies. He annulled all the resolutions of the Assembly, or rather of the Third Estate ; he decreed the maintenance of the Orders, determined the limits of the reforms to be accomplished, threatened the States-General with dissolution if they did not obey, and ordered all the deputies to separate for the time being. Upon this the nobility and clergy obediently left the hall, but the deputies of " the Third " kept their places. Then it was that Mirabeau uttered his beautiful and famous speech, in which he said that the King was only their mandatory, that they held their authority of the people, and having taken the oath they could not separate without having framed a Constitution. Being here by the will of the people they would leave only by the force of the bayonet.

Now, it was exactly this force which the Court no longer possessed. Necker had already told them, in February, and very truly, that obedience was nowhere to be found, and that they could not be sure even of the troops.

As to the people of Paris, we have seen in what kind of humour they were on April 27. Every moment a general rising of the people against the rich was feared in Paris, and a few ardent revolutionaries had not hesitated to go into the gloomy faubourgs in search of reinforcements against the Court. Even at Versailles, on the eve of the Royal Session, the people had almost killed a clerical deputy, the Abbé Maury, as well as d'Esprémenil, a deputy of " the Third," who had come over from the nobility. On the day of the Royal Session the Keeper of the Seals and the Archbishop of Paris were so " hooted, abused and scoffed at, so overwhelmed with shame and rage," that the King's secretary, Passeret, who accompanied the minister, " died of the shock the same day." On the 24th, the Bishop of Beauvais was nearly killed by a blow on the head from a stone. On June 25, the crowd hissed the deputies of the nobility and clergy. All the windows were broken in the palace of the Archbishop of Paris. " The troops refused to fire on the people," says Arthur Young bluntly. The King's threat was therefore meaningless. The people's attitude was too menacing for the Court to resort to bayonets, and this is why Louis XVI. uttered this exclamation, " After all . . . let them stay ! "

As to the Assembly of the Third Estate itself, was it not deliberating under the watchful eyes and menaces of the people who filled the galleries ? As early as June 17, when the Third Estate declared itself a National Assembly, that memorable decision was arrived at amidst the acclamations of the galleries and of the two or three thousand persons who surrounded the Hall of Assembly. The list of the three hundred deputies of " the Third " who were opposed to it went the round of Paris, and there was even some talk of burning their houses. And when the oath was being taken in the Tennis Court, and Martin Dauch opposed it, Bailly, the president of the Assembly, prudently made him escape by a back door to avoid facing the people gathered at the front of the hall, and for several days he had to remain in hiding.

Without this pressure put upon the Assembly by the people, it is quite possible that the brave deputies of " the Third," whose names are remembered in history, might never have succeeded in overcoming the resistance of the timorous who had ranged themselves with Malouet.

As to the people of Paris, they made open preparations for the revolt, which was their reply to the military *coup d'état* prepared by the Court against Paris for July 16.

CHAPTER X

PREPARATIONS FOR THE COUP D'ETAT

The 14th of July—Middle classes distrust people—Royalists prepare *coup d'état*—Middle classes urge people to arm—People seize Bastille—Middle classes restore order—King and feudal rights—Effect of Royal Session—Atmosphere of conspiracy at Court—Foundation of Breton Club—Mirabeau and people—Necker tries to avert famine—Incompetence of National Assembly—Royalist plotting continues—Petition of Assembly

THE accepted account of July 14 runs as follows : The National Assembly was sitting. At the end of June, after two months of parleying and hesitations, the Three Orders were at last united. The power was slipping from the grasp of the Court, which began, therefore, to prepare a *coup d'état*. Troops were summoned and massed round Versailles ; they were to disperse the Assembly and bring Paris to its senses.

On July 11, the accepted version goes on to say, the Court decided to act. Necker was dismissed and exiled, Paris heard of this on the 12th, and the citizens formed a procession, which passed through the streets carrying a statue of the dismissed minister. At the Palais Royal, Camille Desmoulins made his famous speech ending with an appeal to arms. The faubourgs rose and 50,000 pikes were forged in thirty-six hours ; on the 14th the people marched upon the Bastille, which presently lowered its drawbridge and surrendered. The Revolution had gained its first victory.

Such is the usual account, which is repeated at the Republic's festivals. It is, however, only a half-truth. It is true so far as the dry statement of facts is concerned ; but it does not tell what should be told about the part played by the people in the rising; nor yet about the true connection between the two elements of the movement, the people and the middle classes. For in the Paris insurrection leading to July 14, as all through the Revolution, there were two separate currents of different origin: the political movement of the middle classes and the popular movement of the masses. At certain moments during the great days of the Revolution, the two movements joined hands in a temporary alliance, and then they gained their great victories over the old *régime*. But the middle classes always distrusted their temporary ally, the people, and gave clear proof of this in July 1789. The alliance was concluded unwillingly by the middle classes; and on the morrow of the 14th, and even during the insurrection itself, they made haste to organise themselves, in order that they might be able to bridle the revolted people.

Ever since the Réveillon affair, the people of Paris, suffering from scarcity, seeing bread grow dearer day by day, and deceived by empty promises, had been trying to revolt. But not feeling themselves supported, even by those of the middle classes who had become prominent in the struggle with royal authority, they could only chafe the bit. In the meantime, the Court party, led by the Queen and the princes, decided to strike a great blow, which would put an end to the Assembly and to the popular agitation in Paris. They concentrated troops whose attachment to the King and Queen they stimulated by every means, and openly prepared a *coup d'état* against the Assembly and against Paris. Then the Assembly, feeling themselves threatened, gave free rein to those of their members and friends in Paris who wanted " the appeal to the people "; that is to say, the appeal for a popular rising. And the people of the faubourgs, desiring nothing better, responded to the appeal. They did not wait for the dismissal of Necker, but began to rise as early as July 8, and even on June 27. Taking advantage of this the middle classes urged the people to open insurrection, and allowed them to arm themselves. At the same time they took care to be armed, too, so that they could control the popular outbreak and prevent its going " too far." But as the insurrection gathered force, the people, contrary to the will of the middle classes, seized the Bastille, the emblem and support of the royal power ; whereupon the middle classes, having meanwhile organised their militia, lost no time in suppressing the men with pikes and re-establishing order.

That is the twofold movement which has to be described.

We have seen that the purpose for holding the Royal Session of June 23 was to declare to the States-General that they were not the power they wished to be ; that the absolute power of the King remained unimpaired ; that there was nothing for the States-General to change in it ; * and that the two privileged orders, the nobility and the clergy, would of themselves enact whatever concessions they should deem useful for a more just distribution of the taxes.   The benefits which were to be granted to the people *would come therefore from the King in person*, and those benefits would be the abolition of statute labour, in great part already accomplished, of mortmain and of *franc-fief*, restriction of the game laws, the substitution of a regular enlistment instead of drawing lots for the militia, the suppression of the word *taille* and the organisation of the provincial authorities.   All this, however, belonged to the realm of empty promises, or indeed was but the mere naming of reform, for all that these reforms implied, all the substance for making these changes, had still to be provided ; and how could it be provided without laying the axe to the privileges of the two superior orders ?   But the most important point in the royal speech, since the whole revolution was soon to turn upon the matter, was the King's declaration concerning the inviolability of the feudal rights.   He declared that the tithes, redemptions, rents of all kinds and seigneurial and feudal rights were property rights absolutely and for ever inviolable.

By such a pronouncement the King was evidently placing the nobility on his side against the Third Estate.   But to make a promise of this extent was to circumscribe the Revolution in advance, in such a way as to render it powerless to

* Necker's original project allowed the Assembly a right to push the Revolution as far as the establishment of a charter, in imitation of the English, says Louis Blanc ; they took care to exclude from all joint deliberations the form of constitution to be given by the next States-General (*Histoire de la Révolution française*, 4vo, vol. i. p. 120).

accomplish any substantial reform in the finances of the State and in the entire internal organisation of France. It meant maintaining intact the old France, the old *régime*, and we shall see later how, in the course of the Revolution, *royalty and the maintenance of feudal rights*—the old political form and the old economic form—came to be associated in the mind of the nation.

It must be admitted that this manœuvre of the Court succeeded up to a certain point. After the Royal Session the nobility accorded the King, and especially the Queen, an ovation at the palace, and the next day there remained only forty-seven nobles who adhered to the two other Orders. Only a few days later, when the rumour spread that a hundred thousand Parisians were marching on Versailles, the people at the palace were in a state of general consternation at hearing this news, and on an order from the King, confirmed by the weeping Queen—for the nobility no longer relied upon the King—most of the nobles rejoined the representatives of the clergy and the Third Estate. But even then they scarcely concealed their hope of soon seeing those rebels dispersed by force.

Meanwhile, all manœuvrings of the Court, all its conspiracies, and even all conversations of such-and-such a prince or noble, were quickly made known to the revolutionaries. Everything reached Paris by a thousand secret ways of communication carefully established, and the rumours coming from Versailles helped to increase the ferment in the capital. The moment always arrives when those in power can no longer depend even upon their servants, and such a moment had come at Versailles. Thus, while the nobility were rejoicing over the little success gained by the Royal Session, some middle-class revolutionaries were founding at Versailles itself a club, the Breton Club, which soon became a great rallying centre and was later on the famous club of the Jacobins. To this club the servants, even those of the King and Queen, went to report what was said behind closed doors at the Court. Some Breton depu- ties, among them Le Chapelier, Glezen and Lanjuinais, were the founders of this Breton Club, and Mirabeau, the Duke d'Aiguillon, Sieyès, Barnave, Pétion, the Abbé Grégoire and Robespierre were members of it.

Since the States-General had been sitting at Versailles the greatest excitement prevailed in Paris. The Palais Royal, with its gardens and *cafés*, had become an open-air club, whither ten thousand persons of all classes went every day to exchange news, to discuss the pamphlets of the hour, to renew among the crowd their ardour for future action, to know and to understand one another. Here flocked together the lower middle classes and the intellectuals. All the rumours, all the news collected at Versailles by the Breton Club, were immediately communicated to this open-air club of the Parisians. Thence the rumours and news spread to the faubourgs, and if sometimes on the way fiction was added to fact, it was, as is often the case with popular legends, truer than the truth itself, since it was only forestalling, and revealing under the guise of legend, the secret springs of action, and intuitively judging men and things often more correctly than do the wise. Who better than the obscure masses of the faubourgs knew Marie-Antoinette, the Duchess de Polignac, the perfidious King and the treacherous princes ? Who has understood them better than the people did ?

Ever since the day following the Royal Session, the great city was simmering with revolt. The Hôtel de Ville had sent congratulations to the Assembly. The Palais Royal had forwarded an address couched in militant language. For the famished people, despised and rejected until then, the popular triumph was a gleam of hope, and insurrection represented in their eyes the means of procuring the bread they needed. At the time when the famine was growing more and more severe, and even the supply of bad flour, yellow and burnt, reserved for the poor, continually failed, the people knew that in Paris and the vicinity there was enough food to feed everybody, and the poor said to one another that without an insurrection the monopolists would never leave off starving the people.

But, as the murmurs of the people in their dark quarters grew louder, the Paris middle classes and the representatives of the people at Versailles became more and more alarmed about a possible rising in the provinces. Better the King and Court than the people in revolt.* The very day the three Orders were united, June 27, after the first victory of the Third Estate, Mirabeau, who until then was appealing to the people, separated himself completely from them, and advocated the separation of the representatives from them. He even warned the members to be on their guard against " seditious auxiliaries." In this we can already see the future programme of " the Gironde " evolving in the Assembly. Mirabeau wished the Assembly to contribute " to the maintenance of order, to the public tranquillity, to the authority of the laws and their ministers." He went even further. He wanted the deputies to rally round the King, saying that the King meant well ; if it happened that he did any wrong, it was only because he was deceived and badly advised !

The Assembly loudly applauded this speech. " The truth is," says Louis Blanc very aptly, " that far from wishing to overturn the throne, the middle classes were already trying to shelter themselves behind it. Deserted by the nobility, it was in the ranks of his commons, at one time so obstinate, that Louis XVI. would have found his most faithful and most alarmed servitors. He was ceasing to be the King of gentlemen, he was becoming the King of the property-owners."

This primordial defect in the Revolution weighed it down, all the time, as we shall see, up to the moment when reaction got the upper hand.

The distress in the city, however, increased from day to day. It is true that Necker had taken measures to avert the dangers of a famine. On September 7, 1788, he had suspended

* Those who make speeches on the anniversaries of the Revolution prefer to keep silent on this delicate subject, and speak of the touching unanimity which they pretend to have existed between the people and their representatives. But Louis Blanc has already pointed out the fears of the middle classes as the 14th of July drew near, and modern research only confirms this point of view. The additional facts which I give here, concerning the days from the 2nd to the 12th of July, show also that the insurrection of the people of Paris followed up to the 12th its own line of conduct, independent of the middle-class members of the Third Estate.

the exportation of corn, and he was protecting the importation by bounties; seventy million livres were expended in the purchase of foreign wheat. At the same time he gave widespread publicity to the decree of the King's Council of April 23, 1789, which empowered judges and officers of the police to visit private granaries to make an inventory of the grain, and in case of necessity to send the grain to market. But the carrying out of these orders was confided to the old authorities and—no more need be said !

Now in July the Government was giving bounties to those who brought wheat to Paris; but the imported wheat was secretly re-exported, so that it could be brought in again and so obtain the bounty a second time. In the provinces, monopolists were buying up the corn with a view to these speculations; they bought up even the standing crops.

It was then that the true character of the National Assembly was revealed. It had been worthy of admiration, no doubt, when it took the oath in the Tennis Court, but above all things it still maintained towards the people a middle-class attitude. On July 4, when the report of the " Committee of Subsistence " was presented, the Assembly discussed the measures to be taken for guaranteeing food and work to the people. They talked for hours and made proposition after proposition. Pétion proposed a loan, others proposed authorising the provincial assemblies to take the necessary measures, but nothing was decided, nothing undertaken. And, when one of the members raised the question of the speculators and denounced some of them, he had the entire Assembly against him. Two days later, July 6, Bouche announced that the culprits were known, and that a formal accusation would be made the next day. " A general panic took possession of the Assembly," says Gorsas, in the *Courrier de Versailles et de Paris*, which he had just started. But the next day came and not a word more was uttered on this subject. The affair was suppressed in the interim. Why ? For fear—as subsequent events go to prove—of compromising revelations.

In any case, so much did the Assembly fear the popular outbreak, that on the occasion of a riot in Paris, on June 30, after the arrest of the eleven French Guards who had refused to load their muskets to fire on the people, the Assembly voted an address to the King, conceived in the most servile terms and protesting its " profound attachment to the royal authority." *

However grudgingly the King might have consented to give the middle classes the smallest share in the Government, they would have rallied to him and helped with all their power of organisation to keep the people down. But—and let this serve as a warning in future revolutions—in the life of the individual, of parties, and even of institutions, there is a logic which is beyond any one's power to change. The royal despotism could not come to terms with the middle classes, who demanded from it their share in the Government. It was logically destined to fight them, and once the battle began it had to succumb and yield its place to representative government—the form which was best suited to the rule of the middle classes. On the other hand, without betraying its natural supporters, the nobility, it could not make terms with democracy, the people's party, and it did its best to defend the nobles and their privileges, to see itself later on betrayed in return by those self-same persons, privileged from their birth.

Meanwhile information concerning the plots of the Court was coming from all quarters, both to the partisans of the Duke of Orléans, who used to meet at Montrouge, as well as to the revolutionaries, who frequented the Breton Club. Troops were concentrating at Versailles, and on the road from Versailles to Paris. In Paris itself they took possession of the most important points in the direction of Versailles. Thirty-five thousand men were said to be distributed within this compass, and twenty thousand more were to be added to them in a few days. The princes and the Queen, it was rumoured, were planning to dissolve the Assembly, to crush Paris in case of a rising, to arrest and kill, not only the principal leaders

* " The National Assembly deplores the troubles which are now agitating Paris. . . . It will send a deputation to the King to beg him of his grace to employ for the re-establishment of order the infallible means of the clemency and kindness that are so native to his heart, with the confidence which his good people will always deserve."

and the Duke of Orléans, but also those members of the Assembly, such as Mirabeau, Mounier and Lally-Tollendal, who wished to transform Louis XVI. into a constitutional monarch. Twelve members, said La Fayette later on, were to be immolated. The Baron de Breteuil and Marshal de Broglie had been summoned to put this project into execution—both of them quite ready to do it. " If it is necessary to burn Paris, Paris will be burnt," said the former. As to Marshal de Broglie, he had written to the Prince de Condé that a whiff of grape-shot would soon " disperse these argufiers and restore the absolute power which is going out, in place of the republican spirit which is coming in." *

It must not be believed that those rumours were only idle tales, as some reactionary historians have asserted. The letter of the Duchess de Polignac, addressed on July 12 to Flesselles, the Provost of the Merchants, which was found later on, and in which all the persons implicated were mentioned under assumed names, is sufficient proof of the plot hatched by the Court for July 16. If there could still be any doubt on this matter, the words addressed to Dumouriez at Caen on July 10 by the Duchess de Beuvron, in the presence of sixty exulting nobles, should suffice to prove it :

" Well, Dumouriez," said the Duchess, " do you not know the great news ? Your friend Necker is turned out, and the result is that the King reascends the throne and the Assembly is dispersed. Your friends, ' the forty-seven,' are at this very moment in the Bastille, perhaps, with Mirabeau, Turgot, and a hundred or so of those insolent fellows of the Third Estate, and for certain Marshal de Broglie is in Paris with thirty thousand men." †

The Duchess was mistaken. Necker was not dismissed until the 11th, and Broglie took care not to enter Paris.

But what was the Assembly doing then ? It was doing what Assemblies have always done, and always will do. It decided on nothing. What could it decide ?

The very day that the people of Paris began to rise, that

* Louis Blanc, *Histoire de la Révolution française*.
† Dumouriez, *Mémoires*, vol. ii. p. 35.

is, on July 8, the Assembly charged no other than Mirabeau, the people's tribune, with the drawing up of a humble petition to the King, and while praying the King to withdraw the troops the Assembly filled their petition with the grossest adulation. It spoke of a people who dearly loved their King, and thanked Heaven for the gift bestowed upon them in his love. How many times similar words and flatteries will be addressed to the King by the representatives of the people during the progress of the Revolution? The fact is that the Revolution cannot be understood at all if these repeated efforts on the part of the propertied classes to win over Royalty to their side as a buckler against the people are passed by unnoticed. All the dramas which will be enacted later on, in 1793, within the Convention, were already contained in germ in this petition from the National Assembly, signed but a few days before July 14.

CHAPTER XI

PARIS ON THE EVE OF THE FOURTEENTH

Revolution centred in Paris, not in Assembly—Paris ready to rise—Districts organise people—Arrest of soldiers of Gardes françaises—*Scarcity of bread—Fury of people increases—Dismissal of Necker—Camille Desmoulins appeals to arms—Struggle begins—Tocsin rung—People procure food and arms — Permanent Committee instituted — Formation of National Guard—Middle classes try to disarm people*

THE attention of the historians is generally absorbed by the National Assembly. The representatives of the people assembled at Versailles seem to personify the Revolution, and their last words or acts are chronicled with pious devotion. Nevertheless, it was not there that the passionate heart of the Revolution was throbbing during those July days: it was throbbing in Paris.

Without Paris, without her people, the Assembly was naught. If the fear of Paris in revolt had not restrained the Court, the Assembly would have been most certainly dispersed, as has been seen so many times since—on the 18th Brumaire and December 2 in France, and also recently in Hungary and in Russia. No doubt the deputies would have protested ; no doubt they would have uttered some fine speeches, and some of them perhaps might have tried to raise the provinces ; but without a people ready to rise, without a preliminary revolutionary work accomplished among the masses, without an appeal to the people for revolt made direct from man to man and not by manifestoes, a representative Assembly can do little when it has to face an established government backed by its legions of functionaries and its army.

Fortunately Paris was awake.   Whilst the National Assembly

slumbered in fancied security, and on July 10 tranquilly resumed the discussion on the scheme for a Constitution, the people of Paris, to whom the boldest and most clear-sighted of the middle classes had at last appealed, prepared for insurrection. Details of the military trap which the Court was preparing for the 16th were repeated in the faubourgs. Everything was known, even the King's threat to retire to Soissons and deliver up Paris to the army; and Paris, *la grande fournaise*, organised itself in its various sections to answer force by force. The " seditious auxilliaries " with which Mirabeau had threatened the Court had been appealed to indeed, and in the gloomy wineshops of the suburbs the Paris proletarians discussed the means of " saving the country." They armed themselves as best they could.

Hundreds of patriotic agitators, " unknown persons," of course, did everything to keep up the ferment and to draw the people into the streets. Squibs and fireworks were, according to Arthur Young, one of the means used; they were sold at half-price, and whenever a crowd collected to see the fireworks let off at a street corner, some one would begin to harangue the people—tell them news of the Court plots. " Lately a company of Swiss would have crushed all this; a regiment would do it now if led with firmness; but let it last a fortnight, and an army will be wanting," * said Arthur Young on the eve of July 14.

In fact, by the end of June the people of Paris were in full ferment and preparing for insurrection. At the beginning of the month there had already been riots on account of the dearness of corn, writes Hardy, the English bookseller; and if Paris remained calm until the 25th, it was only because, until the Royal Session, the people were always hoping that the Assembly would do something. But since the 25th, Paris understood already that no other hope remained but insurrection.

One party of Parisians marched that day towards Versailles, ready to fight the troops. In Paris itself, bands were formed " prepared to proceed to the direst extremities," as we read

* Young, *Travels in France*, p. 184 (London, 1892).

in the secret Notes addressed to the Minister of Foreign Affairs, which were published by Chassin.* " The people have been in commotion all night, they have made bonfires and let off a prodigious number of rockets in front of the Palais Royal and the General Comptroller's Office. They were shouting, ' Long live the Duke of Orléans ! ' "

The same day, the 25th, soldiers of the French Guards deserted their barracks, fraternising and drinking with the people, who carried them off to various quarters, shouting through the streets as they passed : " *A bas la calotte !* "

Meanwhile the " districts " of Paris, that is, the primary bodies of electors, especially those of the workmen's quarters, assembled regularly and took measures for organising resistance in Paris. The " districts " were kept in touch with each other, and their representatives made repeated efforts to constitute an independent municipal body. Even on the 25th Bonneville appealed to arms at an Assembly of the electors, and proposed that they should form themselves into a Commune, quoting historical precedent to give weight to his proposal. The next day, after having met first in the Museum, Rue Dauphine, the representatives of the " districts " at last transferred themselves to the Hôtel de Ville, and on July 1 they were already in their second session, a verbatim report of which is given by Chassin.† Thus they constituted the " Permanent Committee," which we shall see acting on the day of July 14.

On June 30, a simple incident, the arrest of eleven soldiers of the *Gardes françaises*, who had been sent to the Abbaye prison for refusing to load their muskets, sufficed to cause a serious riot in Paris. When Loustalot, editor of the *Révolutions de Paris*, mounted a chair in front of the Café Foy in the Palais Royal, and harangued the crowd on this matter, four thousand men went immediately to the Abbaye and set the arrested soldiers at liberty. The jailers, seeing the crowd arrive, realised that resistance was useless, and handed over the prisoners ; and the dragoons, riding full gallop to cut down the people,

halted, thrust back their sabres into their sheaths, and fraternised with the crowd. A shudder ran through the Assembly
when they learned next day of this fraternisation of the troops
and the rioters. " Are we to be the tribunes of a people in
revolt ? " these gentlemen asked one another.

But revolt was already growing in the outskirts of Paris.
At Nangis the people had refused to pay the taxes, so long as
they were not fixed by the Assembly, and as there was a
scarcity of bread (only two bushels of wheat were sold to each
buyer) and the people were in an uproar, the market was
surrounded by dragoons. But notwithstanding the presence
of the troops there were several riots at Nangis and in other
little towns on the outskirts. " The people quarrel with the
bakers," says Young, " and then run away with the bread and
wheat for nothing." *

The *Mercure de France* (July 27) even mentions some
attempts made in several places, especially at Saint-Quentin,
to cut the green crops, so great was the scarcity.

In Paris, on June 30, the patriots were already enrolling
themselves at the Café du Caveau for insurrection, and when
they heard the next day that Broglie had taken command of
the army, the people, say the secret reports, openly declared
and posted up everywhere that " should the troops fire a single
shot they would put everything to fire and sword." " Many
other things much stronger than that were said," adds the
official. " Wise men dare not show themselves."

On July 2 the fury of the populace broke out against the
Count d'Artois and the Polignacs. There was talk of killing
them and sacking their palaces. There was talk also of seizing
upon all the cannon distributed through Paris. The crowds
in the streets were larger and the fury of the people inconceivable, say the same reports. " This very day," said Hardy,
the bookseller, in his journal, " a raging multitude was on the
point of setting out from the Palais Royal to rescue the deputies
of the Third Estate, who it was said were exposed to the danger
of being assassinated by the nobles." The people now began
to talk of seizing on the arms at the Hôtel des Invalides.

* Arthur Young, p. 189.

The fury inspired by hunger kept pace with the fury against the Court. Consequently, on July 4 and 6, fearing an attack on the bakers, parties of *Gardes françaises* had to be sent out to patrol the streets and superintend the distribution of bread.

On July 8, a prelude to the insurrection broke out in Paris itself, at the camp of twenty thousand unemployed workmen engaged by the Government in road-making at Montmartre. Two days after, on the 10th, blood was already flowing, and on the same day they began to set fire to the toll-gates. The one in the Chaussée d'Antin was burnt, and the people took advantage of this by letting in provisions and wine free of duty.

Would Camille Desmoulins ever have made his appeal to arms on the 12th if he had not been sure that the people would listen to him, if he had not known that Paris was already in revolt, that only twelve days before Loustalot had stirred up the crowd over a matter of less importance, and that Paris and the faubourgs were even then merely waiting for the signal for some one to begin and it would flame into insurrection ?

The impetuosity of the princes, who were certain of success, precipitated the *coup d'état* planned for the 16th, and the King was compelled to act before reinforcements for the troops had arrived at Versailles.*

Necker was dismissed on the 11th, the Count d'Artois shaking his fist in the minister's face as he passed into the council chamber of the ministers, and the King, with his usual duplicity, pretending to know nothing about it, although he had already signed the dismissal. Necker submitted to his master's orders without a word. He even fell in with his plans, and arranged for his departure for Brussels in such a way that it passed unnoticed at Versailles.

Paris only learned about it towards noon the next day, Sunday, the 12th. Every one had been expecting this dismissal, which was to be the beginning of the *coup d'état*. The people were already repeating the saying of the Duke de Broglie,

* *Vide* the Letters of Salmour, the Envoy from Saxony, to Stutterheim, on July 19 and August 20 (Archives of Dresden), cited by Flammermont ; *La journée du 14 Juillet* 1789, by Pitra (Publications de la Société de l'Histoire de la Révolution française, 1892).

who, with his thirty thousand soldiers massed between Paris and Versailles, was "answerable for Paris," and as sinister rumours were circulating all the morning concerning the massacres prepared by the Court, "all revolutionary Paris" rushed in a body to the Palais Royal. Just then the courier had arrived bringing news of Necker's exile. The Court had decided to open hostilities. . . . Whereupon Camille Desmoulins, coming out of one of the *cafés* in the Palais Royal, the Café Foy, with a sword in one hand and a pistol in the other, mounted upon a chair and made his appeal to arms. Breaking a branch from a tree, he took, as is known, a green leaf as a badge, a rallying-sign. And his cry, " There is not a moment to lose, haste to arms ! " spread through the faubourgs.

In the afternoon an immense procession, carrying the busts of the Duke of Orléans and Necker, veiled in crape (it was said that the Duke of Orléans also had been banished), passed through the Palais Royal, along the Rue Richelieu, and turned towards the Place Louis XV. (now Place de la Concorde), which was occupied by troops—Swiss, French Infantry, Hussars and Dragoons—under the command of the Marquis de Besenval. The troops soon found themselves surrounded by the people. They tried to keep them back with sabre-thrusts ; they even fired upon them, but before an innumerable crowd that pushed and jostled, pressing in and breaking through their ranks on every side, the soldiers were forced to retire. From other sources we learn that the French Guards fired a few shots at the " Royal German " regiment, which adhered to the King, and that the Swiss refused to fire on the people. Besenval, who seems not to have had much confidence in the Court, withdrew, therefore, before an overwhelming torrent of the people and went to camp on the Champ-de-Mars.*

Thus the struggle began. But what would be the final

---

* " The French Guards, having sided with the populace, fired upon a detachment of the Royal German regiment, posted on the boulevard, under my windows. Two men and two horses were killed," wrote Simolin, Plenipotentiary of Catherine II. in Paris, to the Chancellor Osterman, on July 13. And he added : " Yesterday and the day before they burned the *barrière blanche* and that of the Faubourg Poissonnière " (Conches, *Lettres de Louis XVI.*, &c., p. 223).

outcome of it if the troops, still faithful to the King, received orders to march on Paris ? In this eventuality, the middle classes decided to accept, with reluctance, the supreme measure, the appeal to the people. The tocsin was rung throughout Paris, and the faubourgs began to forge pikes.*

By degrees armed men began to appear in the streets. All night long men of the people compelled the passers-by to give them money to buy powder. The toll-gates were in flames. All the gates on the right bank, from the Faubourg Saint-Antoine to that of Saint-Honoré, as well as those at Saint-Marcel et Saint-Jacques, were burnt, and provisions and wine entered Paris freely. All night the tocsin rang and the middle classes trembled for their possessions, because men armed with pikes and cudgels spread themselves through every quarter and plundered the houses of some monopolists, known to be enemies of the people, and knocking at the doors of the rich they demanded money and arms.

The next day, the 13th, the people went first of all to the places where there was food. They attacked the monastery of Saint-Lazare, with cries of " Bread, bread ! " Fifty-two carts were laden with flour, which, instead of being emptied then and there, were dragged to the Halles, so that the food might be used by every one. It was to the Halles that the people also sent the provisions let into Paris without paying duty.†

At the same time the people seized the prison of La Force, where debtors were imprisoned, and the liberated prisoners went about the city thanking the people ; but an outbreak of prisoners in the Châtelet was quelled, apparently by some of the middle classes who had armed in hot haste and were already

---

* Of these 50,000 were made, as well as " all kinds of small arms, at the expense of the town," says Dusaulx ("L'œuvre de sept jours," p. 203).

† " From all parts there came to the Hôtel de Ville an infinite number of carriages, chariots and carts, stopped at the gates of the town, and loaded with all sorts of supplies, plates and dishes, furniture, food-stuffs, &c. The people, who only clamoured for arms and ammunition, . . . came to us in crowds and became more insistent every minute." It was July 13 (Dusaulx, " L'œuvre de sept jours," in *Mémoires sur la Bastille,* published by H. Monin, Paris, 1889, p. 397).

patrolling the streets. By six o'clock the middle-class militia were already formed and marching towards the Hôtel de Ville, and at ten o'clock that evening, says Chassin, they were on duty.

Taine and his followers, faithful echoes of the fears of the middle class, try to make us believe that, on the 13th, Paris was in the hands of thieves. But this allegation is contradicted by all contemporary evidence. There were, no doubt, wayfarers stopped by men with pikes, who demanded money to procure arms; and there were also, on the nights between the 12th and 14th, armed men who knocked at the doors of the well-to-do to ask for food and drink, or for arms and money.

It is also averred that there were attempts at pillage, since two credible witnesses mention persons executed at night, between the 13th and 15th, for attempts of that kind.* But here, as elsewhere, Taine exaggerates.

Whether the modern middle-class Republicans like it or not, it is certain that the revolutionaries of 1789 did appeal to the " compromising auxiliaries " of whom Mirabeau spoke. They went to the hovels on the outskirts to find them. And they

---

* The citations given by M. Jules Flammermont, in a note in his work on the Fourteenth (*La journée du 14 Juillet* 1789), are conclusive on this subject—more conclusive than his text, which seems to us up to a certain point to contradict itself on pages clxxxi. and clxxxii. " In the afternoon," says the Count de Salmour, " the guard of the middle classes, already formed, began to disarm all the vagabonds. It is they and the armed middle-class men who, by their vigilance, saved Paris again this night. . . . The night passed quietly and with much order : thieves and vagabonds were arrested, and for the more serious offences they were hanged on the spot " (Letter of the Count de Salmour, dated July 10, 1789, in the Archives of Dresden). The following passage from a letter of Dr. Rigby, which M. Flammermont gives as a note, p. clxxiii., says the same thing : " As night came on very few of the persons who had armed themselves the preceding evening were to be seen. Some, however, had refused to give up their arms, and proved in the course of the night how just were the suspicions of the inhabitants concerning them, for they began to plunder ; but it was too late to do it then with impunity. They were soon discovered and apprehended, and we were told the following morning that several of these unhappy wretches, who had been taken in the act, had been executed " (Dr. Rigby's Letters, pp. 56–57). On reading these pages we admit there is some truth in the testimony of Morellet, according to which, " on the night between the 13th and 14th some excesses were committed against persons and property."

were quite right to do so, because even if there were a few cases of pillaging, most of these " auxilliaries," understanding the seriousness of the situation, put their arms at the service of the general cause, much more than they used them to gratify their personal hatreds or to alleviate their own misery.

It is at any rate certain that cases of pillage were extremely rare. On the contrary, the spirit of the armed crowds became very serious when they learned about the engagement that had been entered into by the troops and the middle classes. The men with the pikes evidently looked upon themselves as the defenders of the town, upon whom a heavy responsibility rested. Marmontel, a declared enemy of the Revolution, nevertheless notices this interesting feature. " The thieves themselves, seized with the general terror [?], committed no depredations. The armourers' shops were the only ones broken open, and only arms were stolen," he says in his *Mémoires*. And when the people brought the carriage of the Prince de Lambesc to the Place de la Grève to burn it, they sent back the trunk and all the effects found in the carriage to the Hôtel de Ville. At the Lazarite Monastery the people refused money and took only the flour, arms and wine, which were all conveyed to the Place de la Grève. " Nothing was touched that day, either at the Treasury or at the Bank," remarks the English Ambassador in his account.

What is quite true is the fear felt by the middle classes at the sight of these men and women, ragged, pinched with hunger and armed with clubs and pikes " of all shapes." The terror inspired by these spectres of famine thronging the streets was such that the middle classes could not get over it. Later on, in 1791 and 1792, even those among them who wanted to put an end to Royalty preferred reaction rather than make a fresh appeal to the popular revolution. The memory of the famished people swarming in the streets of whom they had caught a glimpse on July 12, 13 and 14 haunted them.

" Arms ! " was the cry of the people after they had found a little bread. They sought everywhere for them, without finding any, while night and day in the faubourgs pikes of every kind were being forged from any iron that came to hand.

The middle classes, meanwhile, without losing a moment, were constituting their executive power in the municipality at the Hôtel de Ville, and their militia.

We know that the elections for the National Assembly took place in two degrees; but the elections over, the electors of the Third Estate, to whom were added some of the electors of the clergy and of the nobility, had continued to meet at the Hôtel de Ville, since June 27, with the authorisation of the Town Council and the " Ministers for Paris." Now these electors took the lead in organising the middle-class militia. We have already seen them holding their second sitting on July 1.

On July 12 they instituted a Permanent Committee, presided over by Flesselles, the Provost of the Merchants, and they decided that each of the sixty districts should choose two hundred well-known citizens, capable of bearing arms, which should form a body of militia numbering 12,000 men, to watch over the public safety. This militia was to be increased in four days to a total of 48,000 men; meanwhile the same Committee was trying to disarm the people.

In this way, Louis Blanc says very truly, the middle classes obtained for themselves a Pretorian Guard of 12,000 men and at the risk of supporting the Court they wanted to disarm the mass of the people.

Instead of the green badge of the earlier days, this militia had now to wear the red and blue cockade, and the Permanent Committee took measures to prevent the people, who were arming themselves, from invading the ranks of this militia. It was decreed that any one with arms and wearing the red and blue cockade, without having been registered in one of the districts, should be brought for judgment before the Committee. The general commandant of this National Guard had been nominated by the Permanent Committee on the night of July 13 and 14; he was a noble, the Duke d'Aumont. He would not accept the post, and another nobleman, the Marquis de la Salle, who had been nominated second in command, took his place.

In short, while the people were forging pikes and arming

themselves, while they were taking measures to prevent the ammunition from being sent out of Paris, while they were seizing the bread-stuffs and sending them to the Halles or to the Place de la Grève, while on the 14th they were constructing barricades to prevent the troops entering Paris, and had seized the arms at the Hôtel des Invalides and were marching in a body towards the Bastille to compel it to capitulate, the middle classes were mainly preoccupied in taking measures for keeping the newly acquired power entirely in their own hands. They constituted the middle-class Commune of Paris, which tried to restrain the popular movement, and at the head of this Commune they placed Flesselles, the Provost of the Merchants, who was corresponding with the Duchess de Polignac about checking the insurrection in Paris. We know, indeed, that on the 13th, when the people went to ask Flesselles for arms, he sent them boxes containing old linen instead of muskets, and the next day he used all his influence to prevent the people from taking the Bastille.

Thus began on the side of the adroit middle-class leaders the system of betraying the Revolution, which, as we shall see, developed so much during the next few years.

CHAPTER XII

THE TAKING OF THE BASTILLE

" A la Bastille ! "—Importance of Bastille—Popular hatred of prisons—Guns taken from Hôtel des Invalides—Deputations sent to de Launey—Attack on Bastille begins—Defenders fire on people—Another deputation sent—Firing continues—Cannon arrives for people—Garrison capitulates—Deaths of de Launey and Flesselles—First victory of people

FROM the dawn of July 14, the attention of the Paris insurrection was directed upon the Bastille, that gloomy fortress with its solid towers of formidable height which reared itself among the houses of a populous quarter at the entrance of the Faubourg Saint-Antoine. Historians are still inquiring how the thoughts of the people came to be turned in this direction, and some of them suggest that it was the Permanent Committee at the Hôtel de Ville, who wanted to furnish an objective for the insurrection in directing it against this emblem of royalty. There is nothing, however, to confirm this supposition, whilst several important facts contradict it. It is more probable that the popular instinct, which, ever since the 12th or 13th, understood that in the plans of the Court to crush the people of Paris the Bastille would play an important part, decided in consequence to get possession of it.

We know, indeed, that in the west the Court had Besenval camped with his thirty thousand men in the Champ-de-Mars, and that in the east it relied for support upon the towers of the Bastille, with their cannon trained on the revolutionary Faubourg Saint-Antoine and its principal thoroughfare, as well as on that other great artery, the Rue Saint-Antoine, which leads to the Hôtel de Ville, the Palais Royal and the Tuileries. The importance of the Bastille was, therefore, only too evident, and from the morning of the 14th, according to the *Deux amis de la liberté*, the words " *A la Bastille !* " flew from mouth to mouth from one end of the town to the other.*

It is true that the garrison of the Bastille numbered only one hundred and fourteen men, of whom eighty-four were pensioners and thirty Swiss, and that the Governor had done nothing towards victualling the place ; but this proves only that the possibility of a serious attack on the fortress had been regarded as absurd. The people, however, knew that the Royalist plotters counted on the fortress, and they learned from inhabitants of the quarter that ammunition had been transferred from the arsenal to the Bastille on the night between the 12th and 13th. They perceived, also, that the Governor, the Marquis de Launey, had already placed his cannon in position on the morning of the 14th, so that the people could be fired on if they massed themselves in the direction of the Hôtel de Ville.

It must also be said that the people had always detested prisons, such as the Bicêtre, the donjon of Vincennes and the Bastille. During the riots of 1783, when the nobility protested against arbitrary imprisonments, the minister Bréteuil decided to abolish incarceration at Vincennes. This famous donjon was then transformed into a granary, and to conciliate public opinion Bréteuil permitted visitors to inspect the terrible *oubliettes*. There was much talk, says Droz, about the horrors that were to be seen there, and of course it was also said that in the Bastille there were even worse things to be seen.†

In any case, it is certain that on the evening of the 13th some musket shots were being exchanged between the detachments of armed Parisians, who passed close to the fortress and its

---

* In several of the *cahiers* the electors had already demanded " that the Bastille be pulled down and destroyed "—Cahiers des Halles ; also those of Les Mathurins, Cordeliers, Sépulcre, &c., cited by Chassin (*Les élections et les cahiers de Paris*, vol. ii. p. 449 *et seq.*). The electors had cause for their demand, as, after the Réveillon affair, the order had been given to fortify the Bastille. Therefore, already on the night of June 30 there was some talk of seizing this fortress (*Récit de l'élargissement . . . des gardes françaises*, cited by Chassin. p. 452 note).

† Droz, *Histoire de Louis XVI.*, vol. i. p. 417.

defenders, and that on the 14th, from the earliest hours of the morning, the crowds, more or less armed, who had been moving about the streets all through the preceding night, began to assemble in the thoroughfares which led to the Bastille. Already during the night the rumour ran that the King's troops were advancing from the side of the Barrière du Trône, in the Faubourg Saint-Antoine, and the crowds moved off eastwards and barricaded the streets north-east of the Hôtel de Ville.

A successful attack on the Hôtel des Invalides gave the people an opportunity of arming themselves and provided them with some cannon. Since the previous day middle-class men, delegated by their districts, had been calling at the Hôtel des Invalides to ask for arms, saying that their houses were in danger of being plundered by the thieves, and Baron de Besenval, who commanded the royal troops in Paris, happening to be at the Invalides, promised to obtain authorisation for this from Marshal de Broglie. The authorisation had not yet arrived when, on the 14th, by seven o'clock in the morning—the pensioners, commanded by Sombreuil, being at their guns with match in hand ready to fire—a mob of seven or eight thousand men suddenly poured out of the three neighbouring streets at a quick pace. Helping one another, " in less than no time " they crossed the fosse, eight feet in depth and twelve feet wide, which surrounded the esplanade of the Hôtel des Invalides, swarmed over the esplanade and took possession of twelve pieces of cannon, 24-, 18- and 10-pounders, and one mortar. The garrison, already infected with a " seditious spirit," made no defence, and the mob, spreading everywhere, soon found their way into the cellars and the church, where they discovered 32,000 muskets concealed, as well as a certain quantity of powder.* These muskets and cannon were used the same day in the taking of the Bastille. As to the powder, on the previous day the people had already stopped thirty-six barrels which were being sent to Rouen ; these had been carried off to the Hôtel de Ville, and all night long powder had been distributed to the people, who were arming themselves.

* I here follow the letter of the Count de Salmour, as well as Mathieu Dumas, both quoted by M. Flammermont.

The removal of the guns by the mob from the Hôtel des Invalides was done very slowly. At two o'clock in the afternoon it was not yet completed. There would therefore have been quite enough time to bring up troops and disperse the people, especially as infantry, cavalry, and even artillery were stationed close by at the Military School and in the Champ-de-Mars. But the officers of these troops did not trust their soldiers ; and besides, they must themselves have hesitated when they were confronted with this innumerable multitude, composed of persons of every age and every condition, of which more than 200,000 had flooded the streets for the last two days. The people of the faubourgs, armed with a few muskets, pikes, hammers, axes, or even with simple cudgels, were moving about in the streets, thronging in crowds to the Place Louis XV. (now the Place de la Concorde) surrounding the Hôtel de Ville and the Bastille, and filling the thoroughfares between. The middle classes of Paris were themselves seized with terror on seeing these masses of armed men in the street.

Hearing that the approaches to the Bastille were invaded by the people, the Permanent Committee at the Hôtel de Ville, of which mention has been made, sent on the morning of the 14th some persons to parley with de Launey, the Governor of the fortress, to beg him to withdraw the cannon levelled on the streets, and not to commit any act hostile to the people ; in return, the Committee, usurping powers they did not possess, promised that the people " would not set on foot any vexatious proceedings against the place." The delegates were received very affably by the Governor, and even stayed to breakfast with him until nearly midday. De Launey was probably trying to gain time while waiting for definite orders from Versailles, which did not come, as they had been intercepted in the morning by the people. Like all the other military chiefs, de Launey must have realised that it would be difficult for him to stand against the whole people of Paris assembled in the streets, and so he temporised. For the time being he ordered the cannon to be drawn back four feet and closed the embrasures with wooden planks, so that the people should not see through them.

About midday the district of Saint-Louis-la-Culture on its own account sent two delegates to speak in its name to the Governor; one of them, the advocate Thuriot de la Rosière, obtained from the Marquis de Launey the promise that he would not give the order to fire if he was not attacked. Two more deputations were sent to the Governor by the Permanent Committee at one and three o'clock; but they were not received. Both of them demanded of the Governor the surrender of the fortress to a body of the middle-class militia, which would guard it jointly with the soldiers and the Swiss.

Luckily, all these compromises were baffled by the people, who understood that the Bastille must be captured, cost what it might. Being in possession of the muskets and the cannon from the Hôtel des Invalides, their enthusiasm was steadily increasing.

The mob thronged the streets adjacent to the Bastille, as well as the different courtyards which surrounded the fortress itself. Presently a fusillade began between the people and the soldiers posted on the ramparts. Whilst the Permanent Committee were striving to allay the ardour of the assailants and making arrangements for proclaiming at the Place de la Grève that de Launey had promised not to fire if they refrained from attacking him, the crowds, shouting "We want the Bastille! Down with the bridges!" rushed towards the fortress. It is said that on seeing from the top of the walls the whole Faubourg Saint-Antoine and the street leading to it quite black with people marching against the Bastille, the Governor, who had ascended thither with Thuriot, almost swooned. It appears even that he was on the point of surrendering the fortress immediately to the Committee of Militia, but that the Swiss opposed it.*

The first drawbridges of that exterior part of the Bastille which was called the Forecourt (*l'Avancée*) were soon battered down, thanks to one of those audacious deeds of some few persons who are always forthcoming at such moments. Eight or ten men, with the help of a tall, strong fellow, Pannetier, a grocer, took advantage of a house that was built against the

* Letter of De Hue to his brothers, German text, quoted by Flammermont, p. cxcviii. note.

exterior wall of the Forecourt to climb this wall, astride of which they moved along as far as a guard-house standing close to the little drawbridge of the Forecourt, and thence they leaped into the first court of the Bastille proper, the Government Court in which was the Governor's house. This court was unoccupied, the soldiers having retreated with de Launey into the fortress itself, after the departure of Thuriot.

The eight or ten men, having dropped into this courtyard, with a few blows of an axe lowered first the little draw-bridge of the Forecourt and opened its gate, and after-wards the larger one. More than three hundred men then rushed into the Government Court, and ran to the other two drawbridges, the greater and the lesser, which, when lowered, served to cross the wide fosse of the actual fortress. These two bridges, of course, had been raised.

Here took place the incident which wrought the fury of the people of Paris to its full pitch, and afterwards cost de Launey his life. When the crowd thronged into the Government Court, the defenders of the Bastille began to fire upon them, and there was even an attempt to raise the great drawbridge of the Forecourt, so as to prevent the crowd from leaving the Government Court and obviously with the intention of either imprisoning or massacring them.* Thus, at the very moment when Thuriot and Corny were announcing to the people in the Place de la Grève that the Governor had promised not to fire, the Government Court was being swept by the musketry of the soldiers posted upon the ramparts, and the guns of the Bastille began to hurl cannon-balls into the adjoin-ing streets. After all the parleying which had taken place that morning, this opening fire upon the people was evidently inter-preted as an act of treason on the part of De Launay, whom the people accused of having lowered the two first drawbridges

---

* This attempt was made, it is now said, not by order of de Launey, but spontaneously by some soldiers, who had gone out to buy pro-visions and were returning. A highly improbable thing, it seems to me, for three or four soldiers to attempt, isolated as they were, in the midst of that crowd. Besides, what would have been the good of imprisoning the crowd if it was not intended to use the prisoners as hostages against the people?

of the Forecourt, for the purpose of drawing the mob under the fire from the ramparts.*

It was then about one o'clock. The news that the cannon of the Bastille were firing on the people spread through Paris and produced a two-fold effect. The Permanent Committee of the Paris militia hastened to send another deputation to the Commandant, to ask him if he would receive there a detachment of militia who would guard the Bastille jointly with the troops. But this deputation never reached the Commandant, for a close fusillade was going on all the time between the soldiers and their assailants, who, crouched along some of the walls, were firing at the soldiers serving the guns. Besides, the people knew that the deputations from the Committee would only throw cold water on the attack. " It is no longer a deputation they want ; it is the siege of the Bastille ; it is the destruction of this horrible prison ; it is the death of the Governor for which they are loudly clamouring "—reported the deputies when they returned.

This did not prevent the Committee at the Hôtel de Ville from sending a third deputation. M. Ethis de Corny, Procureur of the King and of the town, and several citizens were charged once more to allay the people's ardour, to check the assault, and to parley with de Launey, for the purpose of persuading him to receive a guard from the Committee into the fortress. The intention of preventing the people taking possession of the Bastille was evident.†

---

* Various explanations have been given of this sudden opening of hostilities. As the people who had thronged into the Court de l'Orme and the Government Court began to plunder the Commandant's house and those of the soldiers' quarters, it was said that this had decided the defenders of the Bastille to open fire. For the military, however, the taking of the Forecourt by assault, which gave the people access to the drawbridges of the fortress and even to the gates, was quite sufficient reason. But it is also possible that the order to defend the Bastille to the last was at that moment transmitted to de Launey. We know that one order was intercepted, which does not prove that no other was delivered. It is, in fact, supposed that de Launey had received this order.

† " They were charged to induce all persons found near the Bastille *to withdraw to their respective districts in order that they might there be at once admitted into the Paris militia ;* to remind de Launey of the promises he had made to M. Thuriot de la Rozière and to M. Bellon . . ."

As to the people, as soon as the news of the firing spread through the town, they acted without any one's orders, guided by their revolutionary instinct. They dragged the cannon which they had taken from the Hôtel des Invalides to the Hôtel de Ville, and about three o'clock, when Corny's deputation was returning to report their failure, they met about three hundred French Guards, and a number of armed men belonging to the middle class under the command of an old soldier named Hulin, marching to the Bastille, followed by five pieces of artillery. The firing by this time had been going on for more than three hours. The people, not in the least dismayed by the great number killed and wounded,* were maintaining the siege by resorting to various expedients. One of these was the bringing up of two cartloads of straw, to which they set fire, using the smoke as a screen to facilitate their attack on the two entrances, the greater and lesser drawbridges. The buildings of the Government Court were already in flames.

The cannon arrived just at the moment they were wanted. They were drawn into the Government Court and planted in front of the drawbridges and gates at a distance of only 90 feet.

It is easy to imagine the effect that these cannon in the hands of the people must have produced on the besieged. It was evident that the drawbridges must soon go down, and that the gates would be burst open. The mob became still more threatening and was continually increasing in numbers.

The moment soon came when the defenders realised that to resist any longer was to doom themselves to certain destruction. de Launey decided to capitulate. The soldiers, seeing that

(Flammermont, *loc. cit.*, p. clviii.). Having entered the Forecourt, which was full of people armed with muskets, axes, &c., the deputation spoke to the soldiers on the walls. These latter demanded that the people should first withdraw from the Government Court, whereupon the deputation tried to induce the people to do so (*cf.* Boucheron, cited by Flammermont, p. ccxiv. note). Fortunately the people were wise enough not to comply with their wishes. They continued the assault. They understood so well that it was no longer any time for parleying, that they treated the gentlemen of the deputation rather badly, and even talked of killing them as traitors (*loc. cit.*, p. ccxvi. note, and *Procès-verbal des électeurs*).

* Eighty-three killed on the spot, fifteen dead of their wounds, thirteen disabled and sixty injured.

they would never get the better of the whole of Paris which was
coming to besiege them, had some time before advised capitulation, and so about four o'clock, or between four and five, the
Governor ordered the white flag to be hoisted and the drums
to beat the *chamade* (the order to cease fire), and descend from
the battlements.

The garrison capitulated and demanded the right of marching out with their arms. It may be that Hulin and Elie, standing close to the great drawbridge, would have agreed to these
terms in the name of the people; but the people would have
none of them. A furious cry of " Down with the bridges ! "
was raised. At five o'clock, therefore, the Commandant passed
out through one of the loopholes near the lesser drawbridge a
note in which it was said, " We have twenty-thousand-weight
of gunpowder; we shall blow up the whole quarter, with the
garrison, if you do not accept the terms of capitulation."
However, even if de Launey thought of so doing, the garrison
would never have permitted him to put this threat into effect.
At any rate, the fact is that de Launey himself gave up the key
that opened the entrance of the lesser drawbridge.

Immediately, the mass of the besiegers took possession of the
fortress. They disarmed the Swiss and the Invalides, and
seized de Launey, who was dragged towards the Hôtel de Ville.
On the way the mob, furious at his treachery, heaped every
kind of insult on him ; twenty times he was nearly killed, despite
the heroic efforts of Cholat and another.* These two men
protected him with their own bodies, but, when only a hundred
steps from the Hôtel de Ville, he was dragged out of their hands
and decapitated. De Hue, the Commandant of the Swiss,
saved his life by declaring that he was devoted to the Town and
the Nation, and by drinking to them, but three officers of the
Bastille staff and three soldiers were slain. As to Flesselles,
the Provost of the Merchants, who was in correspondence with
Besenval and the Duchess de Polignac, and who had, as
appears by a passage in one of his letters, many other secrets to
hide that were very compromising for the Queen, the people

* Was not this other Maillard ? We know that it was he who
arrested de Launey.

were about to execute him when an unknown man shot him dead. Did this unknown man think that dead men tell no tales ?

As soon as the bridges of the Bastille had been lowered the crowd rushed into the courtyards and began to search the fortress and free the prisoners entombed in the *oubliettes*. There was great emotion, and tears were shed at the sight of the phantoms who issued from their cells, bewildered by the light of the sun and by the sound of the many voices that welcomed them. These poor martyrs of royal despotism were carried in triumph by the people through the streets of Paris. The whole town was soon delirious with joy on hearing that the Bastille was in the hands of the people, and their determination to keep their conquest was redoubled. The *coup d'état* of the Court had failed.

In this way the Revolution began. The people had won their first victory. A material victory of this kind was essential. It was necessary that the Revolution should endure a struggle and come out from it triumphant. Some proof of the strength of the people had to be given, so as to impress their enemies, to arouse courage throughout France, and to push forward everywhere towards revolt, towards the conquest of liberty.

CHAPTER XIII

THE CONSEQUENCES OF JULY 14 AT VERSAILLES

Fête at Versailles—State of Court—Conduct of people—
Middle classes—King visits Paris—His plans of armed resistance come to nothing—Insurrection in Paris spreads—Emigration of nobles—Foulon and others put to death

WHEN a revolution has once begun, each event in it not merely
sums up the events hitherto accomplished ; it also contains
the chief elements of what is to come ; so that the contemporaries of the French Revolution, if they could only have
freed themselves from the momentary impressions, and separated
the essential from the accidental, might have been able, on the
morrow of July 14, to foresee whither events as a whole were
thenceforth trending.

But even on the evening of the 13th, the Court attached no
importance to the movement in Paris.

That evening there was a *fête* at Versailles. There was
dancing in the Orangery, and glasses were filled to drink to the
coming victory over the rebellious capital ; and the Queen,
her friend the Duchess de Polignac and the rest of the Court
beauties, with the princes and princesses, were lavishing
favours on the foreign soldiers in their barracks to stimulate
them for the coming fight.* In their madness and terrible
frivolity, no one in that world of shams and conventional lies,
which constitute every Court, perceived that it was too late to
attack Paris, that the opportunity for doing so was lost. And

---

* Mirabeau, in his speech before the Assembly, which resumed its
sitting on the 15th at eight o'clock in the morning, spoke as if this
fête had taken place the day before. He was alluding, however, to
the *fête* of the 13th.

Louis XVI. was no better informed on the matter than the Queen and the princes. When the Assembly, alarmed by the people's rising, hurried to him on the evening of the 14th, to beg him in servile language to recall the ministers and send away the troops, he replied to them in the language of a master certain of victory. He believed in the plan that had been suggested to him of putting some reliable officers at the head of the middle-class militia and crushing the people with their help, after which he would content himself with sending some equivocal orders about the retirement of the troops. Such was that world of shams, of dreams more than of reality, in which both King and Court lived, and in which, in spite of brief intervals of awakening, they continued to live up to the moment of ascending the steps of the scaffold.

How clearly they were revealing their characters even then ! The King hypnotised by his absolute power, and always ready on account of it to take exactly the step which was to lead him to the catastrophe. Then he would oppose to events inertia— nothing but inertia, and finally yield, for form's sake, just at the moment when he was expected to resist obstinately. The Queen, too, corrupt, depraved to the very heart as absolute sovereign, hastening the catastrophe by her petulant resistance, and then suddenly yielding the next moment, only to resume, an instant after, the childish tricks of a courtesan. And the princes ? Instigators of all the most fatal resolutions taken by the King, and cowards at the very first failures of them, they left the country, flying immediately after the taking of the Bastille to resume their plottings in Germany or Italy. How clearly all these traits of character were revealed in those few days between July 8 and 15.

On the opposite side we see the people, filled with ardour, enthusiasm and generosity, ready to let themselves be massacred that Liberty might triumph, but at the same time asking to be led ; ready to allow themselves to be governed by the new masters, who had just installed themselves in the Hôtel de Ville. Understanding so well the Court schemes, and seeing with the utmost clearness through the plot which had been growing into shape ever since the end of June, they allowed themselves to be entangled in the new plot—the plot of the propertied classes, who were soon to thrust back into their slums the hungry people, " the men with the pikes " to whom they had appealed for a few hours, when it was necessary to set the force of popular insurrection against that of the army.

And finally, when we consider the conduct of the middle classes during these early days, we see already foreshadowed the great dramas of the Revolution which were to come. On the 14th, in proportion as Royalty gradually lost its menacing character, it was the people who, in a corresponding degree, inspired terror in the representatives of the Third Estate assembled at Versailles. In spite of the vehement words uttered by Mirabeau concerning the *fête* at the Orangery, the King had only to present himself before the Assembly, recognise the authority of the delegates, and promise them inviolability, for the whole of the representatives to burst into applause and transports of joy. They even ran out to form a guard of honour round him in the streets, and made the streets of Versailles resound with cries of " *Vive le Roi !* " And this at the very moment when the people were being massacred in Paris in the name of this same King, and while at Versailles the crowd was insulting the Queen and the Duchess de Polignac, and the people were asking themselves if the King was not at one of his old tricks.

In Paris the people were not deceived by the promise to withdraw the troops. They did not believe a word of it. They preferred to organise themselves in a huge insurgent commune, and this commune, like a commune of the Middle Ages, took all the necessary measures of defence against the King. The streets were torn up in trenches and barricades, and the people's patrols marched through the town, ready to sound the tocsin at the first alarm.

Nor did the King's visit to Paris greatly reassure the people. Seeing himself defeated and abandoned, he decided to go to Paris, and to the Hôtel de Ville, to be reconciled with his capital, and the middle classes tried to turn this visit into a striking act of reconciliation between themselves and the King. The middle-class revolutionaries, of whom very many belonged to the Freemasons, made an " arch of steel " with their swords for the King on his arrival at the Hôtel de Ville ; and Bailly, elected Mayor of Paris, fastened in the King's hat the tricolour cockade. There was talk even of erecting a statue to Louis XVI. on the site of the demolished Bastille, but the mass of the people preserved an attitude of reserve and mistrust, which were not dispelled even after the visit to the Hôtel de Ville. King of the middle classes as much as they liked, but not a King of the people.

The Court, for its part, knew very well that after the insurrection of July 14 there would never be peace between royalty and the people. They induced the Duchess de Polignac to leave for Switzerland, despite the tears of Marie-Antoinette, and the following day the princes began to emigrate. Those who had been the life and soul of the defeated *coup d'état* made haste to leave France. The Count d'Artois escaped in the night, and so much was he in fear for his life that, after stealing secretly through the town, he took a regiment and two cannon for escort the rest of the way. The King promised to rejoin his dear emigrants at the first opportunity, and began to make plans of escaping abroad, in order to re-enter France at the head of an army.

In fact, on July 16, all was ready for his departure. He was to go to Metz, place himself at the head of the troops, and march on Paris. The horses were already put to the carriage which were to convey Louis XVI. to the army, then concentrated between Versailles and the frontier. But de Broglie refused to escort the King to Metz, and the princes were in too great a hurry to be off, so that the King, as he said himself afterwards, seeing himself abandoned by the princes and the nobles, relinquished his project of an armed resistance, which the history of Charles I. had suggested to him, and went to Paris to make his submission instead.

Some Royalist historians have tried to cast a doubt on the preparation by the Court of a *coup d'état* against the Assembly and Paris. But there are plenty of documents to prove the reality of the plot. Mignet, whose moderation is well known, and who had the advantage of writing soon after the events, had not the slightest doubt on this point, and later researches have confirmed his position. On July 13, the King was to have revived the declaration of June 23, and the Assembly was to have been dissolved. Forty thousand copies of this declaration were already printed for sending throughout France. The commander of the army massed between Versailles and Paris had been given unlimited powers for the massacre of the people of Paris and for extreme measures against the Assembly in case of resistance.

A hundred million of State notes had been manufactured to provide for the needs of the Court. Everything was ready, and when they heard that Paris had risen, the Court considered this rising as an outbreak which aided their plans. A little later on, when it was known that the insurrection was spreading, the King was still on the point of setting out and leaving to his ministers the task of dispersing the Assembly with the help of foreign troops. It was the ministers who dared not put this plan into execution when they saw the tide rising. This is why so great a panic seized the Court after July 14, when they heard of the taking of the Bastille and the execution of de Launey, and why the Duchess de Polignac, the princes, and so many other nobles, who had been the leading spirits of the plot, afraid of being denounced, had to emigrate in a hurry.

But the people were on the alert. They vaguely understood what the emigrants were going to seek on the other side of the frontier, and the peasants arrested the fugitives, among whom were Foulon and Berthier.

We have already made mention of the misery which reigned in Paris and the environs, and of the monopolists, into whose crimes the Assembly refused to inquire too closely. The chief of these speculators in the people's misery was said to be Foulon, who had made an immense fortune as financier and in his position as contractor for the army and navy. His detestation of the people and the revolution was also well known. Broglie wanted him to be minister when he was preparing the *coup d'état* for July 16, and if the crafty financier refused this post, he had not been sparing of his counsel. His advice was to get rid, at one blow, of all those who had acquired influence in the revolutionary camp.

After the taking of the Bastille, when he learned how de Launey's head had been carried through the streets, he knew that it was best for him to follow the princes and emigrate; but as this was not an easy thing to do, owing to the watchfulness of the District Commune, he took advantage of the death of one of his servants to pretend that he was dead and buried, while he quitted Paris and took refuge in a friend's house at Fontaine-bleau.

There he was discovered and arrested by the peasants, who avenged their long endurance of misery upon him. With a bundle of grass tied on his shoulders, in allusion to the grass he had promised to make the people of Paris eat, the wretched monopolist was dragged to Paris by an infuriated crowd. At the Hôtel de Ville Lafayette tried to save him, but the angry people hanged him on a lamp-iron.

His son-in-law, Berthier, equally guilty in the *coup d'état*, and contractor for the Duke de Broglie's army, was arrested at Compiègne and also dragged to Paris, where they were going to hang him likewise, but, struggling to save himself, he was over-powered and trampled to death.

Other guilty individuals who were on the way to foreign lands were arrested in the north and north-east and brought back to Paris.

The terror excited in the breasts of the Court's familiar friends by these executions on the people's side can easily be imagined. Their pride and their resistance to the Revolution were shattered; they wished only to be forgotten.

CHAPTER XIV

THE POPULAR RISINGS

Necessity of popular risings outside Paris—Effect of taking of Bastille over-estimated—Difference between French and English peasant risings—Importance of peasant insurrection

PARIS, by frustrating the plans of the Court, had struck a mortal blow at royal authority. Besides this, the appearance in the streets of people in rags, as an active force in the Revolution, was giving a new character, a new tendency of equality to the whole movement. The rich and powerful understood perfectly the meaning of what had been going on in Paris during those days, and the emigration, first of the princes, then of the favourites and the monopolists, accentuated the victory. The Court was already seeking the aid of the foreigner against revolutionary France.

If, however, the insurrection had been confined to the capital, the Revolution could never have developed to the extent of resulting in the demolition of ancient privileges. The insurrection at the centre had been necessary to strike at the central Government, to shake it down, to demoralise its defenders. But to destroy the power of the Government in the provinces, to strike at the old *régime* through its governmental prerogatives and its economic privileges, a widespread rising of the people was necessary in cities, towns and villages. This is exactly what came about in the course of July throughout the length and breadth of France.

The historians, who all, whether consciously or not, have followed very closely the *Deux amis de la liberté*, have generally represented this movement of the towns and rural districts as a result of the taking of the Bastille. The news of this success is supposed to have roused the country parts. The châteaux were burned, and this rising of the peasants diffused so much terror that the nobles and clergy abdicated their feudal rights on August 4.

This version is, however, only half true. As far as the towns are concerned, it is correct that a great number of urban risings took place under the influence of the taking of the Bastille. Some of them, as at Troyes on July 18, at Strasbourg on the 19th, at Cherbourg on the 21st, at Rouen on the 24th, and at Maubeuge on the 27th, followed close upon the Paris insurrection, whilst the others went on during the next three or four months, until the National Assembly had voted the municipal law of December 14, 1789, which legalised the constitution of a democratic middle-class municipal government to a considerable extent independent of the Central Government.

With regard to the peasants, it is clear that with the then existing slowness of communications, the space of twenty days which passed between July 14 and August 4 are absolutely insufficient to account for the effect of the taking of the Bastille on the rural districts and the subsequent effect of the peasants' insurrection on the decisions of the National Assembly. In fact, to picture events in such a fashion is to belittle the profound importance of the movement in the country.

The insurrection of the peasants for the abolition of the feudal rights and the recovery of the communal lands which had been taken away from the village communes, since the seventeenth century, by the lords, lay and ecclesiastical, is the very essence, the foundation of the great Revolution. Upon it the struggle of the middle classes for their political rights was developed. Without it the Revolution would never have been so thorough as it was in France. The great rising of the rural districts which began after the January of 1789, even in 1788, and *lasted five years*, was what enabled the Revolution to accomplish the immense work of demolition which we owe to it. It was this that impelled the Revolution to set up the first landmarks of a system of equality, to develop in France the republican spirit, which since then nothing has been able to suppress, to proclaim the great principles of agrarian communism, that we shall see emerging in 1793. This rising, in fact, is what gives the true character to the French Revolution, and distinguishes it radically from the Revolution of 1648–1657 in England.

There, too, in the course of those nine years, the middle classes broke down the absolute power of royalty and the political privileges of the Court party. But beyond that, the distinctive features of the English revolution was the struggle for the right of each individual to profess whatever religion he pleased, to interpret the Bible according to his personal conception of it, to choose his own pastors—in a word, the right of the individual to the intellectual and religious development best suited to him. Further, it claimed the right of each parish, and, as a consequence, of the townships, to autonomy. But the peasant risings in England did not aim so generally, as in France, at the abolishing of feudal dues and tithes, or the recovery of the communal lands. And if Cromwell's hosts demolished a certain number of castles which represented true strongholds of feudalism, these hosts unfortunately did not attack either the feudal pretensions of the lords over the land, or even the right of feudal justice, which the lords exercised over their tenants. What the English revolution did was to conquer some precious rights for the individual, but it did not destroy the feudal power of the lord, it merely modified it whilst preserving his rights over the land, rights which persist to this day.

The English revolution undoubtedly established the political power of the middle classes, but this power was only obtained by sharing it with the landed aristocracy. And if the revolution gave the English middle classes a prosperous era for their trade and commerce, this prosperity was obtained on the condition that the middle classes should not profit by it to attack the landed privileges of the nobility. On the contrary, the middle classes helped to increase these privileges, at least in value. They helped the nobility to take legal possession of the communal lands by means of the Enclosure

Acts, which reduced the agricultural population to misery, placed them at the mercy of the landowners, and forced a great number of them to migrate to the towns, where, as proletarians, they were delivered over to the mercy of the middle-class manufacturers. The English middle classes also helped the nobility to make of their immense landed estates sources, not only of revenue often fabulous, but also of political and local juridical power, by re-establishing under new forms the right of manorial justice. They helped also to increase their revenues tenfold by allowing them through the land laws, which hamper the sale of estates, to monopolise the land, the need of which was making itself felt more and more among a population whose trade and commerce were steadily increasing.

We now know that the French middle classes, especially the upper middle classes engaged in manufactures and commerce, wished to imitate the English middle classes in their revolution. They, too, would have willingly entered into a compact with both royalty and nobility in order to attain to power. But they did not succeed in this, because the basis of the French Revolution was fortunately much broader than that of the revolution in England. In France the movement was not merely an insurrection to win religious liberty, or even commercial and industrial liberty for the individual, or yet to constitute municipal authority in the hands of a few middle-class men. It was above all a *peasant* insurrection, a movement of the people to regain possession of the land and to free it from the feudal obligations which burdened it, and while there was all through it a powerful individualist element —the desire to possess land individually—there was also the communist element, the right of the whole nation to the land—a right which we shall see proclaimed loudly by the poorer classes in 1793.

This is why it would be a strange reduction of the importance of the agrarian insurrection in the summer of 1789 to represent it as an episode of brief duration brought about by enthusiasm over the taking of the Bastille.

CHAPTER XV

THE TOWNS

Condition of municipal institutions—Feudal rights still exist —Need of municipal reform—Townspeople revolt—New municipality voted—Importance of communalist movement— Paris Commune—Other cities follow—Troubles at Strasbourg —New corporation constituted—Middle classes freed from feudalism—Riots in Troyes, Amiens and other cities—Significance of popular action during Revolution

In the eighteenth century the municipal institutions had fallen to utter decay, owing to the numerous measures taken by royal authority against them for two hundred years.

Since the abolition of the plenary assembly of the townspeople, which formerly had the control of urban justice and administration, the affairs of the large cities were going from bad to worse. The posts of "town councillors" introduced in the eighteenth century had to be bought from the commune, and, often enough, the patent so purchased was for life.* The councils met seldom, in some towns about once in six months, and even then the attendance was not regular. The registrar managed the whole business, and as a rule did not fail to make those interested in it pay him handsomely. The attorneys and advocates, and still more the governor of the province, continually interfered to obstruct all municipal autonomy.

Under these conditions the affairs of the city fell more and more into the hands of five or six families, who shared a good deal of the revenues among themselves. The patrimonial revenues which some towns had retained, the proceeds of the *octrois*, the city's trade and the taxes all went to enrich them.

* Babeau, *La ville sous l'ancien régime*, p. 153 *et seq.*

Besides this, mayors and officials began to trade in corn and meat, and soon became monopolists. As a rule, the working population hated them. The servility of the officials, councillors and aldermen towards " Monsieur l'Intendant " (the Governor) was such that his whim became law. And the contributions from the town towards the governor's lodging, towards increasing his salary, to make him presents, for the honour of holding his children at the baptismal font, and so forth, went on growing larger—not to mention the presents which had to be sent every year to various personages in Paris.

In the towns, as in the country, the feudal rights still existed. They were attached to property. The bishop was still a feudal lord, and the lords, both lay and ecclesiastical—such, for instance, as the fifty canons of Brioude—maintained not only honorary rights, or even the right of intervening in the nomination of aldermen, but also, in some towns, the right of administering justice. At Angers there were sixteen manorial tribunals. Dijon had preserved, besides the municipal tribunals, six ecclesiastical courts—" the bishopric, the chapter, the monks of Saint-Bénigne, La Sainte-Chapelle, La Chartreuse and the commandery of La Madeleine." All of these were waxing fat in the midst of the half-starved people. Troyes had nine of these tribunals, beside " two royal mayoral courts." So that the police did not always belong to the towns, but to those who administered " justice." In short, it was the feudal system in full swing.[*]

But what chiefly excited the anger of the citizens was that all kinds of feudal taxes, the poll tax, the twentieths, often the *taille* and the "voluntary gifts" (imposed in 1758 and abolished only in 1789), as well as the *lods et ventes* (which were the dues levied by the lord on all sales and purchases made by his vassals), weighed heavily upon the homes of the citizens, and especially on those of the working classes. Not so heavily, perhaps, as in the country, but still very eavily when added to all the other urban taxes.

---

* *Vide* Babeau, *La Ville*, pp. 323, 331, &c. Rodolphe Reuss, *L'Alsace pendant la Révolution*, vol. i., gives the *cahier* of the Strasbourg Third Estate, very interesting in this connection.

What made these dues more detestable was that when the town was making the assessment hundreds of privileged persons claimed exemption. The clergy, the nobles and officers in the army were exempt by law, as well as the " officers of the King's household," " honorary equerries," and others who paid for those offices without service, to flatter their own vanity and to escape from the taxes. An indication of their titles inscribed over the door was enough to excuse their paying anything to the town. One can readily imagine the hatred that these privileged persons inspired in the people.

The entire municipal system had, therefore, to be reformed. But who can tell how many years it would have lasted yet, if the task of reforming it had been left to the Constituent Assembly. Happily enough, the people undertook to do it themselves, the more so that during the summer of 1789 a fresh cause of discontent was added to all those which have just been enumerated. This cause was the famine—the exorbitant price of bread, for lack of which bread the poorer classes were suffering in most of the towns. Even in those places where the municipality did its best to lower the price of it by purchasing corn, or by proclaiming a fixed price, bread was always scarce, and the hungry people formed in long queues outside the bakers' doors.

But in many of the towns the mayor and the aldermen followed the example of the Court and the princes, and speculated themselves in the dearth. This is why, after the news of the taking of the Bastille, as well as of the executions of Foulon and Berthier, had spread into the provinces, the townspeople began to revolt more or less everywhere. First, they exacted a fixed price on bread and meat ; they destroyed the houses of the principal monopolists, often of the municipal officials ; they took possession of the Town Hall and nominated by election on the popular vote a new municipality, without heeding the limitations fixed by law or the legal rights of the old municipal body, or yet the offices purchased by the " councillors." A movement of the highest revolutionary importance was thus set on foot, for the town affirmed, not only its autonomy, but also its determination to take an active part in the general government of the nation. It was, as Aulard has aptly remarked, a communalist movement of the very greatest importance,* in which the province imitated Paris, where, as we have seen, the Commune had been established on July 13. It is evident that this movement was far from being general. It displayed itself clearly only in a certain number of cities and small towns, chiefly in the east of France. But everywhere the old municipality of the ancient *régime* had to submit to the will of the people, or, at least, to the will of the electorate in the local assemblies.

Thus was accomplished, at the outset, in July and August, the great Communalist Revolution, which the Constituent Assembly legalised later on by the municipal laws of December 14, 1789, and June 21, 1790. Obviously this movement gave the Revolution a powerful access of life and vigour. The whole strength of the Revolution concentrated, as we shall see, in 1792 and 1793, in the municipalities of the towns and villages, of which the revolutionary Commune of Paris was the prototype.

The signal for this reconstruction came from Paris. Without waiting for the municipal law, which some day would be voted by the Assembly, Paris gave herself a Commune. Her Municipal Council, her Mayor (Bailly), and the Commander of her National Guard (Lafayette) were elected. Better still, her sixty districts were organised—" sixty republics," as Montjoie happily terms them : for if these districts did delegate authority to the assembled representatives of the Commune and to the Mayor, they at the same time retained some of it. " Authority is everything," said Bailly, " and there is none at the centre." " Each district is an independent power," declare with regret the friends of the rule and compass, without understanding that this is how revolutions are made.

While the National Assembly had to struggle against its own dissolution, and had its hands full of so many things, when could it have been able to enter on the discussion of a law concerning the reorganisation of the Courts of Justice ? It hardly got as far as that at the end of ten months of its existence.

* Aulard, *Histoire politique de la Révolution française*, 2nd edition, 1903.

But " the district of the Petits-Augustins decided on its own account," says Bailly, in his *Mémoires*, " that justices of the peace should be established."   And the district proceeded then and there to elect them.   Other districts and other cities, Strasbourg especially, did the same, and when the night of August 4 arrived and the nobility had to abdicate their rights of seigneurial justice, they had lost it already in several towns, where new judges had been appointed by the people.   The Constituent Assembly had thus nothing else to do but incorporate the accomplished fact in the Constitution of 1791.

Taine and all the admirers of the administrative order of the somnolent ministers are shocked no doubt at the thought of these districts forestalling the Assembly by their votes and pointing out to it the will of the people by their decisions ; but it is in this way human institutions develop when they are not the product of bureaucracy.   In this way all the great cities were built up ; we can see them still being thus built. Here a group of houses and a few shops beside them ; this will be an important point in the future city ; there a track, as yet scarcely discernible, and that one day will be one of its great streets.   This is the " anarchic " evolution, the only way pertaining to free Nature.   It is the same even with institutions when they are the organic product of life, and this is why revolutions have such immense importance in the life of societies.   They allow men to start with the organic reconstructive work without being hampered by an authority which, perforce, always represents the past ages.

Let us therefore glance at some of these communal revolutions.

In 1789 news spread with what would seem to us almost inconceivable slowness.   Thus at Château-Thierry on July 12, and at Besançon on the 27th, Arthur Young did not find a single *café* or a single newspaper.   The news that was being talked about was a fortnight old.   At Dijon, nine days after the great rising in Strasbourg and the taking of the Town Hall by the insurgents, no one knew anything about it.   Still the news that was coming from Paris, even when it came in the form of legend, could not but stimulate the people to rise.

All the deputies, it was said, had been put in the Bastille ; and as to the "atrocities" committed by Marie-Antoinette, every one was discussing them with perfect assurance.

At Strasbourg the troubles began on July 19, as soon as the news of the taking of the Bastille and the execution of de Launey spread through the town. The people had already a grudge against the municipal council for their slowness in communicating to the people's "representatives"—that is, to the electors—the results of their deliberations over the *cahier de doléances*, the "writ of grievances," drawn up by the poorer classes. The people, therefore, attacked the house of Lemp, the Mayor (or *Ammeister*), and destroyed it.

Through the organ of its "Assembly of Burgesses" the people demanded measures—I quote from the text—"for assuring the political equality of the citizens, and their influence in the elections of the administrators of the public property and of the freely elected judges freely eligible." *

They insisted upon no notice being taken of the existing law, and upon electing by universal suffrage a new town council, as well as all the judges. The Magistracy, or Municipal Government, on its side had no great wish to do this, "and opposed the observance of several centuries to the proposed change." Whereupon the people gathered to besiege the Town Hall, and a storm of stones began to fall in the apartment where negotiations were taking place between the Magistracy and the revolutionary representatives, and to this argument the Magistracy at once yielded.

Meanwhile, seeing poor and starving persons assembling in the streets, the well-to-do middle classes armed themselves against the people, and going to the house of Count Rochambeau, the governor of the province, they asked his permission for the respectable citizens to carry arms, and to form themselves into a police, jointly with the troops, a request which the officer in command, "imbued with aristocratic ideas," unhesitatingly refused, as de Launey had done at the Bastille.

---

* *Lettre des représentants de la bourgeoisie aux députés de Strasbourg à Versailles,* July 28, 1789 (R. Reuss, *L'Alsace pendant la Révolution française,* Paris, 1881, "Documents," xxvi).

The next day, a rumour having spread in the town that the Magistracy had revoked their concessions, the people went again to attack the Town Hall, demanding the abolition of the town-dues and subsidies (*octrois* and *bureaux des aides*). Since this had been done in Paris, it could very well be done in Strasbourg. About six o'clock masses of " workmen, armed with axes and hammers," advanced from three streets towards the Town Hall. They smashed open the doors with their hatchets, broke into the vaults, and in their fury destroyed all the old papers accumulated in the offices. " They have wreaked a blind rage upon the papers : they have been all thrown out of the windows and dest~oyed," wrote the new Magistracy. The double doors of all the archives were forced open in order to burn the old documents, and in their hatred of the Magistracy the people even broke the furniture of the Town Hall and threw it out into the streets. The Record Office, " the depôt of estates in litigation," met with the same fate. At the tax-collector's office the doors were broken open and the receipts carried off. The troops stationed in front of the Town Hall could do nothing ; the people did as they liked.

The Magistracy, seized with terror, hurriedly lowered the prices of meat and bread : they fixed the six-pound loaf at twelve sous.* Then they opened amicable negotiations with the twenty *tribus* (or guilds) of the city for the elaboration of a new municipal constitution. They had to hurry, as rioting still went on in Strasbourg and in the neighbouring districts, where the people were turning out the " established " provosts of the communes, and were nominating others at will, while formulating claims to the forests and claiming other rights directly opposed to legally established property. " It is a moment when every one believed himself in a fair way to obtain the restoration of pretended rights," said the Magistracy in the letter dated August 5.

On top of this the news of the night of August 4 in the Assembly arrived at Strasbourg on the 11th, and the disturbance

---

* Wheat was then 19 livres the sack. The prices rose at the end of August to 28 and 30 livres, so that the bakers were forbidden to bake cakes or fancy bread.

became still more threatening, all the more as the army made common cause with the rebels. Whereupon the old Corporation resolved to resign.* The next day, August 12, the three hundred aldermen in their turn resigned their "offices," or rather their privileges. New aldermen were elected, and they appointed the judges.

Thus, on August 14, a new Corporation was constituted, a provisional Senate, which was to direct the affairs of the city until the Assembly at Versailles should establish a new municipal constitution. Without waiting for this constitution Strasbourg had in this way given herself a Commune and judges to her liking.

The old *régime* was thus breaking up at Strasbourg, and on August 17 M. Dietrich congratulated the new aldermen in these terms :

"Gentlemen, the revolution which has just taken place in our town will mark the epoch of the return of the confidence that should unite the citizens of the same commune. This august assembly has just been freely elected by their fellow citizens to be their representatives. . . . The first use that you have made of your powers has been to appoint your judges. . . . What strength may grow from this union!" Dietrich, moreover, proposed to decree that August 14, the day of the revolution in Strasbourg, should be an annual civic *fête*.

An important fact stands out in this revolution. The middle classes of Strasbourg were freed from the feudal system. They had given themselves a democratic municipal government. But they had no intention of giving up the feudal (patrimonial) rights which belonged to them over certain surrounding lands. When the two deputies from Strasbourg in the National Assembly were pressed by their fellows to abdicate their rights, during the night of August 4, they refused to do so. And when later on one of these two deputies, Schwendt, urged the matter before the Strasbourg middle classes, begging them not to oppose the current of the Revolution, his constituents persisted nevertheless in claiming their feudal rights. Thus

* Reuss, *L'Alsace*, p. 147.

we see forming in this city, since 1789, a party which will rally round the King, " the best of kings," " the most conciliatory of monarchs," with the purpose of preserving their rights over " the rich seignories," which belonged to the city under feudal law. The letter * in which the other Strasbourg deputy, Türckheim, sent in his resignation after escaping from Versailles on October 5, is a document of the highest interest in this connection ; one sees there already how and why the Gironde will rally under its middle-class flag the " defenders of property " as well as the Royalists.

What happened at Strasbourg gives us a clear enough idea of what was going on in the other large towns. For instance, at Troyes, a town about which we have also sufficiently complete documents, we see the movement made up of the same elements. The people, with the help of the neighbouring peasants, rebelled since July 18, after they had heard about the burning of the toll-gates at Paris. On July 20, some peasants, armed with pitchforks, scythes and flails, entered the town, probably to seize the wheat they needed for food and seed, which they expected to find there in the warehouses of the monopolists. But the middle classes formed themselves into a National Guard and repulsed the peasants, whom they already called " the brigands." During the ten or fifteen days following, taking advantage of the panic which was spreading, five hundred " brigands " were talked of as coming from Paris to ravage everything ; the middle classes organised their National Guard, and all the small towns armed themselves likewise. But the people were ill-pleased at this. On August 8, probably on hearing news of the night of August 4, the people demanded arms for all volunteers, and a maximum price for bread. The municipality hesitated. Whereupon the people deposed the members on August 19, and, as had been done at Strasbourg, a new municipality was elected.

The people overran the Town Hall, seized the arms and distributed them among themselves. They broke into the Government salt-stores ; but here, too, they did not plunder, " they only caused the salt to be served out at six sous."

* Published by Reuss.

Finally, on September 9, the disturbance, which had never ceased since August 19, reached its culminating-point. The people seized upon the Mayor (Huez), whom they accused of having tried to defend the trading monopolists, and killed him. They sacked his house, and also a notary's, and the house of the old Commandant Saint-Georges, who a fortnight before had given the order to fire on the people, as well as that of the lieutenant of the mounted police, who had caused a man to be hanged during the preceding riot ; and they threatened, as they had done in Paris after July 14, to sack many others. After this, for about a fortnight, terror reigned among the upper middle classes. But they managed during that time to reorganise their own National Guard, and on September 26 they ended by getting the upper hand of the unarmed people.

As a rule the anger of the people was directed much more against the representatives of the middle classes who monopolised the food-stuffs than against the nobility who monopolised the land. Thus at Amiens, as at Troyes, the insurgent people almost killed three merchants ; whereupon the middle classes hastened to arm their militia. We may even say that this formation of militias in the towns, which was carried out everywhere in August and September, would probably have never taken place if the popular rising had been confined to the country parts, and had been directed solely against the nobility.

At Cherbourg on July 21, at Rouen on the 24th, and in many other towns of less importance, almost the same thing happened. The hungry people rose with cries of " Bread ! Death to the monopolists ! Down with the toll-gates ! " which meant free entrance of all supplies coming in from the country. They compelled the municipality to reduce the price of bread, or else they took possession of the mono-polists' storehouses and carried off the grain ; they sacked the houses of those who were known to have trafficked in the price of bread-stuffs. The middle classes took advantage of this movement to turn out the old municipal government imbued with feudalism, and to set up a new municipality elected on a democratic basis. At the same time, taking advantage of the panic produced by the rising of the " lower classes " in the towns, and of the " brigands " in the country, they armed themselves and organised their Municipal Guard. After that they "restored order," executed the popular leaders, and very often went into the country to restore order there, where they fought with the peasants and hanged the " leaders " of the revolted peasantry.

After the night of August 4, these urban insurrections spread still more. Indications of them are seen everywhere. The taxes, the town-dues, the levies and excise were no longer paid. "The collectors of the *taille* are at their last shift," said Necker, in his report of August 7. "The price of salt has been compulsorily reduced one-half in two of the revolted localities," the collection of taxes " is no longer made," and so forth. "An infinity of places " was in revolt against the treasury clerks. The people would no longer pay the indirect tax ; as to the direct taxes, they are not refused, but conditions were laid down for their payment. In Alsace, for instance, " the people generally refused to pay anything until the exempts and privileged persons had been added to the lists of tax-payers."

In this way the people, *long before the Assembly*, were making the Revolution on the spot ; they gave themselves, by revolutionary means, a new municipal administration, they made a distinction between the taxes that they accepted and those which they refused to pay, and they prescribed the mode of equal division of the taxes that they agreed to pay to the State or to the Commune.

It is chiefly by studying this method of *action* among the people, and not by devoting oneself to the study of the Assembly's legislative work, that one grasps the genius of the Great Revolution—the Genius, in the main, of all revolutions, past and to come.

CHAPTER XVI

THE PEASANT RISING

Peasants begin to rise—Causes of risings—Châteaux destroyed
—Rising in Alsace—Franche-Comté—Castres—Auvergne—
Characteristics of rising—Middle classes and their fears—
Picardy revolts — Terror throughout France — National
Assembly meets

Ever since the winter of 1788, and especially since March 1789,
the people, as we have said, no longer paid rent to the lords.
That in this they were encouraged by the revolutionaries of
the middle classes is undoubtedly true; there were many
persons among the middle classes of 1789 who understood
that without a popular rising they would never have the upper
hand over the absolute power of the King. It is clear, also,
that the discussions in the Assembly of the Notables, wherein
the abolition of the feudal rights was already spoken about,
encouraged the rising, and that the drawing up in the parishes
of the *cahiers*, which were to serve as guides for the assemblies
of electors, tended in the same direction. Revolutions are
never the result of despair, as is often believed by young
revolutionists, who think that good can come out of an excess of
evil. On the contrary, the people in 1789 had caught a glimpse
of the light of approaching freedom, and for that reason they
rose with good heart. But to hope was not enough, to act was
also necessary; the first rebels who prepare a revolution must
be ready to give their lives, and this the people did.

Whilst rioting was being punished by pillory, torture and
hanging, the peasants were already in revolt. From November,
1788, the Governors of the provinces were writing to the
ministers that if they wished to put down all the riotings it
was no longer possible to do so. Taken separately, none was of

great importance ; together, they were undermining the very foundations of State.

In January 1789, writs of plaints and grievances (the *cahiers de doléances*) were drawn up, the electors were elected, and from that time the peasants began to refuse to furnish statute labour to the lords and the State.   Secret associations were formed among them, and here and there a lord was executed by the " Jacques Bonhommes."   In some places the tax-collectors were received with cudgels ; in others, the lands belonging to the nobles were seized and tilled.

From month to month these risings multiplied.   By March the whole of the east of France was in revolt.   The movement, to be sure, was neither continuous nor general.   An agrarian rising is never that.   It is even very probable, as is always the case in the peasant insurrections, that there was a slackening n the outbreaks at the time of field work in April, and afterwards at the beginning of the harvest time.   But as soon as the first harvests were gathered in, during the second half of July 1789, and in August, the risings broke out with fresh force, especially in the east, north-east and south-east of France.

Documents bearing with exactitude on this rising are wanting.   Those that have been published are very incomplete, and the greater part bear traces of a partisan spirit.   If we take the *Moniteur*, which, we know, only began to appear on November 24, 1789, and of which the ninety-three numbers, from May 8 to November 23, 1789, were compiled later on in the Year IV.,* we find in them a tendency to show that the whole movement was the work of the enemies of the Revolution—of heartless persons who took advantage of rustic ignorance. Others go so far as to say that it was the nobles, the lords, or, indeed, even that it was the English, who had incited the peasants to rise.   As for the documents published by the Committee for Investigations in January 1790, they tend rather to represent the whole affair as the result of an unfortunate chance—the work of " brigands," who had devastated the

---

* Moreover, the numbers from November 24, 1789, to February 3, 1790, were also retouched in the Year IV.

country parts, and against whom the middle classes had taken up arms, and whom they had exterminated.

We know to-day how false this representation is, and it is certain that if a historian took the trouble to study carefully the documents in the archives, a work of the highest value would result from it, a work the more necessary as the risings of the peasants continued until the Convention abolished feudal rights, in August 1793, and until the village communes were granted the right of resuming the communal land which had been taken from them during the two preceding centuries. For the time being, this work among the archives not being done, we must confine ourselves to what can be gleaned from some local histories from certain memoirs, and from a few authors, always explaining the rising of 1789 by the light which the better-known movements of the following year sheds on this first outbreak.

That the dearth of food counted for much in these risings is certain. But their chief motive was the desire to get possession of the land and the desire to get rid of the feudal dues and the tithes.

There is, besides, one characteristic trait in these risings. They appear only sporadically in the centre of France and in the south and west, except in Brittany. But they are very general in the east, north-east and south-east. The Dauphiné, the Franche-Comté and the Mâconnais are especially affected by them. In the Franche-Comté nearly all the châteaux were burned, says Doniol ; * three out of every five were plundered in Dauphiné. Next in proportion comes Alsace, the Nivernais, the Beaujolais, Burgundy and the Auvergne. As I have remarked elsewhere, if we trace on a map the localities where these risings took place, this map will in a general way present a striking resemblance to the map " of the three hundred and sixty-three," published in 1877, after the elections which gave to France the Third Republic. It was chiefly the eastern part of France which espoused the cause of the Revolution, and this same part is still the most advanced in our own day.

Doniol has remarked very truly that the source of the risings

* *La Révolution française*, p. 48.

was already set forth in the *cahiers*, which were written for the elections of 1789. Since the peasants had been asked to state their grievances, they were sure that something would be done for them. Their firm belief that the King to whom they addressed their complaints, or the Assembly, or some other power, would come to their aid and redress their wrongs, or at least let them take it upon themselves to redress these wrongs—this was what urged them to revolt as soon as the elections had taken place, and before even the Assembly had met. When the States-General began to sit, the rumours which came from Paris, vague though they were, necessarily made the peasants believe that the moment had come for obtaining the abolition of feudal rights and for taking back the land.

The slightest encouragement given to them, whether on the part of the revolutionaries or from the side of the Orléanists, by no matter what kind of agitators, coupled with the disquieting news which was coming from Paris and from the towns in revolt, sufficed to make the villages rise. There is no longer the slightest doubt that use was made more than once of the King's name, and of the Assembly's, in the provinces. Many documents, indeed, allude to the circulation among the villages of false decrees of the King and of the Assembly. In all their risings, in France, in Russia and in Germany, the peasants have always tried to decide the hesitating ones—I shall even say to persuade themselves by maintaining that there was some force ready to back them up. This gave them cohesion, and afterwards, in case of defeat and of proceedings being taken against them, there was always a safe excuse. They had thought, and the majority thought so sincerely, that they were obeying the wishes, if not the orders, of the King or of the Assembly. Therefore, as soon as the first harvests were reaped in the summer of 1789, as soon as people in the villages began to eat again after the long months of scarcity, and the rumours arriving from Versailles began to inspire hope, the peasants rose. They turned upon the châteaux in order to destroy the charter-rooms, the lists and the title-deeds; and houses were burned down if the masters did not relinquish with a good grace the feudal rights recorded in the charters, the rolls and the rest.

In the neighbourhood of Vesoul and Belfort the war on the country houses began on July 16, the date when the château of Sancy, and then those of Luce, Bithaine and Molans, were plundered. Soon all Loraine had risen. " The peasants, believing that the Revolution was going to bring in equality of wealth and rank, were especially excited against the lords," says the *Courrier français.** At Saarlouis, Forbach, Sarreguemines, Phalsbourg and Thionville the excise officers were driven away and their offices pillaged and burnt. Salt was selling at three sous the pound. The neighbouring villages followed the example of the towns.

In Alsace the peasant rising was almost general. It is stated that in eight days, towards the end of July, three abbeys were destroyed, eleven châteaux sacked, others plundered, and that the peasants had carried off and destroyed all the land records. The registers of feudal taxes, statute-labours and dues of all sorts were also taken away and burnt. In certain localities flying columns were formed, several hundred and sometimes several thousand strong, of peasants gathered from the villages round about ; they marched against the strongest châteaux, besieged them, seized all the old papers and made bonfires of them. The abbeys were sacked and plundered for the same reason, as well as houses of rich merchants in the towns. Everything was destroyed at the Abbey of Mürbach, which probably offered resistance.†

In the Franche-Comté the first riots took place at Lons-le-Saulnier as early as July 19, when the news of the preparations for the *coup d'état* and Necker's dismissal reached that place, but the taking of the Bastille was still unknown, says Sommier.‡ Rioting soon began, and at the same time the middle classes armed its militia (all wearing the tricolour cockade) to resist

* P. 242 et seq.

† According to Strobel (*Vaterländische Geschichte des Elsass*), the rising took place generally in this way : a village rose, and straightway a band was formed composed of the inhabitants of various villages, which went in a body to attack the châteaux. Sometimes these bands concealed themselves in the woods.

‡ *Histoire de la Révolution dans le Jura* (Paris, 1846), p. 22. The bent of men's minds in the Jura is revealed in a song given in the *Cahier d'Aval*.

" the incursions of the brigands who infest the kingdom." *
The rising soon spread to the villages. The peasants divided
among themselves the meadows and woods of the lords. Besides this, they compelled the lords to renounce their right over
land which had belonged formerly to the communes. Or else,
without any formalities, they retook possession of the forests
which had once been communal. All the title-deeds held by
the Abbey of the Bernardins in the neighbouring communes
were carried off.† At Castres the risings began after August 4.
A tax of *coupe* was levied in kind (so much per *setier*) in this town
on all wheats imported into the province. It was a feudal tax,
granted by the King to private individuals. As soon, therefore,
as they heard in Castres the news of the night of August 4, the
people rose, demanding the abolition of this tax ; and immediately the middle classes, who had formed the National Guard,
six hundred strong, began to restore " order." But in the
rural districts the insurrection spread from village to village,
and the châteaux of Gaix and Montlédier, the Carthusian
Convent of Faix, the Abbey of Vielmur and other places were
plundered and the records destroyed.‡

In the Auvergne the peasants took many precautions to put
the law on their side, and when they went to the châteaux to
burn the records, they did not hesitate to say to the lords that
they were acting by order of the King.§ But in the eastern
provinces they did not refrain from declaring openly that the

* Sommier, pp. 24–25.

† Edouard Clerc, *Essai sur l'histoire de la Franche-Comté,* 2nd edition
(Besançon, 1870).

‡ Anacharsis Combes, *Histoire de la ville de Castres et de ses environs
pendant la Révolution française* (Castres, 1875).

§ M. Xavier Roux, who published in 1891, under the title *Mémoire
sur la marche des brigandages dans le Dauphiné en* 1789, the complete
depositions of an inquiry made in 1879 on this subject, attributes the
whole movement to a few leaders : " To call upon the people to rise
against the King would have had no results," says this writer ; " they
attained their end in a roundabout way. A singularly bold plan was
adopted and carried out over the whole province. It is summed up
in these words : to stir up the people against the lords in the name of
the King ; the lords once crushed, the throne was to be attacked,
which, then being defenceless, could be destroyed " (p. iv. of the introduction). Well, we take from M. Roux himself this admission, that all
the inquiries made have never led" to the disclosure of a single leader's
name " (p. v.). The whole people were included in this conspiracy.

time had come when the Third Estate would no longer permit the nobles and priesthood to rule over them. The power of these two classes had lasted too long, and the moment had come for them to abdicate. For a large number of the poorer nobles, residing in the country and perhaps loved by those round them, the revolted peasantry showed much personal regard. They did them no harm ; but the registers and title-deeds of · feudal landlordism they never spared. They burned them, after compelling the lord to swear that he would relinquish his rights.

Like the middle classes of the towns, who knew well what they wanted and what they expected from the Revolution, the peasants also knew very well what they wanted ; the lands stolen from the communes should be given back to them, and all the dues begotten by feudalism should be wiped out. The idea that the rich people as a whole should be wiped out, too, may have filtered through from that time ; but at the moment the *jacquerie* confined its attention to *things*, and if there were cases where the persons of some lords were ill-treated, they were isolated cases, and may generally be explained by the fact that they were speculators, men who had made money out of the scarcity. If the land-registers were given up and the oath of renunciation taken, all went off quietly : the peasants burned the registers, planted a May-tree in the village, hung on its boughs the feudal emblems, and then danced round the tree.*

Otherwise, if there had been resistance, or if the lord or his steward had called in the police, if there had been any shooting —then the château was completely pillaged, and often it was set on fire. Thus, it is reckoned that thirty châteaux were plundered or burnt in the Dauphiné, nearly forty in the Franche-Comté, sixty-two in the Mâconnais and the Beaujolais, nine only in the Auvergne, and twelve monasteries and five châteaux in the Viennois. We may note, by the way, that the peasants made no distinctions for political opinions. They attacked, therefore, the houses of " patriots " as well as those of " aristocrats."

* Sometimes in the south they hung up also this inscription : " By order of the King and of the National Assembly, a final quittance of rents " (Mary Lafon, *Histoire politique du Midi de la France*, 1842–1845, vol. iv. p. 377).

What were the middle classes doing while these riots were going on ?

There must have been in the Assembly a certain number of men who understood that the rising of the peasants at that moment represented a revolutionary force ; but the mass of the middle classes in the provinces saw only a danger against which it was necessary to arm themselves. What was called at the time *la grande peur* (" the great fear ") seized, in fact, on a good many of the towns in the region of the risings. At Troyes, for example, some countrymen armed with scythes and flails had entered the town, and would probably have pillaged the houses of the speculators, when the middle classes, " all who were honest among the middle classes," * armed themselves against " the brigands " and drove them away. The same thing happened in many other towns. The middle classes were seized with panic. They were expecting " the brigands." Some one had seen " six thousand " on the march to plunder everything, and the middle classes took possession of the arms which they found at the Town Hall or at the armourers', and organised their National Guard, for fear lest the poor folk of the town, making common cause with " the brigands," might attack the rich.

At Péronne, the capital of Picardy, the inhabitants had revolted in the second half of July. They burnt the toll-gates, threw the Custom House officers into the water, carried off the receipts from the Government offices and set free all the prisoners. All this was done before July 28. " After receiving the news from Paris on the night of the 28th," wrote the Mayor of Péronne, " Hainault, Flanders and all Picardy have taken up arms ; the tocsin is ringing in all the towns and villages." Three hundred thousand middle-class men were formed into permanent patrols—and all this to be ready for two thousand " brigands," that, they said, were overrunning the villages and burning the crops. In reality, as some one aptly remarked to Arthur Young, all these " brigands " were nothing more than peasants,† who were, indeed, rising, and, armed with pitchforks, cudgels and scythes, were compelling the lords to abdicate their

---

* *Moniteur*, i. 378.   † *Travels in France*, p. 225.

feudal rights, and were stopping passers-by to ask them if they were " for the nation." The Mayor of Péronne has also aptly said : " We are willing to be in the Terror. Thanks to the sinister rumours, we can keep on foot an army of three millions of middle-class men and peasants all over France."

Adrien Duport, a well-known member of the Assembly and of the Breton Club, even boasted of having armed in this way the middle classes in a great many towns. He had two or three agents, " resolute but not well-known men," who avoided the towns, but on arriving at a village would announce that " the brigands were coming." " There are five hundred, a thousand, three thousand of them," said these emissaries, " they are burning all the crops round about, so that the people may starve." Thereupon the tocsin would be rung and the villages would arm themselves. And by the time that the sinister rumour reached the towns, the numbers would have grown to six thousand brigands. They had been seen about a league off in such a forest ; then the townspeople, especially the middle classes, would arm themselves and send patrols into the forest—to find nothing there. But the important point was that the peasants were thus being armed. Let the King take care ! When he tries to escape, in 1791, he will find the armed peasants in his way.

We can imagine the terror which these risings inspired all through France ; we can imagine the impression that they made at Versailles, and it was under the domination of this terror that the National Assembly met on the evening of August 4 to discuss what measures should be taken to suppress the *jacquerie*.

CHAPTER XVII

AUGUST 4 AND ITS CONSEQUENCES

Night of August 4—Aristocracy pretends to relinquish feudal
rights—Assembly begs King to take action—D'Aiguillon and
de Noailles take up cause of peasants—Their great speeches
—Le Guen de Kérangall—Scene in Assembly—Extent of
actual concessions—Effect of news in provinces—Middle
classes take up arms against peasants.

THE night of August 4 is one of the great dates of the Revolution. Like July 14 and October 15, 1789, June 21, 1791,
August 10, 1792, and May 31, 1793, it marked one of the great
stages in the revolutionary movement, and it determined the
character of the period which follows it.

The historic legend is lovingly used to embellish this night,
and the majority of historians, copying the story as it has been
given by a few contemporaries, represent it as a night full of
enthusiasm and saintly abnegation.

With the taking of the Bastille, the historians tell us, the
Revolution had gained its first victory. The news spread to
the provinces, and provoked everywhere somewhat similar
insurrections. It penetrated to the villages, and, at the instigation of all kinds of vagabonds, the peasants attacked their
lords and burnt the châteaux. Whereupon the clergy and
nobility, filled with a patriotic impulse, seeing that they had
as yet done nothing for the peasant, began to relinquish their
feudal rights during this memorable night. The nobles, the
clergy, the poorest parish priest and the richest of the
feudal lords, all renounced upon the altar of their country
their secular prerogatives. A wave of enthusiasm passed
through the Assembly ; all were eager to make their sacrifice.
" The sitting was a holy feast, the tribune an altar, the Assembly

Hall a temple," says one of the historians, who are usually calm enough. "It was a Saint Bartholomew of property," say the others. And when the first beams of day broke over France on the morrow the old feudal system no longer existed. "France was a country born anew, having made an *auto-da-fé* of all the abuses of its privileged classes."

That is the legend. It is true that a profound enthusiasm thrilled the Assembly when two nobles, the Viscount de Noailles and the Duke d'Aiguillon, put the demand for the abolition of feudal rights, as well as of the various privileges of the nobility, and when two bishops—those of Nancy and of Chartres —spoke demanding the abolition of the tithes. It is true that the enthusiasm went on ever increasing, and that during this all-night sitting nobles and clergy followed one another to the tribune and disputed who should first give up their seignorial courts of justice. Pleas were to be heard, made by the privileged persons, for justice—free, unbought, and equal for all. Lords, lay and ecclesiastic, were seen relinquishing their game laws. The Assembly was carried away by its enthusiasm, and in this enthusiasm nobody remarked the clause for *redeeming* the feudal rights and tithes, which the two nobles and the two bishops had introduced into their speeches—a clause terrible even in its vagueness, since it might mean all or nothing, and did, in fact, postpone, as we shall see, the abolition of feudal rights for four years—until August 1793. But which of us in reading the beautiful story of that night, written by its contemporaries, has not been carried away by enthusiasm in his turn ? And who has not passed over those traitorous words, "*rachat au denier* 30" (redemption at a thirty-years' purchase), without understanding their terrible import ? This is also what happened in France in 1789.

The evening sitting of August 4 had at first begun with panic, not with enthusiasm. We have just seen that a number of châteaux had been burnt or plundered during the previous fortnight. Beginning in the east, the peasant insurrection spread towards the south, the north and the centre ; it threatened to become general. In a few places the peasants had acted savagely towards their masters, and the news which came in from the provinces exaggerated what had happened. The nobles ascertained with alarm that there was not any force on the spot capable of checking the riots.

The sitting opened, therefore, with the reading of a scheme for issuing a proclamation against the risings. The Assembly was invited to pronounce an energetic condemnation of the rioters and to command most emphatically respect for property, whether feudal or not, while waiting for the Assembly to legislate on the matter.

"It appears that property, of no matter what nature, is the prey of the most culpable brigandage," said the Committee of Inquiry. "On all sides châteaux are burnt, convents destroyed and farms given over to pillage. The taxes and seignorial dues all are done away with. The laws are powerless, the magistrates are without authority. . . ." And the report demanded that the Assembly should censure severely the disturbances and declare "that the old laws (the feudal laws) were in existence until the authority of the nation had abrogated or modified them, that all the customary dues and payments should be paid as in the past, until it should have been ordained otherwise by the Assembly."

"They are not brigands who do that!" exclaimed the Duke d'Aiguillon; "in several provinces the whole of the people have entered into a league to destroy the châteaux to ravage the lands, and above all to get possession of the record-rooms where the title-deeds of the feudal properties are deposited." It is certainly not enthusiasm that speaks here : it is more like fear.*

The Assembly proceeded in consequence to beg the King to take stringent measures against the rebellious peasants. This had already been spoken of the day before, August 3. But for some days past a certain number of the nobility—a few more advanced in their ideas than the rest of their class, and who saw more clearly all that was happening : the Viscount de

* "To ravage the lands" would probably mean that in certain places the peasants reaped the harvests belonging to the lords while they were yet green. Besides, it was the end of July, the corn was nearly ripe, and the people, who had nothing to eat, cut the corn belonging to the lords.

Noailles, the Duke d'Aiguillon, the Duke de La Rochefoucauld, Alexandre de Lamotte and some others—were secretly consulting together as to the attitude to be taken towards the *jacquerie*. They had understood that the only means of saving the feudal rights was to sacrifice the honorary rights and prerogatives of little value, and to demand *the redemption* by the peasants of the feudal dues *attached to the land and having a real value*. They commissioned the Duke d'Aiguillon with the development of these ideas, and this is how it was done by the Viscount de Noailles and the Duke d'Aiguillon.

Ever since the Revolution began the country folk had demanded the abolition of the feudal rights.*   At the present time, said the two spokesmen of the liberal nobility, the rural districts, dissatisfied that nothing has been done for them during these three months, are in a state of revolt ; they are no longer under control, and the choice now lies " between the destruction of society and certain concessions." These concessions were formulated by the Viscount de Noailles thus : Equality of all persons under taxation, which should be paid in proportion to the income ; all public expenses to be contributed to by all ; " all the feudal rights to be redeemed by the (village) communes by means of a yearly rent " ; and lastly, " the abolition without redemption of the seignorial statute-labours, of mortmain and other kinds of personal servitude." †   It must also be said that

* " The marks of transport and effusion of generous sentiment which made the picture presented by the Assembly more lively and spirited from hour to hour, scarcely left time for coming to some agreement over the prudential measures thought advisable for carrying into effect those beneficent projects, which had been voted in so many memorials of both provincial and parochial assemblies—wherever the citizens had been able to meet for the last eighteen months—amid touching expressions of opinion and ardent protestations."

† " All the feudal rights were to be redeemable by the communes, either by money or exchange," said the Viscount de Noailles.   " Every one will be subject to all the public charges, all the State charges (*subsides*), without any distinction," said d'Aiguillon.   " I demand the redemption for the ecclesiastical funds," said Lafare, Bishop of Nancy, " and I demand that the redemption be not turned to the profit of the ecclesiastical lord, but that it may be invested usefully for the poor."   The Bishop of Chartres demanded the abolition of the game laws, and renounced those rights for his own part.   Whereupon both nobles and clergy rise at the same time to follow his example. De Richer demanded not only the abolition of the manorial courts of

for some time past the personal services had been no longer paid by the peasants. We have very clear evidence on that head from the governors of the provinces. After the revolt of July it was plain that they would never be paid again, whether the lord renounced them or not.

These concessions, proposed by the Viscount de Noailles, were, however, cut down, both by the nobles and by the middle-class deputies, of whom a great number possessed landed property comprising feudal rights. The Duke d'Aiguillon, who followed de Noailles in the tribune, and whom the above-mentioned nobles had chosen as their spokesman, spoke of the peasants with sympathy; he excused their insurrection, but his conclusion was that "the barbarous remnants of the feudal laws which still exist in France are—there is no need for dissimulation—a *species of property, and all property is sacred.*" "*Equity,*" said he, "*forbids us to exact the renunciation of any property without granting a just indemnity to the owner.*" He also softened down the Viscount de Noailles' phrase about the taxes, by saying that all citizens should contribute "in proportion to their means." And as to the feudal rights, he demanded that all these rights—the personal rights as well as the others—might be redeemed by the vassals "if they so desired," the compensation being "*au denier* 30"—that is, thirty times the annual payment. This was to make redemption a sham, because for land rents it was heavy enough at twenty-five years, and in business transactions rent is generally reckoned at twenty, or even seventeen.

These two speeches were received by the gentlemen of the Third Estate with enthusiasm, and they have come down to posterity as sublime acts of abnegation on the part of the nobility, while in reality the National Assembly, which followed the programme laid down by the Duke d'Aiguillon, created thereby the very conditions of the terrible struggles which later on steeped the Revolution in blood. The few peasants who were in this Assembly did not speak, and nobody called

justice, but also that justice should be dispensed gratuitously. Several priests asked that they might be allowed to sacrifice their perquisites (*casuel*), but that a tax in money should take the place of the tithe.

attention to the small value of the "renunciations" of the
nobles. As to the mass of the deputies of the Third Estate,
who were city men for the most part, and therefore probably had
only a very vague idea about the feudal rights as a whole, as
well as about the significance of the peasant rising, in their
eyes, to renounce the feudal rights, even on terms of redemption, was to make a sublime sacrifice to the Revolution.

Le Guen de Kérangall, a Breton deputy, "dressed as a
peasant," then uttered some beautiful and moving words.
These words, when he spoke of the "infamous parchments"
which registered the obligations of personal servitude, survivals
of serfdom, made, and still make, hearts throb. But he, too,
did not speak against a redemption of all the feudal rights,
including those same "infamous" services, imposed "in times
of darkness and ignorance," the injustice of which he so
eloquently denounced.

It is certain that the spectacle presented by the Assembly
during that night must have been fine—representatives of the
nobility and clergy coming forward to relinquish the privileges
they had exercised without question for centuries. The action
and the word were magnificent when the nobles rose to renounce
their privileges in the matter of taxes, and the priests to renounce their tithes, the poorest curates among them giving up
the *casuel*, the greatest lords giving up their courts of manorial
justice, and all of them relinquishing the hunting rights, asking
for the suppression of the pigeon-houses, which had been such a
plague to the peasants. It was fine to see, also, whole provinces
renouncing privileges which had created for them an exceptional
position in the kingdom. The category of *pays d'états* endowed
with special rights was thus suppressed, and the privileges of
the towns, several of which held feudal rights over the neighbouring country, were abolished. The representatives of the
Dauphiné (where, as we have seen, the rising had been strong
and widespread) having led the way for the abolition of provincial distinctions, the others followed them.

All the eye-witnesses of this memorable sitting have given
glowing descriptions of it. When the nobility accepted in
principle the redemption of the feudal rights, the clergy were

called upon to declare themselves. They accepted fully the redemption of the ecclesiastical feudalities on the condition that the price of redemption should not create personal fortunes amongst the clergy, but that the whole should be employed in works of general utility. A bishop then spoke about the injuries done in the peasants' fields by the packs of hounds kept by the lords, and demanded the abolition of the hunting privileges, and immediately the nobility gave their assent by a loud and impassioned shout. The enthusiasm reached a very high pitch during the sitting, and when the Assembly separated at two o'clock in the morning, every one felt that the foundations of a new society had been laid.

It would not be fair to try to diminish the importance of that night. Enthusiasm of this kind is needed to push on events. It will be needed again when a Social Revolution comes. In a revolution enthusiasm must be provoked, and words which make hearts vibrate must be pronounced. The fact that the nobility, the clergy and the privileged persons of every kind had recognised during that night's sitting the progress of the Revolution, that they decided to submit to it instead of taking up arms against it—this fact by itself was already a conquest of the human mind. It was all the greater as the renunciation was made with enthusiasm. It is true that it was done in the light of the burning châteaux, but how many times had that same light merely provoked in the privileged classes an obstinate resistance, and led to hatred and massacre! That night in August those distant flames inspired other words—words of sympathy for the rebels; and other acts—acts of conciliation.

Ever since July 14, the spirit of the Revolution, born of the ferment which was working through the whole of France, was hovering over everything that lived and felt, and this spirit, created by millions of wills, gave the inspiration that we lack in ordinary times.

But having pointed out the effects of the enthusiasm which only a revolution could inspire, the historian must also consider calmly how far all this enthusiasm did actually go, and what was the limit it dared not pass; he must point out what it gave the people and what it refused to grant them.

Well, that limit can be indicated in very few words. The Assembly only sanctioned in principle and extended to France altogether what the people had accomplished themselves in certain localities. It went no further.

We have seen what the people had already done in Strasbourg and in so many other towns. They had compelled all the citizens, noble and middle-class, to share the taxation, and had proclaimed the necessity of an income tax—and the National Assembly accepted that. The people had abolished all honorary offices, and the nobility agreed to renounce those offices on August 4; by so doing, they again accepted a revolutionary act. The people had also abolished the manorial courts of justice and appointed judges by election; the Assembly accepted this in its turn. Finally, the people had abolished the privileges of the towns and the provincial toll-gates—it was actually done in the eastern provinces—and now the Assembly made a general principle of a fact already accomplished in a part of the kingdom.

For the rural districts the clergy admitted in principle that the tithes should be redeemable; but in how many places were the people paying them! And when the Assembly tried afterwards to exact payment up to 1791, it had to resort to threats of execution to compel the peasants to obey. Let us rejoice, certainly, that the clergy yielded to the abolition of the tithes—under the condition that they should be redeemed—but let us also say that the clergy would have done infinitely better had they not insisted on redemption. What struggles, what hatreds, what bloodshed had been spared if they had given up the tithes and had left the payment of their salaries to the nation or their parishioners. As to the feudal rights, how much strife would have been avoided if the Assembly, instead of accepting the motion of the Duke d'Aiguillon, had simply adopted on August 4, 1789, that of the Viscount de Noailles, which after all was a very modest proposal: the abolition without indemnity of the personal dues, and redemption for the rents attaching to land. But, to arrive at this latter measure, in 1792, how much blood had to flow during three years, not to mention the savage struggles which had to be gone through to attain in 1793 the total abolition of feudal rights without redemption ?

But let us for the moment do as the men of 1789 did. Every one was filled with joy after that sitting. Every one congratulated themselves upon that Saint Bartholomew of feudal abuses, which proves how important it is during a revolution to recognise, or at least to proclaim, a new principle. Couriers were despatched from Paris, carrying the great news to every corner of France : " All the feudal rights are abolished ! " For it was so that the decisions of the Assembly were understood by the people, and it was so stated in the first article of the resolution of August 5. All the feudal rights are abolished ! No more tithes ! No more quit-rents ! No more dues on the sales of inheritance, no more payments in kind, nor statute-labours, nor subsidies ! The game laws are gone ! Done with the pigeon-houses : all game is henceforth free to everybody ! There were to be no more nobles, no privileged persons of any sort : every one was equal before the judge elected by all !

At least this was how the night of August 4 was understood in the provinces. And before the resolutions of August 5 and 11 had been published, before the line of demarcation between what should be redeemed and what should disappear since that day had been marked out—long before those acts and renunciations had been formulated into paragraphs of law, messengers had already brought the good news to the peasant. Henceforth, whether he was shot down or not, he would no longer pay anything.

The peasant insurrection took, therefore, a new force. It spread through the provinces, such as Brittany, which until then had remained quiet. And if the landowners demanded payment of any kind of dues, the peasants went to their châteaux and burnt all the records and land-registers. They did not care to submit to the decrees of August and distinguish between redeemable rights and abolished rights, says Du Châtellier.* Everywhere, all over France, the pigeon-houses and game were destroyed. In the villages the peasants ate their fill therefore,

---

* *Histoire de la Révolution dans les départements de l'ancienne Bretagne*, 8 vols., vol. i. p. 422.

and they also took possession of those lands which, though formerly belonging to the village communities, had been seized by the lords.

It was then that in the east of France one could see what has happened later on more or less all over France—namely, the middle classes interposing against the peasants in favour of the landlords. Liberal historians have passed this by in silence, but it is a fact of the highest importance for the comprehension of the history of the next few years.

We have seen that the peasant rising attained its greatest vigour in the Dauphiné and in eastern France generally. The rich people and the lords fled, Necker complaining that he had to furnish six thousand passports to the richest inhabitants in a fortnight. Switzerland was inundated with them. But the middle-class people who remained armed themselves and organised their militia, and the National Assembly soon voted a draconian measure against the peasants (August 10).* Under the pretext that the insurrection was the work of brigands, it authorised the municipalities to call out the troops, to disarm all men without profession and without domicile, to disperse the bands and to deal with them summarily. The middle classes of the Dauphiné profited largely by these laws. When bands of peasants in revolt passed through Burgundy, burning the châteaux, the middle-class men in the towns and villages leagued themselves against them. One of these bands, says the *Deux amis de la liberté*, was defeated at Cormatin on July 27, when twenty were killed and sixty taken prisoners. At Cluny there were a hundred killed and one hundred and sixty prisoners. The municipality of Mâcon made war in due form upon the peasants, who refused to pay the tithe, and they hanged twenty of them. Twelve peasants were hanged at Douai ; at Lyons the middle classes, while fighting the peasants, killed eighty of them and took sixty prisoners. In the Dauphiné the Provost-Marshal went all over the country hanging the rebellious peasants.† In the Rouergue, the town of Milhaud appealed

* Buchez and Roux, *Histoire parlementaire*, vol. ii. p. 254.

† After the defeat of two large bands of peasants, one of which threatened to attack the châteaux of Cormatin, the other the town of Cluny, and after punishments of a frightful severity had been inflicted,

to the neighbouring towns, inviting them to arm themselves against the brigands and those who refused to pay the taxes.*

In short, we see by these several acts, of which it would be easy to increase the list, that wherever the rising of the peasants was the most violent, there the middle classes undertook to crush it ; and they would have undoubtedly helped considerably to do it if the news which came from Paris after the night of August 4 had not given a new impetus to the insurrection.

The peasant rising apparently slackened only in September or October, perhaps on account of the ploughing ; but in January 1790 we learn, from the account of the Feudalism Committee, that the peasant insurrection had begun again with renewed vigour, probably because of the claims for payment. The peasants were unwilling to submit to the distinction made by the Assembly between the dues attached to the land and the personal services, and they rose in order that they should pay nothing at all.

We shall return to this very important subject in one of the succeeding chapters.

the war went on, but in a scattered way, say Buchez and Roux. " However the Permanent Committee of Mâcon illegally constituted itself into a tribunal, by order of which twenty of these unhappy peasants were executed for the crime of hunger and for having rebelled against the tithe and feudal laws" (p. 244). Everywhere the rising was clearly provoked by acts of minor importance, by disputes with the lord or the chapter about a meadow or a fountain, and in one château, to which the rights of plenary jurisdiction belonged, several vassals were hanged for marauding offences, &c. The pamphlets of the time, which Buchez and Roux consulted, say that the *parlement* (the Court) of Douai ordered twelve leaders of bands to be executed ; the Committee of Electors (middle-class men) at Lyons sent out a flying column of volunteer National Guards. One contemporary pamphlet states that this little army in a single engagement killed eighty of the so-called brigands, and took sixty prisoners. The Provost-Marshal of the Dauphiné, at the head of a body of middle-class militia, marched through the country and executed as he went (Buchez and Roux, vol. ii. p. 245).

* *Courrier parisien*, sitting of August 19, 1789, p. 1729.

CHAPTER XVIII

THE FEUDAL RIGHTS REMAIN

Assembly and feudal privileges—Survivals of serfdom—Obligations to feudal lord—Lords try to back out of their promises—Church tithes abolished in theory but not in practice—Disappointment of peasants—Game laws—Feudal rights—Personal servitude alone abolished—Other dues remain—Redemption of land rendered impossible—Effect of vagueness of Assembly—Article of August 4, 1789, not to be taken literally—Peasants refuse to pay—King the rallying-point of feudalism—Tactics of Assembly—Its *resolutions* finally published by the King

WHEN the Assembly met again on August 5 to draw up, under the form of resolutions, the list of renunciations which had been made during the historic night of the 4th, one could see up to what point the Assembly was on the side of property, and how it was going to defend every one of the pecuniary advantages attached to those same feudal privileges, which it had made a show of abandoning a few hours before.

There were still in France, under the name of *mainmortes, banalités,* * &c., a few survivals of the ancient serfdom. There were still peasants subject to mortmain in the Franche-Comté, the Nivernais and the Bourbonnais. They were serfs in the true sense of the word; they could not sell their goods, nor transmit them by inheritance, except to those of their children who lived with them. They remained therefore attached to the soil.† How many they were we do not exactly know, but

* The common oven, mill, press, &c., belonging to the lord, for the use of which the peasants had to pay, besides suffering much loss of food, grain and wine.

† The fact of being attached to the land is what constitutes the essence of serfdom. Wherever serfdom has existed for several centuries, the lords have also obtained from the State rights over the person of the serf, which made serfdom (in Russia, for example, at the

it is thought that the number given by Boncerf as three hundred thousand *mainmortables* is the most probable.*

Besides these *mainmortables* there were a very large number of peasants and also of free townsmen, who were, nevertheless, still held under personal obligations either to their former lords or else to the lords of the lands they had bought or held on lease.

It is estimated that as a rule the privileged classes—the nobility and clergy—held half the lands of every village, but that besides these lands, which were their property, they still retained various feudal rights over the lands owned by the peasants. Small proprietors were even then very numerous in France, but there were very few of them, adds M. Sagnac, who " held by right of freehold, who did not owe at least a quit-rent, or some other due, in recognition of the seigniory." Nearly all lands paid something, either in money or in a portion of the crops, to some or other lord.

These obligations varied very much, but they may be divided into five classes : (1) The personal obligations, often humiliating—relics of serfdom ; † (2) payments of all sorts in money, in kind or in work, which were due for a real or supposed concession of land ; these were the mortmain and the real statute-labours,‡ the quit-rent, the field-rent, the land-tax, the fines on sales and on inheritance ; (3) various payments resulting from the lords' monopolies ; that is to say, the lords levied certain customs-revenues, certain town-dues, or certain rents from those who used their markets or their measures,

beginning of the eighteenth century) a state closely akin to slavery, and in the current language of the day allowed serfdom to be confounded with slavery.

* Sagnac, *La législation civile de la Révolution française*, pp. 59, 60.

† Arthur Young, writing of these vexatious and ruinous dues, says : " What are these tortures of the peasantry in Bretagne, which they call *chevanchés, quintaines, soule, saut de poisson, baiser de mariées, chansons ; transporte d'œuf sur un charette ; silence des grenouilles, corvée à miséricorde ; milode ; leide ; couponage ; cartilage ; barrage ; forage ; maréchaussé ; bauvin ; ban d'août ; trousses ; gelinage ; civerage ; taillabilité ; vingtain ; sterlage ; bordelage ; minage ; ban de vendanges ; droit d'accapt* . . . ? The very terms . . . are unknown in England, and consequently untranslatable " (*Travels in France*, p. 319 ; London, 1892).

† " Real " opposed to " personal " means here an obligation attached to *things*, that is to say, to the possession of the land.

mills, wine-presses, common ovens and the rest; (4) the fees of justice levied by the lord wherever the court belonged to him, the taxes, fines and so on; and (5) the lord possessed the exclusive right of hunting over his land and those of the neighbouring peasantry, as well as the right of keeping pigeon-houses and rabbit-warrens, which conferred a much-coveted honour with the privilege.

All these rights were vexatious to the last degree, and they cost the peasant dear, even when they mattered little or nothing to the lord. And it is a fact, upon which Boncerf lays stress in his remarkable work, *Les inconvénients des droits féodaux* * that ever since 1776 the impoverished lords, and especially their stewards, began to squeeze the farmers, the tenants and the peasants generally, in order to get out of them as much as possible. In 1786 there was even a pretty wide revision of the land-registers for the purpose of augmenting the feudal dues.

The Assembly, therefore, after pronouncing the abolition of all the survivals of the feudal system, halted when it became a question of wording these renunciations and putting them into the written law.

Thus it seemed as if the lords having sacrificed their *main-mortes*, there was nothing more to be said about it; they had only to put their renunciation into the form of a decree. But even on this question they raised discussions. They tried to establish a distinction between the personal mortmainable serfdom, a condition which should be abolished without indemnity, and the real mortmainable serfdom attached to the land and transmitted with the leasing or purchase of it: serfs of the latter class might redeem themselves. And if the Assembly decided in the end to abolish without indemnity all the rights and dues, feudal as well as manorial, " which pertained to mortmain, real or personal, and to personal services," they managed so as to cast a doubt even on this—especially in every case where it was difficult to separate the rights of *mortmain* from *feudal* rights in general.

There was the same shuffling over the question of the

* P. 52.

Church tithes. It is known that the tithes very often amounted to a fifth or even a quarter of all harvests, and that the clergy claimed a share of the very grasses and nuts which the peasants gathered. These tithes weighed very heavily upon the peasants, especially upon the poorer ones. But then, on August 4, the clergy had declared their renunciation of all tithes in kind, on condition that these tithes should be redeemed by those who paid them. But as they did not indicate the conditions of redemption, nor the rules of procedure under which the redemption should be made, the renunciation in reality was reduced to a simple declaration of principle. The clergy accepted the redemption ; they permitted the peasants to redeem the tithes if they wished to do so, and to debate the price with the holders of the tithes. But, on August 6, when it was proposed to draw up the resolutions concerning the tithes, a difficulty presented itself.

There were tithes which the clergy had sold in the course of the centuries to private individuals, and these tithes were called lay or *enfeoffed*. For such as these redemption was considered absolutely necessary, in order to maintain the right of property for the last purchaser. Worse than that : the tithes paid by the peasants to the clergy themselves were represented to the Assembly by certain speakers, as *a tax* which the nation paid in support of its clergy ; and by degrees, during the discussion, the opinion prevailed that there might be a question of redeeming the tithes if the nation undertook to give a regular salary to the clergy. This discussion lasted five days, until the 11th, and then several priests, backed by the archbishops, declared that they relinquished the tithes to the country, and left themselves to the justice and generosity of the nation.

It was decided, therefore, that the tithes paid to the clergy should be abolished ; but while means were being found for providing from some other source the expenses for religion, the *tithes should be paid as formerly*. As to the enfeoffed tithes, they were to be paid until they were redeemed.

It can be imagined what a terrible disappointment this was for the rural populations, and what a cause of disturbance.

In theory the tithes were suppressed, but in reality they were to be collected as usual. "Until when ?" asked the peasants; and the answer was, "Until we find some other means of paying the clergy!" And as the finances of the kingdom were going from bad to worse, the peasant was justified in asking if the tithes would ever be abolished. The stoppage of work and the revolutionary agitation manifestly prevented the collection of the taxes, whilst the cost of the new law and the new administration tended necessarily to increase the difficulty. Democratic reforms are expensive and it is only with time that a nation in revolution is able to pay the cost of its reforms. Meanwhile the peasant had to pay the tithes, and up to 1791 they were exacted from him in a very harsh way, and as he did not want to pay, law upon law and penalty upon penalty were decreed by the Assembly against the defaulters.

The same remark applies to the game laws. On the night of August 4 the nobles had renounced their hunting rights. But when it came to the formulation of what had been said, it was perceived that this would give the right of hunting to every one. Whereupon the Assembly retracted, and only extended the right of hunting to all proprietors, or rather to the owners of real estate upon their own lands. But here again they left rather vague the formula at which they finally stopped. The Assembly abolished the *exclusive* right of hunting and that of the unenclosed warrens, but they said that every proprietor had the right to destroy and to cause to be destroyed, only upon his inherited land, all kinds of game. Did this authorisation apply to the farmers ? It is doubtful. The peasants, however, did not wait for, nor require, the permission of tricky lawyers. Immediately after August 4 they began everywhere to destroy the game belonging to the lords. After having seen for many years their crops devoured by the game, they themselves destroyed the depredators without waiting for any authorisation.

Finally as to what concerned the essential thing, the great question which so deeply interested more than twenty millions of Frenchmen—the feudal rights—the Assembly, when it was formulating in resolutions the renunciations of the night of August 4, confined itself simply to the enunciation of a principle.

"The National Assembly destroys entirely the feudal system," said the first article of the resolutions of August 5. But the following articles of August 5 to 11 explain that only the personal servitude degrading to honour should disappear entirely. *All the other dues, whatsoever their origin or nature, remained.* They might be redeemed one day, but there was nothing in the resolutions of August to indicate either when or under what conditions that could be done. No limit was imposed. Not the slightest suggestion was made as to the legal procedure by means of which the redemption would be made. Nothing—nothing but the principle, the *desideratum*. And, meanwhile, the peasant had to pay everything, as before.

There was something worse in these resolutions of August 1789. They opened the door to a measure by which redemption would be made impossible, and this was passed by the Assembly seven months later. In February 1790 they made redemption absolutely impossible for the peasant to accept, by imposing the joint redemption of all land rents, personal and real. M. Sagnac has remarked, on page 90 of his excellent work that Demeunier had already proposed on August 6 or 7 a measure of this kind. And the Assembly, as we shall see, made a law in February 1790, after which it became impossible to redeem the dues upon the *land* without redeeming at the same time, in the same lot, the *personal* services, abolished though they were since August 5, 1789.

Carried away by the enthusiasm with which Paris and France received the news of that all-night sitting of August 4, the historians have not given sufficient prominence to the extent of the restrictions which the Assembly put against the first clause of its decree by means of clauses voted in the sittings from August 5 to 11. Even Louis Blanc, who furnishes, however, in his chapter *La propriété devant la Révolution,** the ideas necessary for the appreciation of the tenor of the resolutions passed in August, seems to hesitate at destroying the beautiful legend, and he glosses over the restrictions, or

* Book II. chap. i.

else tries even to excuse them in saying that "the logical sequence of facts in history is not so rapid, indeed far from it, as that of the ideas in the head of a thinker." But the fact remains that this vagueness, these doubts, these hesitations, which the Assembly flung to the peasants when they asked for measures, clear and precise, to abolish the old abuses, became the cause of the terrible struggles which were evolved during the four following years. It was not until after the expulsion of the Girondins that the question of the feudal rights came up again boldly and in its entirety, in the sense of Article 1 of the resolution of August 4.*

It is no use now, and at a distance of a hundred years, to declaim against the National Assembly. Indeed, the Assembly did all that could have been hoped for from an assembly of property owners and well-to-do middle-class men; perhaps it did even more. It gave forth a principle, and by so doing it invited, so to say, a further step. But it is very important to take into account these restrictions, for if the article which declared the total destruction of the feudal system is taken literally, we cannot fail to understand completely the four years of the Revolution which follow, and still more the struggles which broke out in the very midst of the Convention in 1793.

The resistance to these resolutions was immense. If they could not satisfy the peasants and if they became the signal for a powerful recrudescence of the peasant risings, to the nobles,

---

* Buchez and Roux (*Histoire parlementaire de la Révolution française*, vol. ii. p. 243) see in the abdications of August 4 only concessions rendered necessary by the debates on the "Declaration of the Rights of Man." The majority being in favour of this declaration, their vote would have infallibly carried with it the abolition of privileges. It is also interesting to note how Madame Elisabeth announced the night of August 4 to her friend, Madame de Mombelles: "The nobility," she writes, "with an enthusiasm worthy of the French heart, have renounced everything, the feudal rights and their hunting rights. Fishing will also be comprised, I believe. The clergy have likewise renounced the tithes and perquisites and the possibility of holding several benefices. This decree has been sent into all the provinces. *I hope this will put an end to the burning of the châteaux.* They have burned seventy." (Conches, *loc. cit.* p. 238.)

the higher clergy and the King these resolutions signified the spoliation of Church and nobility. From that day began the hidden agitation, which was fomented unceasingly and with an ever-growing ardour against the Revolution. The Assembly believed it could safeguard the rights of landed property, and in ordinary times a law of that kind might have attained this end. But in the villages people understood that the night of August 4 had dealt a tremendous blow at all feudal rights, and that the resolutions of August 5 to 11 had stripped the landlords of them, even though redemption of these rights was imposed upon the peasants. The general spirit of these resolutions, which included the abolition of the tithes, the rights of hunting and other privileges, clearly indicated to the people that the interests of the people are superior to the rights which property-owners may have acquired in the course of history. They contained the condemnation, in the name of justice, of all the hereditary privileges of feudalism. And henceforth nothing could rehabilitate those rights in the mind of the peasant.

The peasants understood that those rights were condemned and they rightly declined to buy them out. They just simply ceased to pay. But the Assembly, having neither the courage to abolish the feudal rights altogether, nor the inclination to work out a method of redemption that would be acceptable to the peasants, created in that way the equivocal conditions which were to bring forth civil war throughout France. On the one hand, the peasants understood that they need not buy anything, nor pay anything ; that the Revolution had only to go on in order to abolish the feudal rights without redemption. On the other hand, the rich people understood that the resolutions of August had as yet abolished nothing except the mortmain and the sacrificed hunting rights ; so that, by rallying themselves to the counter-revolution, and to the King as its representative, they would perhaps succeed in maintaining their feudal rights and in keeping the land that they and their ancestors had, under various pretexts, robbed from the village communes.

The King, probably by the advice of his counsellors, had

thoroughly understood the part assigned to him in the counter-revolution as a rallying-point for the defence of feudal privileges, and he hastened to write to the Archbishop of Arles to tell him that he would never give, except under compulsion, his sanction to the resolutions of August. "The sacrifice of the two first orders of the State is fine," he said; "but I can only admire it; I will never consent to the spoliation of my clergy and my nobility. I will not give my sanction to decrees which would despoil them."

And he continued to refuse his assent until he was led a prisoner to Paris by the people. And even when he gave it, he did everything, in conjunction with the property-owning clergy, nobles and middle classes, to couch his sanction in such a form as to render the resolutions of the Assembly dead letters.

My friend, James Guillaume, who has been so kind as to read my manuscript, has made a note on the question of the sanction of the resolutions (*arrêtés*) of August 4, which I here reproduce in entirety:

The Assembly at the time exercised both *constituent* and *legislative* power: and it had several times declared that its enactments, as a constituent power, were independent of the royal authority; only the *laws* had need of the King's sanction (they were called *decree* before the sanction, *law* after it).

The acts of August 4 were of a *constituent* nature: the Assembly had worded them as resolutions (*arrêtés*), but it did not think for a moment that it was necessary to obtain a permission from the King to state that the privileged persons had renounced their privileges. The character of these resolutions—or of this *resolution*, for sometimes they speak of it in the plural and sometimes in the singular—is indicated in the 19th and last Article, which says: "The National Assembly will occupy itself, immediately *after the constitution*, with drawing up the *laws* necessary for the development of the *principles* which it has *determined* by the present *resolution*, which will be forthwith sent by Messieurs the Deputies into all the provinces," &c. It was on August 11 that the publication of the resolutions was definitely adopted; at the same time the Assembly accorded to the King the title of "Restorer of French Liberty," and ordered that a *Te Deum* should be sung in the chapel of the palace.

On the 12th the president (Le Chapelier) went to ask the King when he would receive the Assembly for the *Te Deum;* the King replied that it would be on the 13th at noon. On the 13th the whole of the Assembly went to the palace; the president made a speech; he did not in the least ask for sanction; he explained to the King what the Assembly had done, and announced to him the title that had been accorded to him: Louis XVI. replied that he accepted the title with gratitude; he congratulated the Assembly and expressed his confidence in it. Then the *Te Deum* was sung in the chapel.

It mattered little that the King had written secretly to the arch-bishop to express a different sentiment: just then only public actions mattered.

Therefore *there was not the least public opposition* from the King, during the early days, against the resolutions of August 4.

But on Saturday, September 12, concerned at the disturbances which were agitating all France, the party of the " patriots " judged that, to put an end to them, it was necessary to make a solemn proclamation of the resolutions of August 4, and to this end the majority decided *that the resolutions should be presented for the King's sanction,* in spite of the opposition made to this decision by the counter-revolutionists, who would have preferred not to mention them further.

However, on Monday the 14th the patriots perceived that there might be some misunderstanding over this word " *sanction.*" Just at that point the Assembly discussed the " suspensive veto " of the King, and Barnave remarked that the veto could not be applied to the reso-lutions of August 4. Mirabeau spoke to the same effect. " The resolutions of August 4," he said, " were enacted by the constituent power, since when they cannot be subjected to sanction. The resolutions of August 4 are not laws, but principles and constitutional bases. Consequently, when you sent for sanction the acts of August 4, it was *for promulgation only* that you should have forwarded them." Le Chapelier, indeed, proposed to replace the word " sanction " in all concerning these resolutions by the word " promulgation," and added: " I maintain that it is useless to receive royal sanction for what his Majesty has already given authentic approbation to, as much by the letter, which he sent me when I had the honour to be the spokesman of the Assembly. (when president), as by the solemn acts of grace and the *Te Deum* sung in the King's Chapel."

It was proposed, therefore, to decree that the Assembly should suspend its order of the day (the question of the veto) until the promul-gation of the resolutions of August 4 had been made by the King.

(Great noise and disorder.) The sitting was ended without arriving at any decision.

On the 15th there was a fresh discussion, without results. On the 16th and 17th other things were discussed, the succession to the Throne occupying attention.

At last, on the 18th, the King's reply arrived. He approved the general spirit of the articles of August 4, but there were some of them to which he could only give a conditional assent; and he concluded in these terms: "Therefore, I approve the greater number of these articles, and I will sanction them *when they shall be worded as laws*." This dilatory reply produced great discontent; it was repeated that the King had been asked only to *promulgate*, which he could not refuse to do. It was decided that the president should go to the King to beg him to order the promulgation at once. Confronted by the threatening language of the speakers in the Assembly, Louis XVI. knew that he must yield; but while yielding he cavilled over the words: he sent back to the president (Clermont Tonnerre) on the evening of September 20 a reply saying: "You have asked me to invest with my sanction the resolutions of August 4 . . . I have communicated to you the criticisms to which they seem to me to be susceptible . . . You ask me now to promulgate these same decrees; *promulgation* belongs to *laws*. . . . But I have already said that I approved of the general spirit of these resolutions. . . . I am going to order their *publication* throughout the kingdom. . . . I do not doubt but that I shall be able to invest with my sanction all the laws which you will decree upon the various matters contained in these resolutions."

If the resolutions of August 4 contained only principles, or theories, if we seek in them vainly for practicable *measures*, &c., it is so, because such must be the character of these *resolutions*, so clearly marked by the Assembly in Article 19. On August 4 the Assembly had proclaimed, in principle, the destruction of the feudal system; and it was added that the Assembly *would make* the *laws*, for the application of the *principle*, and that they would make these laws *when the Constitution should be completed*. We may reproach the Assembly for this method if we wish; but we must acknowledge that it deceived no one, and in no way broke its word by not making the laws *immediately*, since it had promised to make them *after the Constitution*. But, once the Constitution was completed, the Assembly had to dissolve and bequeath its work to the Legislative Assembly.

This note by James Guillaume throws a new light upon the

tactics of the Constituent Assembly. When the war against the châteaux had raised the question of feudal rights the Assembly had two courses before it. Either it could elaborate some scheme of laws upon feudal rights, schemes which would have taken months, or rather years, to discuss, and, seeing the diversity of opinions held by the representatives on this subject, would have ended only in dividing the Assembly. Or else the Assembly might have confined itself to proposing *only some principles*, which should serve as bases for the enactment of future laws.

It was this second alternative which was ordained by the Assembly. It hastened to compile in several sittings the *resolutions* which the King was finally obliged to publish. And in the provinces these declarations of the Assembly had the effect of so shaking the feudal system that, four years after, the Convention was able to vote for the complete aboliton of the feudal rights without redemption. Whether this was foreseen or not we do not know, but this alternative was, after all, preferable to the first.

CHAPTER XIX

DECLARATION OF THE RIGHTS OF MAN

Meaning and significance of Declaration—Modelled on Declaration of Independence—Its defects—Its influence—"Preamble to the Constitution"—Defiance of feudalism

A few days after the taking of the Bastille the Constitution Committee of the National Assembly met to discuss the "Declaration of the Rights of Man and of the Citizen." The idea of issuing such a declaration, suggested by the famous Declaration of Independence of the United States, was perfectly right. Since a revolution was in course of accomplishment, and a complete change in the relations between the various ranks of society would result from it, it was well to state its general principles before this change was expressed in the form of a Constitution. By this means the mass of the people would be shown how the revolutionary minorities conceived the revolution, and for what new principles they were calling on the people to struggle.

It would not be fine phrases merely; it would be a brief summary of the future that it was proposed to conquer; and under the solemn form of a declaration of rights, made by an entire people, this summary would be invested with the significance of a national oath. Proclaimed in a few words, the principles that they were going to put into practice would kindle the people's courage. It is always ideas that govern the world, and great ideas presented in a virile form have always taken hold of the minds of men. In fact the young North American republicans, at the time when they were intending to conquer their independence, had issued just such declarations, and ever since, the Declaration of Independence of the United States had become the charter, one might almost say the Decalogue, of the young North American nation.*

Consequently, as soon as the Assembly nominated (on July 9) a committee for the preparatory work of the Constitution, it was found necessary to draw up a Declaration of the Rights of Man, and the work was begun after July 14. The committee took for their model the Declaration of Independence of the United States, which had already become famous, since 1776, as a statement of democratic belief.† Unfortunately the defects in it were also copied ; that is to say, like the American Constitutionalists assembled in the Congress of Philadelphia, the National Assembly kept out of its declaration all allusions to the economic relations between citizens ; it confined itself to affirming the equality of all before the law, the right of the nation to give itself whatever government it wished, and the constitutional liberties of the individual. As to property, the French Declaration took care to affirm its "inviolable and sacred" character and it added that "nobody could be deprived

---

* "When in the course of human events," said the Declaration of Independence of the United States, "it becomes necessary for one people to dissolve the political bands which have connected them with another, and to assume among the Powers of the Earth the separate and equal station to which the Laws of Nature and of Nature's God entitle them, a decent respect to the opinions of mankind requires that they should declare the causes which impel them to the separation.

"We hold these Truths to be self-evident, that all men are created equal, that they are endowed by their Creator with certain unalienable Rights, that among these are Life, Liberty and the Pursuit of Happiness—that to secure these rights, Governments are instituted among men, deriving their just powers from the consent of the governed, *that whenever any form of government becomes destructive of these ends it is the right of the people to alter or to abolish it,* and to institute new government, laying its foundation on such principles, and organising its powers in such form, as to them shall seem most likely to effect their safety and happiness" (Declaration made in Philadelphia, July 4, 1776). This declaration certainly does not correspond to the communist aspirations proclaimed by numerous groups of citizens. But it expresses and indicates exactly their ideas concerning the political form which they wished to obtain, and it inspired the America s with a proud spirit of independence.

† James Guillaume has recalled this fact in his work, *La déclaration des droits de l'homme et du citoyen*, Paris, 1900, p. 9. The Reporter of the Constitutional Committee had indeed mentioned this fact. To be assured of this one has only to compare the texts of the French drafts with those of the American declaration given in J. Guillaume's book.

of his property if it were not that public necessity, *legally established*, clearly exacted it, and under the condition of a *just* and *previous* indemnity." This was to repudiate the right of the peasants to the land and to the abolition of the exactions of feudal origin.

The middle classes put forth in this way their liberal programme of equality before the law in judicial matters and of government controlled by the nation and existing only by its will. And, as in all minimum programmes, this signified implicitly that the nation must not go further ; it must not touch upon the rights of property established by feudalism and despotic royalty.

It is probable that during the discussions raised by the drawing-up of the Declaration of the Rights of Man, some ideas of a social and equalising character were brought forward. But they must have been set aside. In any case we find no trace of them in the Declaration of 1789.* Sieyès' proposal that " if men are not equal in *means*, that is in riches, intellect, and strength, &c., it does not follow that they may not be equal in *rights* " †—even this idea, so modest in its claim, is not to be found in the Declaration of the Assembly. Instead of the foregoing words of Sieyès, the first article of the Declaration was conceived in these terms : " Men are born and live free and equal under the laws. Social distinctions may be established only on grounds of common utility " ; which allows that social distinctions might be established by law in the interest of the community, and, by means of that fiction, opens the door to all inequalities.

Altogether, when reading to-day the " Declaration of the Rights of Man and of the Citizen," we are tempted to ask if this declaration had really the influence over the minds of the period which historians attribute to it. It is evident that Article 1, which affirms the equality of rights for all men ; Article

---

* In America the people of certain States demanded the proclamation of the common right of the whole nation to the whole of the land ; but this idea, detestable from the middle-class point of view, was excluded from the Declaration of Indepndence.

† Article 16 of Sieyès' proposal (*La déclaration des droits de l'homme et du citoyen*, by James Guillaume, p. 30).

6, which says that the law should be " the same for all," and that " all the citizens have a right to co-operate, either person-ally or through their representatives, in its formation " ; Article 10, by virtue of which " no one should be molested for his opinions, provided that their manifestation does not disturb the public order established by law " ; and finally, Article 12, which declares that the public force was " instituted for the advantage of all—not for the special use of those to whom it is entrusted "—these affirmations, made in the midst of a society wherein feudal subjection still existed, and while the Royal family still considered itself the owner of France, worked a complete revolution in the minds of men.

But it is also certain that the Declaration of 1789 would have never had the influence it exercised later on in the course of the nineteenth century if the Revolution had stopped short at the limits of this profession of middle-class liberalism. Luckily the Revolution went much further. And when, two years later, in September 1791, the National Assembly drew up the Constitution, it added to the Declaration of the Rights of Man a " Preamble to the Constitution," which contained already these words : " The National Assembly . . . abolishes irrevocably the institutions that are hurtful to liberty and the equality of rights." And further, " There no longer exists either nobility, or peerage, or hereditary distinctions, or distinctions of orders, or *feudal system*, or *patrimonial courts of justice*, nor are there any titles, denominations and pre-rogatives which were derived from them, nor any order of chivalry, nor any such corporations which required proofs of nobility for entering them, or decorations which supposed distinctions of birth, *nor any other superiority except that of the public functionaries in the exercise of their functions.* There are no longer any guilds, nor corporations of professions, arts and crafts [the middle-class ideal of the State Omnipotent appears in these two paragraphs]. *The law does not recognise any longer either religious vows or any other pledge which would be contrary to natural laws and to the Constitution.*"

When we think that this defiance was flung to a Europe still plunged in the gloom of all-powerful royalty and feudal subjection, we understand why the French Declaration of the Rights of Man, often confounded with the Preamble of the Constitution which followed it, inspired the people during the wars of the Republic and became later on the watchword of progress for every nation in Europe during the nineteenth century. But it must not be forgotten that it was not the Assembly, nor even the middle classes of 1789 who expressed their desires in this Preamble. It was the popular revolution which was forcing them bit by bit to recognise the rights of the people and to break with feudalism—at the cost of what sacrifices we shall see presently.

CHAPTER XX

THE FIFTH AND SIXTH OF OCTOBER 1789

King refuses to sanction Declaration—Middle classes and people in opposition to royalty—Influence of people on upper classes—Power of King's *veto* during Revolution—Assembly refuse King the *veto*, but grant him the *suspensive veto*—Weakness of Assembly—Scarcity of food in Paris—Accusations against royal family and people at Court—Danger of national bankruptcy—Plans for King's escape—Influence of history of Charles I. on Louis XVI.—His terror of Revolution—Plotting continues—Preparations for march on Versailles—Precautions of King—Outbreak of insurrection—March on Versailles—Queen chief object of people's animosity—Entry of women into Versailles—King sanctions Declaration of Rights of Man—Lafayette sets out for Versailles—Terror at Court—End of Monarchy of Versailles

EVIDENTLY to the King and the Court the " Declaration of the Rights of Man and of the Citizen " must have seemed a criminal attempt upon all the laws, human and divine. The King, therefore, bluntly refused to give it his sanction. It is true that, like the " resolutions " passed between August 4 and 11, the Declaration of Rights represented only an affirmation of principles ; it had, therefore, as they said then, a " constituent character " (*un caractère constituant*), and as such it did not need the royal sanction. The King had but to promulgate it.

Now this is what he refused to do under various pretexts. On October 5 he wrote again to the Assembly to say that he wished to see how the maxims of the Declaration would be applied before giving it his sanction.*

* " I do not quite understand the Declaration of the Rights of Man : it contains very good maxims, suitable for guiding your labours. But it contains some principles that require explanations, and are even

He had opposed, as we have seen, by a similar refusal, the resolutions of August 4 to 11, concerning the abolition of the feudal rights, and it can be imagined what a weapon the Assembly made of these two refusals. What! the Assembly was abolishing the feudal system, personal subjection and the pernicious prerogatives of the lords, it was proclaiming the equality of all before the law—and see how the King, but especially the princes, the Queen, the Court, the Polignacs, the Lamballes and all the rest of them, are opposing it! If it were only a matter of speeches in favour of equality, the circulation of which had been prevented! But no, the whole Assembly, including the nobles and the bishops, were all agreed to make a law favourable to the people and to do away with all privileges (for the people who do not pay much heed to legal terms, the " resolutions " were as good as " laws "), and now the Court party are going to prevent these laws coming into force! The King would have accepted them; he came to fraternise with the people of Paris after July 14; but it is the Court, the princes, the Queen, who are opposed to the attempt of the Assembly to secure the happiness of the people.

In the great duel between royalty and the middle classes, the latter thus had got the people on their side. At this moment public opinion was really inflamed against the princes, the Queen, and the upper classes on account of the Assembly, whose labours they began to follow with interest.

At the same time the people themselves were influencing those labours in a democratic sense. Thus the Assembly might perhaps have accepted the scheme of two Chambers " in the English fashion." But the people would not have it. They understood instinctively what learned jurists have since so well explained—that in revolution a second Chamber was impossible : it could only act when the revolution was exhausted and a period of reaction had begun.

Similarly, it was also the people of Paris who were more vehemently opposed to the royal *veto* than those who sat in

liable to different interpretations, which cannot be fully appreciated until the time when their true meaning will be fixed by the laws to which the Declaration will serve as the basis. Signed : Louis."

the Assembly. Here, too, the masses understood the situation quite clearly ; for if, in the normal course of affairs, the power of the King to check a decision of the parliament loses much of its importance, it is quite another thing in a revolutionary period. Not that the royal power becomes less dangerous in the long run ; but in ordinary times a parliament being the organ of privileged persons will seldom pass anything that the King would have to veto in the interest of the privileged classes ; while during a revolutionary period the decisions of a parliament, influenced as they are by the popular spirit of the moment, may often tend towards the destruction of ancient privileges, and, consequently, they will encounter opposition from the King. He will use his *veto*, if he has the right and the strength to use it. This is, in fact, what happened with the Assembly's " resolutions " of August, and even with the Declaration of Rights.

In spite of this, there was in the Assembly a numerous party who desired the absolute *veto*—that is to say, they wished to give the King the possibility of legally preventing any measure he might choose to prevent ; and it took lengthy debates to arrive at a compromise. The Assembly refused the absolute *veto*, but they accepted, against the will of the people, the *suspensive veto*, which permitted the King to suspend a decree for a certain time, without altogether annulling it.

At a distance of a hundred years the historian is naturally inclined to idealise the Assembly and to represent it as a body that was ready to fight for the Revolution. In reality it was not. The fact is that even in its most advanced representatives the National Assembly remained far below the requirements of the moment. It must have been conscious of its own impotence. Far from being homogeneous, it contained, on the contrary, more than three hundred deputies—four hundred according to other estimates ; that is to say, more than one-third, ready to come to terms with royalty. Therefore, without speaking of those members who were pledged to the Court, and there were several of them, how many feared the revolution much more than the royal power ! But the revolution had begun, and there was the direct pressure of the people and the fear of their rage; there was also that intellectual atmosphere which dominates the timorous and forces the prudent to follow the more advanced ones. Moreover the people maintained their menacing attitude, and the memory of de Launey, Foulon and Bertier was still fresh in their minds. In the faubourgs of Paris there was even talk of massacring those members of the Assembly whom the people suspected of having connections with the Court.

Meanwhile the scarcity of food in Paris was always terrible. It was September, the harvest had been gathered in, but still there was a lack of bread. Long files of men and women stood every night at the bakers' doors, and after long hours of waiting the poor often went away without any bread. In spite of th purchase of grain that the Government had made abroad, and the premium paid to those who imported wheat to Paris, bread was scarce in the capital, as well as in all the large towns, and in the small towns near Paris. The measures taken for revictualling were insufficient, and what was done was paralysed by fraud. All the vices of the *ancien régime*, of the centralised State which was growing up since the sixteenth century, became apparent in this question of bread. In the upper circles the refinement of luxury had attained its limits; but the mass of the people, flayed without mercy, had come to the point of not being able to produce its own food on the rich soil and in the productive climate of France !

Besides, the most terrible accusations were being circulated against the princes of the royal family and personages in the highest positions at Court. They had re-established, it was said, the " famine compact," and were speculating on the rise of prices of the bread-stuffs. And these rumours, as it appeared later on, were not quite unfounded.

To complete all, the danger of national bankruptcy was imminent. Interest on State debts had to be paid immediately, but the expenses were increasing, and the Treasury was empty. No one dared now to resort to the abominable means which were habitual under the old *régime* for levying the taxes, when everything in the peasant's home was seized by the tax collector; whilst the peasants, on their side, in the expectation of a more just assessment of the taxes, preferred not to pay, and the rich, who hated the Revolution, with secret joy refrained from paying anything whatever. Necker, again in the Ministry since July 17, 1789, had tried various ingenious expedients for avoiding bankruptcy—but without success. In fact, one cannot well see how bankruptcy could be prevented without either resorting to a forced loan from the rich, or seizing the wealth of the clergy. The middle classes understood it, and became resigned to such drastic measures, since they had lent their money to the State and did not wish to lose it. But the King, the Court and the higher ecclesiastics, would they ever agree to this seizure of their properties by the State?

A strange feeling must have taken possession of men's minds during the months of August and September 1789. At last the desire of so many years was realised. Here was a National Assembly which held in its hands the legislative power. An Assembly which had already proved itself not quite hostile to a democratic, reforming spirit; and now it was reduced to impotence, and to the ridicule attendant on impotency. It could make decrees to avoid bankruptcy, but the King, the Court, the princes would refuse to sanction them. Like so many ghosts of the past, they had the power to strangle the representation of the French people, to paralyse its will, to prolong to infinity the provisional unsettled state of affairs.

More than that: these ghosts were preparing a great *coup*. In the King's household they were making plans for his escape from Versailles. The King would shortly be carried off to Rambouillet, or to Orléans, where he would put himself at the head of the armies, and thence he would threaten Versailles and Paris. Or else he might fly towards the eastern frontier and there await the arrival of the German and Austrian armies which the *émigrés* had promised him. All sorts of influences were thus intermingling at the palace: that of the Duke of Orléans, who dreamed of seizing the throne after the departure of Louis; that of " Monsieur," the brother of Louis XVI., who would have been delighted if his brother, as well as Marie-Antoinette, whom he hated personally, had disappeared.

Since the month of September the Court meditated the escape of the King; but if they discussed many plans, they dared not carry out any one of them. It is very likely that Louis XVI. and his wife dreamed of repeating the history of Charles I., and of waging a regular war against the parliament only with better success. The history of the English King obsessed them: it fascinated them; but they read it, as prisoners awaiting trial read police stories. They drew from it no instruction as to the necessity of yielding in time: they only said to themselves: "Here they ought to have resisted; there it was necessary to plot; there again daring was required!" And so they made plans, which neither they nor their courtiers had the courage to put into execution.

The Revolution held them spell-bound; they saw the monster that was going to devour them, and they dared neither submit nor resist. Paris, which was already preparing to march upon Versailles, filled them with terror and paralysed their efforts. "What if the army falters at the supreme moment, when the battle has begun? What if the commanders betray the King, as so many of them have done already? What would be left to do then if not to share the fate of Charles I. ?"

And yet they plotted. Neither the King nor his courtiers, nor the privileged classes as a whole could understand that the time for compromise was far away; that now the only way was frankly to submit to the new force and to place the royal power under its protection—for the Assembly asked nothing better than to grant its protection to the King. Instead of that, they plotted, and by so doing they impelled those members of the Assembly who were, after all, very moderate, into counter-plots: they drove them towards revolutionary action. This is why Mirabeau and others, who would have willingly worked at the establishing of a moderately constitutional monarchy, had to throw in their lot with the advanced sections. And this is why moderates, like Duport, constituted "the confederation of the clubs," which allowed them to keep the people in a state of ferment, for they felt they would soon have need of the masses.

The march upon Versailles on October 5, 1789, was not as spontaneous as it was supposed to be. Even in a Revolution every popular movement requires to be prepared by men of the people, and this one had its forerunners. Already on August 30 the Marquis of Saint-Huruge, one of the popular orators of the Palais Royal, had wanted to march on Versailles with fifteen hundred men to demand the dismissal of the "ignorant, corrupt and suspected" deputies, who were defending the suspensive *veto* of the King. Meanwhile they threatened to set fire to the châteaux of those deputies, and warned them that two thousand letters had been sent into the provinces to that effect. The gathering was dispersed, but the idea of a march upon Versailles was thrown out, and it continued to be discussed.

On August 31 the Palais Royal sent to the Hôtel de Ville five deputations, one of which was headed by Loustalot, the most sympathetic of republican writers, asking the municipality of Paris to exercise pressure upon the Assembly to prevent its acceptance of the royal *veto*. Some of those who took part in these deputations went to threaten the deputies, others to implore them. At Versailles the crowd, in tears, begged Mirabeau to abandon the defence of the absolute *veto*, justly remarking that if the King had this right he would no longer have need of the Assembly.*

From this time, the idea began to grow that it would be well to have the Assembly and the King at hand in Paris. In fact, since the first days of September, there was open speaking already at the Palais Royal about bringing the King and "M. le Dauphin" to Paris, and for this purpose all good citizens were exhorted to march on Versailles. The *Mercure de France* made mention of it on September 5 (page 84), and Mirabeau spoke of women who would march on Versailles a fortnight before the event.

The banquet given to the Guards on October 3, and the

* Buchez and Roux, p. 368 *et seq.* Bailly, *Mémoires*, ii. 326, 341.

plots of the Court, hastened events. Every one had a fore-boding of the blow which the party of reaction was preparing to strike. Reaction was raising its head; the Municipal Council of Paris, essentially middle class, became bold in reactionary ways. The royalists were organising their forces without troubling much to conceal the fact. The road from Paris to Metz having been lined with troops, the carrying off of the King and his going to Metz were discussed openly. The Marquis de Bouillé, who commanded the troops in the East, as well as de Breteuil and de Mercy were in the plot, of which de Breteuil had taken the direction. For this end the Court collected as much money as possible, and October 5 was spoken of as the possible date of the flight. The King would set out that day for Metz, where he would place himself in the midst of the army commanded by the Marquis de Bouillé. There he would summon to him the nobility and the troops which still held faithful, and would declare the Assembly rebellious.

With this movement in view they had doubled at the palace the number of the body-guards (young members of the aristocracy charged with the guarding of the palace), and the regiment of Flanders had been summoned to Versailles, as well as the dragoons. The regiment came, and on October 1 a great banquet was given by the body-guard to the regiment of Flanders, and the officers of the dragoons and of the Swiss in garrison at Versailles were invited to this banquet.

During the dinner Marie-Antoinette and the Court ladies, as well as the King, did all they could to bring the royalist enthusiasm of the officers to a white heat. The ladies themselves distributed white cockades, and the National cockade was trodden underfoot. Two days later, on October 3, another banquet of the same kind took place.

These banquets precipitated events. The news of them soon reached Paris—exaggerated perhaps on the way—and the people of the capital understood that if they did not march immediately upon Versailles, Versailles would march upon Paris.

The Court was evidently preparing a great blow. Once the King, having left Versailles, was safe somewhere in the midst of his troops, nothing would be easier than to dissolve the Assembly, or else compel it to return to the Three Orders —that is to say, to the position before the Royal Session of June 23. In the Assembly itself there was a strong party of some four hundred members, the leaders of whom had already held confabulations with Malouet for the transference of the Assembly to Tours, far from the revolutionary people of Paris. If this plot of the Court succeeded, then all the hitherto obtained results would be upset. The fruits of July 14 would be lost; lost, too, the results of the rising of the peasants and of the panic of August 4.

What was to be done to prevent such a disaster? *The people had to be roused—nothing less than that would do!* And therein lies the glory of the prominent revolutionists of that moment; they understood the necessity of a popular rising and accepted it, though usually the middle classes recoil before such a measure. To rouse the people—the gloomy, miserable masses of the people of Paris—this is what the revolutionists undertook to do on October 4; Danton, Marat and Loustalot, whose names we have already mentioned, being the most ardent in the task. A handful of conspirators cannot fight an army; reaction cannot be vanquished by a band of men, howsoever determined they may be. To an army must be opposed an army, and, failing an army—the people, the whole people, the hundreds of thousands of men, women and children of a city. They alone can be victorious, they alone have conquered armies by demoralising them, by paralysing their brute force.

On October 5 the insurrection broke out in Paris to the cry of " Bread! Bread! " The sound of the drum beaten by a young girl served to rally the women. Soon a troop of women was formed; it marched to the Hôtel de Ville, forced the doors of the Communal Hall, demanding bread and arms, and, as a march upon Versailles had already been talked of for several days, the cry " To Versailles! " attracted crowds of women. Maillard, known in Paris since July 14 for the part he had taken in the siege of the Bastille, was declared leader of the column, and the women set out.

A thousand diverse ideas no doubt crossed their minds, but that of bread must have dominated all others. It was at Versailles that the conspiracies against the happiness of the people were hatched; it was there that the famine compact had been made, there that the abolition of the feudal rights was being prevented—so the women marched on Versailles. It is more than probable that among the mass of the people the King, like all Kings, was regarded as a good enough creature, who wished the welfare of his people. The royal prestige was then still deeply rooted in the minds of men. But even in 1789 they hated the Queen. The words uttered about her were terrible. " Where is that rip ? Look at her, the dirty whore; we must catch hold of that bitch and cut her throat," said the women, and one is struck by the ardour, the pleasure, I might say, with which these remarks were written down in the inquiry at the Châtelet. Here again the people judged soundly. If the King had said, on learning about the fiasco of the Royal Session on June 23, " After all, let these wretches stay ! "—Marie-Antoinette was wounded to the heart by it. She received with supreme disdain the " plebeian " King when he came on his return from his visit to Paris on July 17, wearing the tricolour cockade, and since then she had become the centre of all the intrigues. The correspondence which later she carried on with Count Fersen about bringing the foreign armies to Paris originated from that moment. Even this night of October 5, when the women invaded the palace —this very night, says the extremely reactionary Madame Campan, the Queen received Fersen in her bedchamber.

The people knew all this, partly through the palace servants; and the crowd, the collective mind of the people of Paris, understood what individuals were slow to comprehend—that Marie-Antoinette would go far in her hatred of the Revolution, and that, in order to prevent all the plottings of the Court, it was necessary that the King and his family, and the Assembly as well, should be kept in Paris under the eye of the people.

At first, on entering Versailles, the women, crushed by

fatigue and hunger, soaked through with the downpour of rain, contented themselves with demanding bread. When they invaded the Assembly they sank exhausted on the benches of the deputies; but nevertheless, by their presence alone these women had already gained a first victory. The Assembly profited by this march upon Versailles to obtain from the King his sanction for the Declaration of the Rights of Man.

After the women had started from Paris, men had also begun to march, and then, about seven o'clock in the evening, to prevent any mishap at the palace, Lafayette set out for Versailles at the head of the National Guards.

Terror seized upon the Court. " It is all Paris, then, that is marching against the palace ? " The Court held a council, but without arriving at any decision. Carriages had already been ordered out to send off the King and his family, but they were discovered by a picket of National Guards, who sent them back to the stables.

The arrival of the middle-class National Guards, the efforts of Lafayette, and above all, perhaps, a heavy rain, caused the crowd which choked the streets of Versailles, the Assembly and the purlieus of the palace, to diminish by degrees. But about five or six in the morning some men and women found at last a little gate open which enabled them to enter the palace. In a few moments they had found out the bedchamber of the Queen, who had barely time to escape to the King's apartment; otherwise she might have been hacked to pieces. The body-guard were in similar danger when Lafayette rode up, just in time to save them.

The invasion of the palace by the crowd was one of those defeats of royalty from which it never recovered. Lafayette obtained from the crowds some cheering for the King when he appeared upon a balcony. He even extracted from the crowd some cheers for the Queen by making her appear on the balcony with her son, and by kissing respectfully the hand of her whom the people called " the Medicis " . . . but all that was only a bit of theatricality. The people had realised their strength, and they used it to compel the King to set out for Paris. The middle classes then tried to make all sorts of royalist demonstrations on the occasion of the entrance of the King into his capital, but the people understood that *henceforth the King would be their prisoner*, and Louis XVI. on entering the Tuileries, abandoned since the reign of Louis XIV., had no illusions about it. " Let every one put himself where he pleases ! " was his reply when he was asked to give orders, and he asked for the history of Charles I. to be brought to him from his library.

The great monarchy of Versailles had come to an end. For the future there would be " Citizen Kings " or emperors who attained the throne by fraud ; but the reign of the " Kings by the Grace of God " was gone.

Once more, as on July 14, *the people*, by solidarity and by their action, had paralysed the plots of the Court and dealt a heavy blow at the old *régime*. The Revolution was making a leap forward.

CHAPTER XXI

FEARS OF THE MIDDLE CLASSES—THE NEW MUNICIPAL ORGANISATION

Unexpected reaction sets in—Exultation of revolutionists—
Their misconception of the situation—Reaction *versus* Revolution—Aims of middle classes—Assembly, afraid of people,
strengthens its position—Council of Three Hundred establishes
its authority—Importance of Bailly and Lafayette—Martial
law voted—Marat, Robespierre and Buzot alone protest—
Intrigues of Duke of Orléans and Count de Pro ence—Mirabeau—Aims of educated middle class—Duport, Charles de
Lameth and Barnavo—Bailly and Lafayette—Alarm of
middle classes at insurrection—Proposal of Sieyès accepted
—Ancient feudal divisions abolished—France divided into
departments—Electoral Assemblies—Difference between *passive* and *active* citizens—General assemblies of village communes forbidden—Importance to Revolution of municipal
centres—Parliaments abolished—Formidable opposition to
new organisation

ONCE more one might have thought that the Revolution would
now freely develop of itself. Royal reaction was vanquished;
"Monsieur and Madame Veto" had given in, and were held
as prisoners in Paris; and the National Assembly would surely
use now the axe in the forest of abuses, hew down feudalism,
and apply the great principles it had proclaimed in the Declaration of the Rights of Man, the mere reading of which had
made all hearts throb.

There was, however, nothing of the sort. Against all
expectations, it was reaction that began after October 5. It
organised its powers, and went on, growing in strength until
the month of June 1792.

After having accomplished its task, the people of Paris
retreated to their hovels; the middle classes disbanded them
and made them leave the streets. And had it not been for

the peasant insurrection, which followed its course until the feudal rights were actually abolished in July 1793, had it not been for the numerous insurrections in the provincial towns which prevented the government of the middle classes from firmly establishing itself, the final reaction, which triumphed in 1794, might have been already triumphant in 1791 or even in 1790.

" The King is at the Louvre, the National Assembly at the Tuileries, the channels of circulation are cleared, the market-place is full of sacks of corn, the National exchequer is being replenished, the mills are turning, the traitors are flying, the shavelings are down, the aristocracy is expiring," thus Camille Desmoulins wrote in the first number of his journal (November 28). But in reality reaction was everywhere raising its head. While the revolutionaries exulted, believing that the Revolution was almost accomplished, the reactionaries knew that the great struggle, the real one, between the past and the future, was only to begin in every provincial town, great and small, in every little village ; that now was the time for them to act in order to get the upper hand in the revolution.

The reactionaries understood something more. They saw that the middle classes, who until then had sought the support of the people, in order to obtain constitutional laws and to dominate the higher nobility, were going, now that they had seen and felt the strength of the people, to do all they could to dominate the people, to disarm them and to drive them back into subjection.

This fear of the people made itself felt in the Assembly, immediately after October 5. More than two hundred deputies refused to go to Paris, and demanded passports for returning to their homes. They met with a refusal, and were treated as traitors, but a certain number of them sent in their resignations all the same : they were not thinking of going so far ! There was now a new series of emigrations, as there had been after July 14. But this time it was not the Court which gave the signal, it was the Assembly.

However, there was in the Assembly   strong nucleus of middle-class representatives who knew how to profit by the first moments of success—to establish the power of their own class upon a solid foundation. Consequntly, even before moving to Paris, the Assembly voted, on October 19, the responsibility of the ministers, as well as of administrative officials before the National representation, and the assessment of all taxes by the Assembly. These two first conditions of a Constitutional Government were thus established. The title of the " King of France " was also changed into " King of the French."

Whilst the Assembly was thus profiting by the movement of October 5 to establish itself as the sovereign power, the middle-class municipality of Paris, *i.e.*, the Council of the Three Hundred, which had set itself up after July 14, also took advantage of events to establish its authority. Sixty directors, chosen from among the Three Hundred, and divided between eight departments—food, police, public works, hospitals, education, land and revenues, taxes and the National Guard—were going to take over all these important branches of administration, and thus to become a respectable power, especially as the municipality had under its orders a National Guard of 60,000 men, drawn solely from well-to-do citizens.

Bailly, the Mayor of Paris, and Lafayette, the chief commander of the National Guard, were becoming important personages. As to the municipal police functions, the middle classes assumed the right of supervision in everything: meetings, newspapers, the selling of literature in the streets, the advertisement posters, and so on ; so as to be able to suppress all that might be hostile to their interests.

And finally, the Council of the Three Hundred, taking advantage of the murder of a baker on October 21, went to the Assembly to beg for martial law, which was voted at once. Henceforth it was sufficient for a municipal official to unfurl the red flag for martial law to be proclaimed ; after that every crowd had to disperse, and the troops, when required by the municipal official, could fire upon the people if they did not disperse after three summonses had been made. If the people dispersed peaceably without resistance, before the last summons, only the ringleaders of the disturbance were arrested and sent to prison for three years—if the crowd was unarmed ; otherwise the sentence was death. But in case of any violence committed by the people, it was death for all concerned in the riot. It was death, too, for any soldier or officer of the National Guard who should stir up any rioting.

A murder committed in the street was thus sufficient excuse for this law to be passed, and, as Louis Blanc has aptly remarked, in the whole press of Paris there was but one voice, that of Marat, to protest against this atrocious law, and to say that in a time of revolution, when a nation had still to break its chains and to fight to the bitter end against its enemies, martial law had no right to exist. In the Assembly, Robespierre and Buzot were the only ones to protest, and these not on a point of principle. It was not advisable, they said, to proclaim martial law before having established a court which could try the criminals for felony against the nation.

Profiting by the slackening of the people's ardour, which necessarily followed after the movement of October 5 and 6, the middle classes began, also in the Assembly, as in the municipality, to organise their new power—not, it is true, without some collisions between the personal ambitions which clashed and conspired against each other.

The Court on its side saw no reason for abdicating ; it conspired and struggled also, and made profit out of the necessitous and ambitious, such as Mirabeau, by enrolling them in its service.

The Duke of Orléans, having been compromised in the movement of October 5, which he had secretly supported, was sent in disgrace, by the Court, as ambassador to England. But then it was " Monsieur," the Count of Provence, the King's brother, who began intriguing to send away the King— " the log " (soliveau), as he wrote to a friend. Once the King had gone, Orléans could pose as a candidate for the throne of France. Mirabeau, always in want, and who, ever since June 23, had acquired a formidable power over the Assembly, was intriguing on his side to get into the Ministry. When his plots were thwarted by the Assembly, which voted that none of its members should accept a place in the Ministry, he threw himself into the arms of the Count of Provence, in the hope of getting into power by his intervention. Finally, he sold himself to the King and accepted from him a pension of fifty thousand francs a month for four months, and the promise of an embassy ; in return for which M. de Mirabeau pledged himself " to aid the King with his knowledge, his power and his eloquence, in whatever Monsieur will judge useful to the State and in the interest of the King." All this, however, only became known later on, in 1792, after the taking of the Tuileries, and, meanwhile, Mirabeau kept, until his death on April 2, 1791, his reputation as a champion of the people.

Historians will never unravel the tissue of intrigues which was then being woven round the Louvre and in the palaces of the princes, as well as round the Courts of London, Vienna and Madrid, and in the various German principalities. Quite a world fermented round the royalty which was perishing. And even in the midst of the Assembly, how many ambitions were struggling to grasp the power ! But after all, these are but incidents of small value. They help to explain certain facts, but they could change nothing in the progress of events, marked out by the very logic of the situation and the forces in the conflict.

The Assembly represented the educated middle classes on their way to conquer and organise the power which was falling from the hands of the Court, the higher clergy, and the great nobles. And it contained in its midst a number of men marching straight towards this end with intelligence and a certain audacity, which increased every time that the people gained a fresh victory over the old *régime*. There was in the Assembly a " triumvirate " composed of Duport, Charles de Lameth, and Barnave, and at Paris there were the Mayor Bailly and the commander of the National Guard, Lafayette, upon whom all eyes were turned. But the real power of the mement was represented by the compact forces of the Assembly which were elaborating the laws to constitute the government of the middle classes.

This was the work which the Assembly resumed with ardour,

as soon as it was installed in Paris and could go on with its work with a certain amount of tranquillity.

This work was begun, as we have seen, the very day after the taking of the Bastille. The middle classes were seized with alarm when they saw the people arming themselves with pikes in a few days, burning the toll-gates, seizing the bread-stuffs wherever they found them, and all the while showing as much hostility to the rich middle classes as towards the "red heels" (*talons rouges*). They made haste to arm them-selves and to organise *their* National Guard—to array the "beaver hats" against the "woollen caps" and the pikes, so that the popular insurrections could be kept in hand. And after the insurrection on October 5, they passed without delay the law about rioting, of which we have just spoken.

At the same time they made haste to legislate in such a way that the political power which was slipping out of the hand of the Court should not fall into the hands of the people. Thus, eight days after July 14, Sieyès, the famous advocate of the Third Estate, had already proposed to the Assembly to divide the French into two classes, of which one only, the *active* citizens, should take part in the government, whilst the other, comprising the great mass of the people under the name of the *passive* citizens, should be deprived of all political rights. Five weeks later the Assembly accepted this division as the basis for the Constitution. The Declaration of Rights, of which the first principle was Equality of Rights for all citizens, was thus flagrantly violated as soon as proclaimed.

Now, on resuming the work of political organisation for France, the Assembly abolished the ancient feudal division into provinces, of which each one preserved certain privi-leges for the nobility and the *parlements*. It divided France into departments, and suspended the ancient *parlements*, *i.e.*, the ancient tribunals, which also possessed certain judicial privileges—and it went on to the organisation of an entirely new and uniform administration, always maintaining the principle of excluding the poorer classes from the Government.

The National Assembly, which had been elected under the old *régime* under a system of elections in two degrees, was nevertheless the outcome of an almost universal suffrage. That is to say, that the *primary assemblies*, which had been convoked in every electoral division, were composed of nearly all the citizens of the locality. These primary assemblies had nominated the *electors*, who made up in each division one *electoral* assembly, and this, in its turn, chose its representative in the National Assembly. It is well to note that after the elections the electoral assemblies continued to meet, receiving letters from their deputies and keeping watch over their votes.

Having now attained power, the middle classes did two things. They extended the prerogatives of the electoral assemblies, by confiding to them the election of the local councils (the *directoires* of each department), the judges and certain other functionaries. They gave them thus a great power. But, at the same time, they excluded from the primary assemblies the mass of the people, whom by this means they deprived of all political rights. They admitted into them only the *active* citizens, that is, those who paid in direct contributions at least three days' work.* The rest became *passive* citizens, who could no longer take part in the primary assemblies, and accordingly had no right to nominate the electors, or the municipality, or any of the local authorities. Besides, they could no longer form part of the National Guard.†

Furthermore, to be eligible as an elector, it was necessary to pay, in direct taxes, the value of *ten* days' work, which made these assemblies entirely middle class. Later on, in 1791, when reaction was emboldened by the massacre on the Champ-de-Mars, the Assembly made an additional restriction : electors must possess landed property. And to be nominated a representative of the people in the National Assembly, it was necessary to pay in direct taxation the value of a *marc* of silver (eight ounces), that is to say, fifty livres.‡

* Each municipality fixed the value, in money, of the day, and it was agreed to take for a basis the day of a journeyman.

† The municipal law of December 14, 1789, not only excluded the *passive* citizens from all the elections of municipal officers (paragraphs 5, 6, 8, &c.), but it also forbade the electoral assemblies to meet "by trades, professions or guilds." They could only meet by quarters, or districts.

‡ The *livre* had the value of about one franc.

And finally, the *permanence* of the electoral assemblies was interdicted. Once the elections were over, these assemblies were not to meet again. Once the middle-class governors were appointed, they must not be controlled too strictly. Soon the right even of petitioning and of passing resolutions was taken away—" Vote and hold your tongue! "

As to the villages, they had preserved, as we have seen, under the old *régime*, in nearly the whole of France, up to the Revolution, the general assembly of the inhabitants, like the *mir* in Russia. To this general assembly belonged the administration of the affairs of the commune, such as the re-division and the use of the communal lands—cultivated fields, meadows and forests, and also the waste lands. But now these general assemblies of the village communes were forbidden by the municipal law of December 22 to 24, 1789. Henceforth only the well-to-do peasants, the *active* citizens, had the right to meet, *once a year*, to nominate the mayor and the municipality, composed of three or four middle-class men of the village.

A similar municipal organisation was given to the towns, where the *active* citizens met to nominate the general council of the town and the municipality, that is to say, the legislative power in municipal matters and the executive power to whom was entrusted the administration of the commune's police and the command of the National Guard.

Thus the movement described as taking place in the towns in July 1789, and which consisted in obtaining by revolutionary means an elective municipal administration at a time when the laws of the old *régime*, still in full force, authorised nothing of the kind—this movement was sanctioned by the municipal and administrative law of December 22 to 24, 1789. And, as we shall see, an immense power was conferred on the Revolution by the creation, at its very outset, of these thirty thousand municipal centres, independent in a thousand matters of the central government, and capable of revolutionary action, when the revolutionaries succeeded in seizing upon them.

It is true that the middle classes surrounded themselves with every precaution in order to keep the municipal power in the hands of the well-to-do members of the community, and the municipalities themselves were placed under the supervision of the councils of the department, which, being chosen by electors in the second degree, thus represented the wealthier section of the middle classes and were the support and the right hand of the counter-revolutionists during the Revolution. On the other hand, the municipality itself, which was elected by the *active* citizens only, also represented the middle classes more than the masses of the people, and in towns like Lyons and so many others it became a centre of reaction. But with all that, the municipalities were not dependent upon the royal power, and it must be recognised that the municipal law of December 1789 contributed to the success of the Revolution more than any other law. During the insurrection against the feudal lords, in August 1789, many municipalities were hostile to the revolted peasants, and we saw how the municipalities of the Dauphiné took the field against the peasants and hanged the rebels without mercy. But in proportion as the Revolution developed, the people came to get hold of the municipalities, and in 1793 and 1794 the municipalities in several parts of France became the real centres of action for the popular revolutionaries.

Another very important step was made by the National Assembly when it abolished the old courts of justice—the *parlements*—and introduced judges elected by the people. In the rural districts, each canton, composed of five or six parishes, appointed, through its *active* citizens, its own magistrates ; and in the large towns this right was given to the electoral assemblies. The old *parlements* naturally strove to maintain their prerogatives. In the south, for instance at Toulouse, eighty members of the *parlements*, supported by eighty-nine gentlemen, even started a movement to restore to the monarch his legitimate authority and " liberty," and to religion " its useful influence." At Paris, Rouen and Metz, and in Brittany the *parlements* would not submit to the levelling power of the Assembly, and they headed conspiracies in favour of the old *régime*.

But they found no support among the people, and they

were compelled to yield to the decree of November 3, 1789, by which they were sent on vacation until a new order was given. The attempts to resist led only to a new decree, on January 11, 1790, by which it was declared that the resistance to the law by the magistrates of Rennes " disqualified them from fulfilling any functions of the active citizen, until, having sent in their request to the legislative body, they had been admitted to take the oath of fidelity to the Constitution, as decreed by the National Assembly and accepted by the King."

The National Assembly, it can be seen, meant to make its decisions concerning the new administrative organisation for France respected. But this new organisation encountered a formidable opposition on the part of the higher clergy, the nobility and the upper middle classes, and it took years of a revolution, much more far-reaching than the middle classes had intended, to break down the old organisation for the admission of the new.

CHAPTER XXII

FINANCIAL DIFFICULTIES—SALE OF CHURCH PROPERTY

Necessity of avoiding bankruptcy—Assembly determine to seize Church property—Value of Church revenue—Its unequal distribution—Proposals of Bishop of Autun—Alarm of wealthy clergy—Delight of middle classes—Expropriation voted—Suppression of monastic orders—Paper currency—Administration of Church property transferred to municipalities—Clergy henceforward deadly enemies of Revolution —Organisation of French Church—Effects of new organisation —Constituent Assembly works essentially for middle class— Need of " wind from the street "

THE greatest difficulty for the Revolution was that it had to make its way in the midst of frightful economic circumstances. State bankruptcy was still hanging threateningly over the heads of those who had undertaken to govern France, and if this bankruptcy came indeed, it would bring with it the revolt of the whole of the upper middle classes against the Revolution. If the deficit had been one of the causes which forced royalty to make the first constitutional concessions, and gave the middle classes courage to demand seriously their share in the Government, this same deficit weighed, like a nightmare, all through the Revolution upon those who were successively pushed into power.

It is true that, as the State loans were not international in those times, France had not the fear of foreign nations coming down upon her in the guise of creditors, to seize upon her provinces, as would be done to-day if a European State in revolution was declared bankrupt. But there were the home money-lenders to be considered, and if France had suspended payment, it would have been the ruin of so many middle-class fortunes that the Revolution would have had against it all the middle class, both upper and lower—in fact every one except the workers and the poorest of the peasantry. So it was that the Constituent Assembly, the Legislative Assembly, the Convention, and, later on, the Directory, had to make unheard-of efforts during a succession of years to avoid bankruptcy.

The solution arrived at by the Assembly at the close of 1789 was that of seizing the property of the Church, putting it up for sale, and in return paying the clergy by fixed salaries. The Church revenues were valued in 1789 at a hundred and twenty million *livres* for the tithes, eighty millions in other revenues brought in by various properties (houses and landed property, of which the value was estimated at a little more than two thousand millions), and thirty millions or thereabout from the subsidy that was added every year by the State ; a total, let us say, of about two hundred and thirty millions a year. These revenues were evidently shared in a most unjust way among the different members of the clergy. The bishops lived in the most refined luxury, and rivalled in their expenditure the richest lords and princes, whilst the priests in the towns and villages " reduced to a suitable portion," lived in poverty. It was proposed, therefore, by Talleyrand, Bishop of Autun, after October 10, to take possession of all Church property in the name of the State, to sell it, to endow the clergy adequately, by giving 1200 livres a year to each priest, plus his lodging, and with the rest to cover part of the public debt, which had mounted to fifty millions in life-interests, and to sixty millions in rents for ever. This measure enabled the deficit to be filled in, the remainder of the salt tax (*gabelle*) to be abolished, and a stop put to the selling of the *charges* or posts of officials and functionaries, which used to be sold to contractors by the State.

This scheme, of course, did not fail to evoke great alarm on the part of those who were landed proprietors. " You are leading us on to an agrarian law ! " they told the Assembly. " Every time you go back to the origin of property, the nation will go back with you ! "—which meant recognising that the foundation of all landed property lay in injustice, usury, fraud or theft.

But the middle classes who did not own land were delighted with this scheme. Bankruptcy was avoided by it, and the *bourgeois* would be enabled to buy property. But as the word " expropriation " frightened the pious souls of the landowners, means were found to avoid it. It was said that the Church property was " put at the disposal of the nation," and it was decided to put it up for public sale to the value of four hundred millions. November 2, 1789, was the memorable date when this immense expropriation was voted in the Assembly by five hundred and sixty-eight voices against three hundred and forty-six. Three hundred and forty-six were against it. And these opposers became, henceforth, the bitter enemies of the Revolution, always agitating to do the greatest possible and imaginable harm to the constitutional *régime* and later on to the Republic.

But the middle classes, taught by the Encyclopedists on the one hand, and haunted on the other hand by the ineluctability of the bankruptcy, did not allow themselves to be daunted. When the enormous majority of the clergy and especially of the monastic orders began to intrigue against the expropriation of the Church property, the Assembly voted, on February 12, 1790, for the suppression of perpetual vows and of the monastic orders of both sexes. Only it did not dare to touch for the time being the religious bodies entrusted with public education and the care of the sick. These were not abolished until August 18, 1792, after the taking of the Tuileries.

We can understand the hatred these decrees excited in the breasts of the clergy, as well as of those—and in the provinces they were very numerous—upon whom the clergy had a hold. So much, however, did the clergy and the religious orders hope to retain the *administration* of their enormous properties, which would be considered in such case merely as guarantees for the State loans, that they did not at first display all their hostility. But this state of affairs could not last. The Treasury was empty, the taxes were not coming in. A loan of thirty millions, voted on August 9, 1789, was not successful; another, of eighty millions, voted on the 27th of the same month, had brought in even much less. Finally, an extraordinary tax of a fourth of the revenue had been voted on September 26 after one of Mirabeau's famous speeches. But this tax was immediately swallowed up in the gulf of interests on old loans, and then followed the idea of a forced paper currency, of which the value would be guaranteed by the national property confiscated from the clergy, and which should be redeemed according as the sale of the lands brought in money.

One can imagine the colossal speculations to which these measures for the sale of the national property upon a large scale gave rise. One can easily guess the element which they introduced into the Revolution. Nevertheless, even now the economists and the historians ask whether there was any other method for meeting the pressing demands of the State. The crimes, the extravagance, the thefts and the wars of the old *régime* weighed heavily upon the Revolution; and starting with this enormous burden of debt, bequeathed to it by the old *régime*, it had to bear the consequences. Under menace of a civil war, still more terrible than that which was already breaking out, under the threat of the middle classes turning their backs upon it—the classes which, although pursuing their own ends, were nevertheless allowing the people to free themselves from their lords, but would have turned against all attempts at enfranchisement if the capital they had invested in the loans was endangered, set between these two dangers, the Revolution adopted the scheme for a paper currency (*les assignats*), guaranteed by the national property.

On December 21, 1789, on the proposition of the districts of Paris,* the administration of the Church property was transferred to the municipalities, which were commissioned to put up for sale four hundred millions' worth of this property. The great blow was struck. And henceforth the clergy, with the exception of some village priests who were real friends of the people, vowed a deadly hatred to the Revolution—a

* *Vide* chap. xxiv.

clerical hatred, which the abolition of monastic vows helped further to envenom. Henceforward all over France we see the clergy becoming the centres of conspiracies made to restore the old *régime* and feudalism. They were the heart and soul of the reaction, which we shall see bursting forth in 1790 and in 1791, threatening to put an end to the Revolution before it had realised anything substantial.

But the middle classes resisted it, and did not allow themselves to be disarmed. In June and July 1790 the Assembly opened the discussion upon a great question—the internal organisation of the Church of France. The clergy being now paid by the State, the legislators conceived the idea of freeing them from Rome, and putting them altogether under the Constitution, The bishoprics were identified with the new departments : their number was thus reduced, and the two boundaries, that of the diocese and that of the department, became identical. This might have been allowed to pass ; but the election of the bishops was by the new law entrusted to the Assemblies of electors—to those same Assemblies which were electing the deputies, the judges and the officers of the State.

This was to despoil the bishop of his sacerdotal character and to make a State functionary of him. It is true that in the Early Churches the bishops and priests were nominated by the people ; but the electoral Assemblies which met for the elections of political representatives and officials were not the ancient assemblies of the people—of the believers. Consequently the believers saw in it an attempt made upon the ancient dogmas of the Church, and the priests took every possible advantage of this discontent. The clergy divided into two great parties : the constitutional clergy who submitted, at least for form's sake, to the new laws and took the oath to the Constitution, and the unsworn clergy who refused the oath and openly placed themselves at the head of a counter-revolutionary movement. So it came about that in every province, in each town, village and hamlet, the question put to the inhabitants was—whether they were for the Revolution or against it ? The most terrible struggles sprang, therefore, into existence in every locality, to decide which of the two parties should get the upper hand. The Revolution was transported from Paris into every village : from being parliamentary it became popular.

The work done by the Constituent Assembly was undoubtedly middle-class work. But to introduce into the customs of the nation the principle of political equality, to abolish the relics of the rights of one man over the person of another, to awaken the sentiment of equality and the spirit of revolt against inequalities, was nevertheless an immense work. Only it must be remembered, as Louis Blanc has remarked, that to maintain and to kindle that fiery spirit in the Assembly, " the wind that was blowing from the street was necessary." " Even rioting," he adds, " in those unparalleled days, produced from its tumult many wise inspirations ! *Every rising was so full of thoughts !* " In other words, it was the street, the man in the street, that each time forced the Assembly to go forward with its work of reconstruction. Even a revolutionary Assembly, or one at least that forced itself upon monarchy in a revolutionary way, as the Constituent Assembly did, would have done nothing if the masses of the people had not impelled it to march forward, and if they had not crushed, by their insurrections, the anti-revolutionary resistance.

CHAPTER XXIII

THE FETE OF THE FEDERATION

End of first period of Revolution—Duel between King and Assembly—King bribes Mirabeau—He finds tools among middle class—Enemies of Revolution among all classes—Period of plots and counter-plots—The *Fête* of the Federation—Meaning of the *fête*—Joy of the people

WITH the removal of the King and the Assembly from Versailles to Paris the first period—the heroic period, so to speak, of the Great Revolution—ended. The meeting of the States-General, the Royal Session of June 23, the Oath of the Tennis Court, the taking of the Bastille, the revolt of the cities and villages in July and August, the night of August 4, and finally the march of the women on Versailles and their triumphal return with the King as prisoner; these were the chief stages of the period.

Now, when both the "legislative" and the "executive" power—the Assembly and the King—settled at Paris, a period of hidden, continuous struggle began between moribund royalty and the new Constitutional power which was being slowly consolidated by the legislative labours of the Assembly and by the constructive work done on the spot, in every town and village.

France had now, in the National Assembly, a constitutional power which the King had been forced to recognise. But, if he recognised it officially, he saw in it only a usurpation, an insult to his royal authority, of which he did not wish to admit any diminution. So he was always on the alert to find a thousand petty means of belittling the Assembly, and for disputing with it the smallest fragment of authority. Even to the last moment he never abandoned the hope of one day reducing to obedience this new power, which he reproached himself for having allowed to grow by the side of his own.

In this struggle every means seemed good to the King. He knew, by experience, that the men of his own surroundings easily sold themselves—some for a trifle, others demanding a high price—and he exerted himself to obtain money, plenty of money, borrowing it in London, so as to be able to buy the leaders of the parties in the Assembly and elsewhere. He succeeded only too well with one of those who stood in the forefront, with Mirabeau, who in return for heavy sums of money became the counsellor of the Court and the defender of the King, and spent his last days in an absurd luxury. But it was not only in the Assembly that royalty found its tools; the great number were outside it. They were found among those whom the Revolution had deprived of their privileges, of the handsome pensions which had been allotted to them in former days, and of their colossal incomes; among the clergy who saw their influence perishing; among the nobles who were losing, with their feudal rights, their privileged position; among the middle classes who were alarmed for the capital they had invested in manufactures, commerce and State loans—among those self-same middle classes who were now enriching themselves during and by means of the Revolution.

They were numerous, indeed, the enemies of the Revolution. They included all those who formerly had lived on the higher ecclesiastics, the nobles and the privileged members of the upper middle class. More than one-half of that active and thinking portion of the nation which contains the makers of its historic life stood in the ranks of these enemies. And if among the people of Paris, Strasbourg, Rouen and many other towns, both large and small, the Revolution found ardent champions—how many towns there were, like Lyons, where the centuries-old influence of the clergy and the economic servitude of the workers were such that the poor themselves supported the priests against the Revolution. How many towns, like the great seaports, Nantes, Bordeaux, Saint-Malo, where the great merchants and all the folk depending on them were already bound up with reaction.

Even among the peasants, whose interests should have lain with the Revolution—how many lower middle-class men there were in the villages who dreaded it, not to mention those peasants whom the mistakes of the revolutionists themselves were to alienate from the great cause. There were too many theorists amongst the leaders of the Revolution, too many worshippers of uniformity and regularity, incapable, therefore, of understanding the multiple forms of landed property recognised by the customary law; too many Voltaireans, on the other hand, who showed no toleration towards the prejudices of the masses steeped in poverty; and above all, too many politicians to comprehend the importance which the peasants attached to the land question. And the result was that in the Vendée, in Brittany and in the south-east, the peasants themselves turned against the Revolution.

The counter-revolutionists knew how to attract partisans from each and all of these elements. A Fourteenth of July or a Fifth of October could certainly displace the centre of gravity of the ruling power; but it was in the thirty-six thousand communes of France that the Revolution had to be accomplished, and that required some time. And the counter-revolutionists took advantage of that time to win over to their cause all the discontented among the well-to-do classes, whose name was legion. For, if the radical middle classes put into the Revolution a prodigious amount of extraordinary intelligence, developed by the Revolution itself—intelligence, subtleness and experience in business were not wanting either among the provincial nobility or the wealthy merchants and clergy, who all joined hands for lending to royalty a formidable power of resistance.

This relentless struggle of plots and counter-plots, of partial risings in the provinces and parliamentary contests in the Constituent Assembly, and later on in the Legislative—this concealed struggle lasted nearly three years, from the month of October 1789 to the month of June 1792, when the Revolution at last took a fresh start. It was a period poor in events of historic import—the only ones deserving mention in that interval being the recrudescence of the peasants' rising in January and February 1790, the *Fête* of the Federation, on July 14, 1790, the massacre at Nancy on August 31, 1790, the flight of the King on June 20, 1791, and the massacre of the people of Paris on the Champ-de-Mars on July 17, 1791.

Of the peasants' insurrections we shall speak in a later chapter, but it is necessary to say something here about the *Fête* of the Federation. It sums up the first part of the Revolution. Its overflowing enthusiasm and the harmony displayed in it show what the Revolution might have been if the privileged classes and royalty, comprehending how irresistible was the change, had yielded with a good grace to what they were powerless to prevent.

Taine disparages the festivals of the Revolution, and it is true that those of 1793 and 1794 were often too theatrical. They were got up *for* the people, not *by* the people. But that of July 14, 1790, was one of the most beautiful popular festivals ever recorded in history.

Previous to 1789 France was not unified. It was an historic entity, but its various parts knew little of each other and cared for each other even less. But after the events of 1789, and after the axe had been laid at the roots of the survivals of feudalism, after several glorious moments had been lived together by the representatives of all parts of France, there was born a sentiment of union and solidarity between the provinces that had been linked together by history. All Europe was moved to enthusiasm over the words and deeds of the Revolution—how could the provinces resist this unification in the forward march towards a better future ? This is what the *Fête* of the Federation symbolised.

It had also another striking feature. As a certain amount of work was necessary for this festival, the levelling of the soil, the making of terraces, the building of a triumphal arch, and as it became evident, eight days before the *fête*, that the fifteen thousand workmen engaged in this work could never finish it in time—what did Paris do ? Some unknown person suggested that every one should go to work in the Champ-de-Mars; and all Paris, rich and poor, artists and labourers, monks and soldiers, went to work there with a light heart. France, represented by the thousands of delegates arrived from the provinces, found her national unity in digging the earth—a symbol of what equality and fraternity among men should one day lead to.

The oath that the scores of thousands of persons present took " to the Constitution, as decreed by the National Assembly and accepted by the King," the oath taken by the King and spontaneously confirmed by the Queen for her son, are of little importance. Every one took his oath with some " mental reservations "; every one attached to it certain conditions. The King took his oath in these words: " I, King of the French, swear to use all the power reserved to me by the constitutional Act of the State to maintain the Constitution decreed by the National Assembly and accepted by me." Which meant that he would indeed maintain the Constitution, but that it would be violated, and that he would not be able to prevent it. In reality, at the very moment the King was taking the oath he was thinking only of how he was to get out of Paris—under the pretence of going to review the army. He was calculating the means of buying the influential members of the Assembly, and discounting the help that should come from the foreigners to check the Revolution which he himself had let loose through his opposition to the necessary changes and the trickery in his dealings with the National Assembly.

The oaths were worth little, but the important thing to note in this *fête*—beyond the proclamation of a new nation having a common ideal—is the remarkable good humour of the Revolution. One year after the taking of the Bastille, Marat had every reason for writing: " Why this unbridled joy ? Why these evidences of foolish liveliness ? The Revolution, as yet, has been merely a sorrowful dream for the people ! " But although nothing had yet been done to satisfy the wants of the working people, and everything had been done, as we shall see presently, to prevent the real abolition of the feudal abuses, although the people had everywhere paid with their lives and by terrible sufferings every progress made in the political Revolution—in spite of all that, the people burst into transports of joy at the spectacle of the new democratic *régime* confirmed at this *fête*.   Just as fifty-eight years later, in February 1848, the people of Paris were to place " three years of suffering at the service of the Republic," so now the people showed themselves ready to endure anything, provided that the new Constitution promised to bring them some alleviation, provided that it held in it for them a little goodwill.

If then, three years later, the same people, so ready at first to be content with little, so ready to wait, became savage and began the extermination of the enemies of the Revolution, it was because they hoped to save, at least, some part of the Revolution by resorting to extreme means.   It was because they saw the Revolution foundering before any substantial economic change had been accomplished for the benefit of the mass of the people.   In July 1790 there was nothing to forecast this dark and savage character.   " The Revolution, as yet, has been only a sorrowful dream for the people."   " It has not fulfilled its promises.   No matter.   *It is moving. And that is enough*."   And everywhere the people's hearts were filled with life.

But reaction, all armed, was watchful, and in a month or two it was to show itself in full force.   After the next anniversary of July 14, on July 17, 1791, it was already strong enough to shoot down the people of Paris on this same Champ-de-Mars.

CHAPTER XXIV

THE "DISTRICTS" AND THE "SECTIONS" OF PARIS

Creation of Communes—Their power—Village Communes—
Municipal Communes—Commune of Paris—Soul of Revolu-
tion—Erroneous conceptions of Communes—Electoral divi-
sions of Paris—Districts useful for organisation of Revolution
—Varied constitution of districts—Germ of Commune—
Lacroix on districts—Independence of districts—Link between
Paris and provincial towns—Sections become instruments of
federation

WE have seen how the Revolution began with popular risings
ever since the first months of 1789. To make a revolution
it is not, however, enough that there should be such risings
—more or less successful. It is necessary that after the risings
there should be left something new in the institutions, which
would permit new forms of life to be elaborated and established.

The French people seem to have understood this need
wonderfully well, and the something new, which was introduced
into the life of France, since the first risings, was the popular
Commune. Governmental centralisation came later, but the
Revolution began by creating the Commune—autonomous to
a very great degree—and through this institution it gained,
as we shall see, immense power.

In the villages it was, in fact, the peasants' Commune which
insisted upon the abolition of feudal dues, and legalised the
refusal to pay them; it was the Commune which took back
from the lords the lands that were formerly communal,
resisted the nobles, struggled against the priests, protected
the patriots and later on the *sans-culottes*, arrested the returning
émigrés, and stopped the runaway king.

In the towns it was the municipal Commune which reconstructed the entire aspect of life, arrogated to itself the right of appointing the judges, changed on its own initiative the apportioning of the taxes, and further on, according as the Revolution developed, became the weapon of sans-culottism in its struggle against royalty and against the royalist conspirators and the German invaders. Later still, in the Year II. of the Republic, it was the Communes that undertook to work out the equalisation of wealth.

And it was the Commune of Paris, as we know, that dethroned the King, and after August 10 became the real centre and the real power of the Revolution, which maintained its vigour so long only as that Commune existed.

The soul of the Revolution was therefore in the Communes, and without these centres, scattered all over the land, the Revolution never would have had the power to overthrow the old *régime*, to repel the German invasion, and to regenerate France.

It would, however, be erroneous to represent the Communes of that time as modern municipal bodies, to which the citizens, after a few days of excitement during the elections, innocently confide the administration of all their business, without taking themselves any further part in it. The foolish confidence in representative government, which characterises our own epoch, did not exist during the Great Revolution. The Commune which sprang from the popular movement was not separated from the people. By the intervention of its "districts," "sections" or "tribes," constituted as so many mediums of popular administration, it remained of the people, and this is what made the revolutionary power of these organisations.

Since the organisation and the life of the "districts" and the "sections" is best known for Paris,* it is of the City of Paris that we shall speak, the more so as in studying the life of the Paris "sections" we learn to know pretty well the life of the thousands of provincial Communes.

From the very beginning of the Revolution, and especially

* The "districts" were described as "sections" after the municipal law of June 1790 was passed.

since events had roused Paris to take the initiative of rebellion in the first days of July 1789, the people, with their marvellous gift for revolutionary organisation, were already organising in view of the struggle which they would have to maintain, and of which they at once felt the import.

The City of Paris had been divided for electoral purposes into sixty districts, which were to nominate the electors of the second degree. Once these were nominated, the districts ought to have disappeared; but they remained and organised themselves, on their own initiative, as permanent organs of the municipal administration, by appropriating various functions and attributes which formerly belonged to the police, or to the law courts, or even to different government departments under the old *régime*.

Thus they rendered themselves necessary, and at a time when all Paris was effervescing at the approach of July 14 they began to arm the people and to act as independent authorities; so much so that the Permanent Committee, which was formed at the Hôtel de Ville by the influential middle classes,* had to convoke the districts to come to an understanding with them. The districts proved their usefulness and displayed a great activity in arming the people, in organising the National Guard, and especially in enabling the capital to repulse an attack upon it.

After the taking of the Bastille, we see the districts already acting as accepted organs of the municipal administration. Each district was appointing its Civil Committee, of from sixteen to twenty-four members, for the carrying out of its affairs. However, as Sigismond Lacroix has said in the first volume of his *Actes de la Commune de Paris pendant la Révolution*,† each district constituted itself " how it liked." There was even a great variety in their organisation. One district, " anticipating the resolutions of the National Assembly concerning judicial organisation, appointed its justices of peace and arbitration." But to create a common understanding between them, " they formed a central corresponding bureau where special delegates met and exchanged communications."

* See chap. xii.   † Vol. i., Paris, 1894, p. vii.

The first attempt at constituting a Commune was thus made *from below upward*, by the federation of the district organisms ; it sprang up in a revolutionary way, from popular initiative. The Commune of August 10 was thus appearing in germ from this time, and especially since December 1789, when the delegates of the districts tried to form a Central Committee at the Bishop's palace.*

It was by means of the " districts " that henceforth Danton, Marat and so many others were able to inspire the masses of the people in Paris with the breath of revolt, and the masses, accustoming themselves to act without receiving orders from the national representatives, were practising what was described later on as Direct Self-Government.†

Immediately after the taking of the Bastille, the districts had ordered their delegates to prepare, in consultation with the Mayor of Paris, Bailly, a plan of municipal organisation, which should be afterwards submitted to the districts themselves. But while waiting for this scheme, the districts went on widening the sphere of their functions as it became necessary.

When the National Assembly began to discuss municipal law, they did so with painful slowness. " At the end of two months," says Lacroix, " the first article of the new Municipality scheme had still to be written." ‡ These delays naturally seemed suspicious to the districts, and from this time began to develop a certain hostility, which became more and more apparent, on behalf of part of the population of Paris and the official Council of its Commune. It is also important to note that while trying to give a legal form to the Municipal Government, the districts strove to maintain their own independence. They sought for unity of action, not in subjection to a Central Committee, but in a federative union.

Lacroix says : " The state of mind of the districts . . .

---

* Most of the " sections " held their general assemblies in churches, and their committees and schools were often lodged in buildings which formerly belonged to the clergy or to monastic orders. The Bishopric became a centra᾿ place for the meetings of delegates from the sections.

† Sigismond Lacroix, *Actes de la Commune*, vol. iii. p. 625.   Ernest Mellié, *Les Sections de Paris pendant la Révolution*, Paris, 1898, p. 9.

‡ Lacroix, *Actes*, vol. ii. p. xiv.

displays itself both by a very strong sentiment of communal unity and by a no less strong tendency towards direct self-government. Paris did not want to be a federation of sixty republics cut off haphazard each in its territory ; the Commune is a unity composed of its united districts. . . . Nowhere is there found a single example of a district setting itself up to live apart from the others . . . But side by side with this undisputed principle, another principle is disclosed . . . which is, that the Commune must legislate and administer for itself, directly, as much as possible. Government by representation must be reduced to a minimum ; everything that the Commune can do directly must be done by it, without any intermediary, without any delegation, or else it may be done by delegates reduced to the *rôle* of special commissioners, acting under the uninterrupted control of those who have commissioned them . . . the final right of legislating and administrating for the Commune belongs to the districts—to the citizens, who come together in the general assemblies of the districts."

We thus see that the principles of anarchism, expressed some years later in England by W. Godwin, already dated from 1789, and that they had their origin, not in theoretic speculations, but in the *deeds* of the Great French Revolution.

There is still another striking fact pointed out by Lacroix, which shows up to what point the districts knew how to distinguish themselves from the Municipality and how to prevent it from encroaching upon their rights. When Brissot came forward on November 30, 1789, with a scheme of municipal constitution for Paris, concocted between the National Assembly and a committee elected by the Assembly of Representatives (the Permanent Committee of the Paris Commune, founded on July 12, 1789), the districts at once opposed it. Nothing was to be done without the direct sanction of the districts themselves,* and Brissot's scheme had to be abandoned. Later on, in April 1790, when the National Assembly began to discuss the municipal law, it had to choose between two proposals : that of an assembly—free and illegal, after all— of delegates from the districts, who met at the Bishop's palace,

* Lacroix, *Actes*, vol. iii. p. iv.

a proposal which was adopted by the majority of the districts and signed by Bailly, and that of the legal Council of the Commune, which was supported by some of the districts only. The National Assembly decided in favour of the first. Needless to say that the districts did not limit themselves to municipal affairs. They always took part in the great political questions of the day. The royal *veto*, the imperative mandate, poor-relief, the Jewish question, that of the "marc of silver" *—all of these were discussed by the districts. As for the "marc of silver," they themselves took the initiative in the matter, by convoking each other for discussion and appointing committees. "They vote their own resolutions," says Lacroix, "and ignoring the official representatives of the Commune, they are going themselves on February 8 (1790) to present to the National Assembly the first *Address of the Paris Commune in its sections*. It is a personal deonstration of the districts, made independently of any official representation, to support Robespierre's motion in the National Assembly against the "marc of silver." †

What is still more interesting is that from this time the provincial towns began to put themselves in communication with the Commune of Paris concerning all things. From this there developed a tendency to establish a *direct link* between the towns and villages of France, outside the National Parliament, and this direct and spontaneous action, which later became even more manifest, gave irresistible force to the Revolution.

It was especially in an affair of capital importance—the liquidation of the Church property—that the districts made their influence felt, and proved their capacity for organisation. The National Assembly had ordained on paper the seizing of the Church property and the putting it up for sale, for the benefit of the nation; but it had not indicated any practical means for carrying this law into effect. At this juncture it was the Paris districts that proposed to serve as intermediaries for the purchase of the property, and invited all the munici-

* *Vide* chap. xxi.
† Lacroix, *Actes*, vol. iii. pp. xii. and xiii.

palities of France to do the same.   They thus found a practical method of applying the law.

The editor of the *Actes de la Commune* has fully described how the districts managed to induce the Assembly to entrust them with this important business: " Who speaks and acts in the name of that great personality, the Commune of Paris ? " demands Lacroix. And he replies: " The Bureau de Ville (Town Council) in the first place, from whom this idea emanated ; and afterwards the districts, who have approved it, and who, having approved it, have got hold of the matter *in lieu* of the Town Council, for carrying it out, *have negotiated* and *treated directly with the State*, that is to say, with the National Assembly, and at last *effected the proposed purchase directly*, all contrarily to a formal decree, but with the consent of the Sovereign Assembly."

What is even more interesting is that the districts, having once taken over this business, also took no heed of the old Assembly of Representatives of the Commune, which was already too old for serious action, and also they twice dismissed the Town Council that wanted to interfere. " The districts," Lacroix says, " prefer to constitute, with a view to this special object, a special deliberate assembly, composed of sixty delegates, and a small executive council of twelve members chosen by these·sixty representatives." *

By acting in this way—and the libertarians would no doubt do the same to-day—the districts of Paris laid the foundations of a new, free, social organisation.†

---

* Lacroix, *Actes*, iv. p. xix.

† S. Lacroix, in his Introduction to the fourth volume of the *Actes de la Commune*, gives a full account of this affair.   But I cannot resist reproducing here the following lines of the " Address to the National Assembly by the deputies of the sixty sections of Paris, relative to the acquisition to be made, in the name of the Commune, of national domains."   When the members of the Town Council wanted to act in this affair of the purchases, instead of the sections, the sections protested and they expressed the following very just idea concerning the representatives of a people : " How would it be possible for the acquisition consummated *by the Commune itself, through the medium of its commissioners, specially appointed ' ad hoc,'* to be less legal than *if it were made by the general representatives. . . . Are you no longer recognising the principle that the functions of the deputy cease in the presence*

We thus see that while reaction was gaining more and more ground in 1790, on the other side the districts of Paris were acquiring more and more influence upon the progress of the Revolution. While the Assembly was sapping by degrees the royal power, the districts and afterwards the " sections " of Paris were widening by degrees the sphere of their functions in the midst of the people. They thus prepared the ground for the revolutionary Commune of August 10, and they soldered at the same time the link between Paris and the provinces.

" Municipal history," says Lacroix, " is made outside official assemblies. It is by means of the districts that the most important acts in the communal life, both political and administrative, are accomplished : the acquisition and selling of the national estates (*biens nationaux*) goes on, as the districts had wished, through the intermediary of their special commissioners ; the national federation is prepared by a meeting of delegates to whom the districts have given a special mandate. . . . The federation of July 14 is also the exclusive and direct work of the districts," their intermediary in this case being an assembly of delegates from the sections for concluding a federative compact.*

It has often been said that the National Assembly represented the national unity of France. When, however, the question of the *Fête* of the Federation came up, the politicians, as Michelet has observed, were terrified as they saw men surging from all parts of France towards Paris for the festival, and the Commune of Paris had to burst in the door of the National Assembly to obtain its consent to the *fête*. " Whether it liked or not, the Assembly had to consent," Michelet adds.

Besides, it is important to note that the movement was born first (as Buchez and Roux had already remarked) from the need of assuring the food-supply to Paris, and to take measures against the fears of a foreign invasion ; that is to say, this movement was partly the outcome of an act of local

of the deputer ? " Proud and true words, unfortunately buried nowadays under governmental fictions.
* Lacroix, vol. i. pp. ii. iv. and 729, note.

administration, and yet it took, in the sections of Paris,* *the character of a national confederation*, wherein all the cantons of the departments of France and all the regiments of the army were represented. The sections, which were created for the individualisation of the various quarters of Paris, became thus the instrument for the federate union of the whole nation.

* S. Lacroix, *Les Actes de la Commune,* 1st edition, vol. vi., 1897, pp. 273 *et seq.*

CHAPTER XXV

THE SECTIONS OF PARIS UNDER THE NEW MUNICIPAL LAW

Commune of Paris—Permanence of sectional assemblies—
Distrust of executive power—Local power necessary to carry
out Revolution—National Assembly tries to lessen power of
districts—Municipal law of May–June 1790—Impotence of
attacks of Assembly—Municipal law ignored—Sections the
centre of revolutionary initiative—Civic committees—Increasing power of sections—Charity-bureaux and charity-
workshops administered by sections—Cultivation of waste
land

OUR contemporaries have allowed themselves to be so won
over to ideas of subjection to the centralised State that the
very idea of communal independence—to call it " autonomy "
would not be enough—which was current in 1789, seems
strange nowadays. M. L. Foubert,* when speaking of the
scheme of municipal organisation decreed by the National
Assembly on May 21, 1790, was quite right in saying that
" the application of this scheme would seem to-day a revolutionary act, even anarchic—so much the ideas have changed " ;
and he adds that at the time this municipal law was considered
insufficient by the Parisians who were accustomed, since July
14, 1789, to a very great independence of their " districts."

The exact delimitation of powers in the State, to which
so much importance is attached to-day, seemed at that time
to the Parisians, and even to the legislators in the National
Assembly, a question not worth discussing and an encroachment
on liberty. Like Proudhon, who said " The Commune will

* *L'idée autonomiste dans les districts de Paris en 1789 et en 1790,* in
the review *La Révolution française,*" Year XIV., No. 8, February 14,
1895, p. 141 *et seq.*

be all or nothing," the districts of Paris did not understand that the Commune was not *all*. "A Commune," they said, "is a society of joint-owners and fellow inhabitants enclosed by a circumscribed and limited boundary, and it has collectively the same rights as a citizen." And, starting from this definition, they maintained that the Commune of Paris, like every other citizen, "having liberty, property, security and the right to resist oppression, has consequently every power to dispose of its property, as well as that of guaranteeing the administration of this property, the security of the individuals, the police, the military force—*all*." The Commune, in fact, must be sovereign within its own territory: the only condition, I may add, of real liberty for a Commune.

The third part of the preamble to the municipal law of May 1790 established, moreover, a principle which is scarcely understood to-day, but was much appreciated at that time. It deals with the direct exercise of powers, without inter-mediaries. "The Commune of Paris"—so says this preamble—"in consequence of its freedom, *being possessed of all its rights and powers, exercises them always itself—directly as much as possible, and as little as possible by delegation.*"

In other words, the Commune of Paris was not to be a governed State, but a people governing itself directly—when possible—without intermediaries, without masters.

It was the General Assembly of the section, and not the elected Communal Council, which was to be the supreme authority for all that concerned the inhabitants of Paris. And if the sections decided to submit to the decision of a majority amongst themselves in general questions, they did not for all that abdicate either their right to federate by means of freely contracted alliances, or that of passing from one section to another for the purpose of influencing their neighbours' decisions, and thus trying by every means to arrive at unanimity.

The " permanence " of the general assemblies of the sections —that is, the possibility of calling the general assembly whenever it was wanted by the members of the section and of discussing everything in the general assembly—this, they said, will educate every citizen politically, and allow him, when it is necessary, " to elect, with full knowledge, those whose zeal he will have remarked, and whose intelligence he will have appreciated." *

The section in permanence—the forum always open—is the only way, they maintained, to assure an honest and intelligent administration.

Finally, as Foubert also says, distrust inspired the sections : *distrust of all executive power.* " He who has the executive power, being the depository of force, must necessarily abuse it." " This is the opinion of Montesquieu and Rousseau," adds Foubert—it is also mine !

The strength which this point of view gave to the Revolution can be easily understood, the more so as it was combined with another one, also pointed out by Foubert. " The revolutionary movement," he writes, " is just as much against centralisation as against despotism." The French people thus seem to have comprehended from the outset of the Revolution that the immense work of transformation laid upon them could not be accomplished either constitutionally or by a central power ; it had to be done by the local powers, and to carry it out they must be free.

Perhaps they also thought that enfranchisement, the conquest of liberty, must begin in each village and each town. The limitation of the royal power would thus be rendered only the more easy.

The National Assembly evidently tried all it could to lessen the power of the districts, and to put them under the tutelage of a communal government, which the national representatives might be able to control. Thus the municipal law of May 27 to June 27, 1790, suppressed the districts. It was intended to put an end to those hotbeds of Revolution, and for that purpose the new law introduced a new subdivision of Paris into forty-eight sections—*active* citizens only being allowed to take part in the electoral and administrative assemblies of the new " sections."

The law had, moreover, taken good care to limit the duties

* Section des Mathurins, quoted by Foubert, p. 155.

of the sections by declaring that in their assemblies they should occupy themselves "with no other business than that of the elections and the administration of the civic oath." * But this was not obeyed. The furrow had been ploughed more than a year before, and the "sections" went on to act as the "districts" had acted. After all, the municipal law was itself obliged to grant to the sections the administrative attributes that the districts had already arrogated to themselves. We find, therefore, under the new law the same sixteen commissioners whom we saw in the districts—elected and charged not only with police and even judicial functions, but also trusted by the administration of the department "with the reassessment of the taxes in their respective sections." † Furthermore, if the Constituent Assembly abolished the "permanence"—that is to say, the permanent right of the sections to meet without a special convocation— it was compelled nevertheless to recognise their right of holding general assemblies, at the demand of fifty active citizens.‡

That was sufficient, and the citizens did not fail to take advantage of it. For instance, scarcely a month after the installation of the new municipality, Danton and Bailly went to the National Assembly, on behalf of forty-three out of the forty-eight sections, to demand the instant dismissal of the ministers and their arraignment before a national tribunal.

The sections parted with none of their sovereign power. Although they had been deprived of it by law, they retained it, and proudly displayed it. Their petition had, in fact,

* Division I., Article 2.   † Division IV., Article 12.

‡ Danton understood thoroughly the necessity of guarding for the sections all the rights which they had attributed to themselves during the first year of the Revolution, and this is why the *General Ruling for the Commune of Paris*, which was elaborated by the deputies of the sections at the Bishopric, partly under the influence of Danton, and adopted on April 7, 1790, by forty districts, abolished the General Council of the Commune. It left all decisions to the *citizens assembled in their sections*, and the sections retained the right of *permanence*. On the contrary, Condorcet, in his "municipality scheme," remaining true to the idea of representative government, personified the Commune in its elected General Council, to which he gave all the rights (Lacroix, *Actes*, 2nd series, vol. i. p. xii.).

nothing municipal about it, but they took action, and that was all. Besides, the sections, on account of the various functions they had assumed, became of such importance that the National Assembly listened to them and replied graciously.

It was the same with the clause of the municipal law of 1790, which entirely subjected the municipalities "to the administration of the department and the district for all that concerned the functions they should have to exercise by delegation from the general administration." * Neither the sections nor the Commune of Paris nor the provincial Communes would accept this clause. They simply ignored it and maintained their independence.

Generally speaking, the sections gradually took upon themselves the part of being centres of revolutionary initiative, which had belonged to the " districts " ; and if their activity relaxed during the reactionary period which France lived through in 1790 and 1791, it was still, as we shall see by the sequel, the sections which roused Paris in 1792 and prepared the revolutionary Commune of August 10.

By virtue of the law of May 21, 1790, each section had to appoint sixteen commissioners to constitute their civic committees, and these committees entrusted at first with police functions only, never *ceased*, during the whole time of the Revolution, extending their functions in every direction. Thus, in September 1790, the Assembly was forced to grant to the sections the right which the Strasbourg sections had assumed in August 1789, namely, 'the right to appoint the justices of the peace and their assistants, as well as the *prud'hommes* (conciliation judges). And this right was retained by the sections until it was abolished by the revolutionary Jacobin government, which was instituted on December 4, 1793.

On the other hand, these same civic committees of the sections succeeded, towards the end of 1790, after a severe struggle, in obtaining the power of administering the affairs of the charity-bureaux, as well as the very important right of inspecting and organising the distribution of relief, which enabled them to replace the charity workshops of the old

* Article 55.

régime by relief-works, under the direction of the sections themselves. In this way they obtained a great deal. They undertook by degrees to supply clothes and boots to the army. They organised milling and other industries so well that in 1793 any citizen, domiciled in a section, had only to present him- or her-self at the sectional workshop to be given work.* A vast powerful organisation sprang up later on from these first attempts, so that in the Year II. (1793–1794) the sections tried to take over completely the manufacture as well as the supply of clothing for the army.

The " Right to Work," which the people of the large towns demanded in 1848, was therefore only a reminiscence of what had existed during the Great Revolution in Paris. But then in 1792–93, it was organised from below, not from above, as Louis Blanc, Vidal and other authoritarians who sat in the Luxembourg from March till June 1848 *intended* it to be.†

There was something even better than this. Not only did the sections throughout the Revolution supervise the supply and the sale of bread, the price of objects of prime necessity, and the application of the maximum when fixed by law, but they also set on foot the cultivation of the waste lands of Paris, so as to increase agricultural produce by market gardening.

This may seem paltry to those who think only of bullets and barricades in time of revolution; but it was precisely by entering into the petty details of the toilers' daily life that the sections of Paris developed their political power and their revolutionary initiative.

But we must not anticipate. Let us resume the current of events. We shall return again to the sections of Paris when we speak of the Commune of August 10.

* Meillé, p 289.
† We must say " intended," because in 1848 nothing was *done* besides talk and discussion.

CHAPTER XXVI

DELAYS IN THE ABOLITION OF THE FEUDAL RIGHTS

The people desire to abolish feudal system—Aims of middle classes—Gradual estrangement of middle classes and people—" Anarchists "—" Girondins "—Importance of feudal question in Revolution—August 4, 1789—Reactionary party gains ground—Honorary rights and profitable rights—Decrees of February 27, 1790—Feudalism still oppresses peasants—Difficulties of peasants

ACCORDING as the Revolution progressed, the two currents of which we have spoken in the beginning of this book, the popular current and the middle-class current, became more clearly defined—especially in economic affairs.

The people strove to put an end to the feudal system, and they ardently desired equality as well as liberty. Seeing delays, therefore, even in their struggle against the King and the priests, they lost patience and tried to bring the Revolution to its logical development. They foresaw that the revolutionary enthusiasm would be exhausted at no far distant day, and they strove to make the return of the landlords, the royal despotism, and the reign of the rich and the priests impossible for all time. And for that reason they wished—at least in very many parts of France—to regain possession of the lands that had been filched from the village communities and demanded agrarian laws which would allow every one to work on the land if he wanted, and laws which would place the rich and the poor on equal terms as regarded their rights as citizens.

They revolted when they were compelled to pay the tithes, and they made themselves masters of the municipalities, so that they could strike at the priests and the landlords. In short, they maintained revolutionary conditions in the greater part of France, whilst in Paris they kept close watch over the law-makers from the vantage-points of the galleries in the Assembly, and in their clubs and meetings of the " sections." Finally, when it became necessary to strike a heavy blow at royalty, the people organised the insurrection and fought arms in hand, on July 14, 1789, and on August 10, 1792.

The middle classes, on their side, worked with all their might to complete " the conquest of power "—the phrase, as is seen, dates from that time. According as the power of the King and the Court crumbled and fell into contempt, the middle classes developed their own. They took up a firm position in the provinces, and at the same time hastened to establish their present and future wealth.

If in certain regions the greater portion of the property confiscated from the *émigrés* and the priests passed in small lots into the hands of the poor (at least this is what may be gathered from the researches of Loutchitzky,*)—in other regions an immense portion of these properties served to enrich the middle classes, whilst all sorts of financial specu-lations were laying the foundations of many a large fortune among the Third Estate.

But what the educated middle classes had especially borne in mind—the Revolution of 1648 in England serving them as a model—was that now was the time for them to seize the government of France, and that the class which would govern would have the wealth—the more so as the sphere of action of the State was about to increase enormously through the formation of a large standing army, and the reorganisation of public instruction, justice, the levying of taxes, and all the rest. This had been clearly seen to follow the revolution in England.

It can be understood, therefore, that an abyss was ever widening between the middle classes and the people in France; the middle classes, who had wanted the revolution and urged the people into it, so long as they had not felt that " the

* *Izvestia (Bulletin)* of the University of Kieff, Year XXXVII., Nos. 3 and 8 (Russian).

conquest of power" was already accomplished to their advantage; and the people, who had seen in the Revolution the means of freeing themselves from the double yoke of poverty and political disability.

Those who were described at that time by the "men of order" and the "statesmen" as "the anarchists," helped by a certain number of the middle class—some members of the Club of the Cordeliers and a few from the Club of the Jacobins—found themselves on one side. As for the "statesmen," the "defenders of property," as they were then called, they found their full expression in the political party of those who became known later on as "the Girondins": that is to say, in the politicians who, in 1792, gathered round Brissot and the minister Roland.

We have told in chap. xv. to what the pretended abolition of the feudal rights during the night of August 4 was reduced by the decrees voted by the Assembly from August 5 to 11, and we now see what further developments were given to this legislation in the years 1790 and 1791.

But as this question of feudal rights dominates the whole of the Revolution, and as it remained unsolved until 1793, after the Girondin chiefs had been expelled from the Convention, I shall, at the risk of a little repetition, sum up once more the legislation of the month of August 1789, before touching upon what was done in the two following years. This is the more necessary as a most regrettable confusion continues to prevail about this subject, although the abolition of the feudal rights was the principal work of the Great Revolution. Over this question the main contests were fought, both in rural France and in the Assembly, and out of all the work of the Revolution, it was the abolition of these rights which best survived, in spite of the political vicissitudes through which France passed during the nineteenth century.

The abolition of the feudal rights certainly did not enter the thoughts of those who called for social renovation before 1789. All they intended to do was to amend the abuses of these rights. It was even asked by certain reformers whether it would be possible "to diminish the seigniorial prerogative," as Necker said. It was the Revolution that put the question of abolition pure and simple of these rights.

"All property, without any exception, shall be always respected"—they made the King say at the opening of the States-General. And it was added that "his Majesty expressly understands by the word property the feudal and seigniorial tithes, levies, rents, rights and dues and, generally speaking, all rights and prerogatives profitable or honorary, attached to the estates and to the fiefs belonging to any person."

None of the future revolutionists protested then against this interpretation of the rights of the lords and the landed proprietors altogether.

"But," says Dalloz—the well-known author of the *Répertoire de jurisprudence*, whom certainly no one will tax with revolutionary exaggeration—"the agricultural populations did not thus interpret the liberties promised to them; everywhere the villages rose up; the châteaux were burned, and the archives and the places where the records of feudal dues were kept were destroyed; and in a great many localities the landlords gave their signatures to documents renouncing their rights." *

Then, in the dismal blaze of the burning châteaux and the peasant insurrection which threatened to assume still greater proportions, took place the sitting of August 4, 1789.

As we have seen, the National Assembly voted during that memorable night a decree, or rather a declaration of principles, of which the first article was "The National Assembly destroys completely the feudal system."

The impression produced by those words was immense. They shook all France and Europe. The sitting of that night was described as a "Saint Bartholomew of property." But the very next day, as we saw already, the Assembly changed its mind. By a series of decrees, or rather of resolutions passed on August 5, 6, 8, 10 and 11, they re-established and placed under the protection of the Constitution all that was essential in the feudal rights. Renouncing, with certain exceptions, the personal services that were due to them, the

* Dalloz, article *Féodalisme*.

lords guarded with all the more care those of their rights, often quite as monstrous, which could in the slightest way be made to represent rents due for the possession or the use of the land—the *real* rights, as the law-makers said (rights over things—*res* in Latin signifying things). These were not only the rents for landed property, but also a great number of payments and dues, in money and in kind, varying with the province, established at the time of the abolition of serfdom and attached thenceforth to the possession of the land. All these exactions had been entered in the *terriers* or landed-estate records, and since then these rights had often been sold or conceded to third parties.

The *champarts*, the *terriers*, the *agriers comptants* and so on * and the tithes too—everything, in short, that had a pecuniary value—*were maintained in full*. The peasants obtained *only the right to redeem these dues*, if some day they would come to an agreement with the landlord about the price of the redemption. But the Assembly took good care neither to fix a term for the redemption nor to determine its rate.

In réality, except that the idea of feudal property was shaken by Article 1 of the resolutions of August 5 to 11, everything which concerned dues reputed to be attached to the use of the *land* remained just as it was, and the municipalities were ordered to bring the peasants to reason if they did not pay. We have seen how ferociously certain of them carried out these instructions.†

* Shares of the produce of the land, taxes on it, court rolls, &c.

† These facts, which are in complete contradiction to the unmeasured praise lavished on the National Assembly by many historians, I first published in an article on the anniversary of the Great Revolution in the *Nineteenth Century*, June 1889, and afterwards in a series of articles in *La Révolte* for 1892 and 1893, and republished in pamphlet form under the title *La Grande Révolution*, Paris, 1893. The elaborate work of M. Ph. Sagnac (*La législation civile de la Révolution française*, 1789-1804: *Essai d'histoire sociale*, Paris, 1898) has since confirmed this point of view. After all, it was not a question of a more correct *interpretation of facts*, it was a question of *the facts themselves*. And to be convinced of this, one has only to consult any collection of the laws of the French State—such as is contained, for instance, in the well-known *Répertoire de jurisprudence*, by Dalloz. There we have, either in full or in a faithful summary, all the laws concerning landed property,

We have seen, furthermore, in the note written by my friend James Guillaume * that the Assembly, by specifying in one of its acts of August 1789 that these were only " resolutions," gave themselves, by this, the advantage of not having to require the King's sanction. But at the same time, the acts were thus deprived of the character of law, so long as their provisions had not been put into the shape of constitutional decrees. No obligatory character was attached to them: legally, nothing had been done.

However, even these " resolutions " seemed too advanced to the landlords and to the King. The latter tried to gain time, so as not to have them promulgated, and on September 18 he was still addressing remonstrances to the National Assembly asking them to reconsider their resolutions. He only decided on their promulgation on October 6, after the women had brought him back to Paris and placed him under the supervision of the people. But then it was the Assembly that turned a deaf ear. They made up their minds to promulgate the resolutions only on November 3, 1789, when they sent them out for promulgation to the provincial *parlements* (courts of justice); so that in reality the resolutions of August 5 to 11 were never actually promulgated.

In such conditions the peasants' revolt had necessarily to go on, and that is what happened. The report of the Feudal Committee, made by Abbé Grégoire in February 1790, stated, in fact, that the peasant insurrection was still going on and that it had gained in strength since the month of January. It was spreading from the East to the West.

But in Paris the party of reaction had already gained much ground since October 6. Therefore, when the National Assembly undertook the discussion of the feudal rights after Grégoire's report, they legislated in a reactionary spirit. In reality the decrees which they passed from February 28 to March 5 and on June 18, 1790, had as consequence the re-

both private and communal, which are not to be found in the histories of the Revolution. From this source I have drawn, and it was by studying the texts of these laws that I have come to understand the real meaning of the Great French Revolution and its inner struggles.

* *See* above, chap. xviii.

establishing of the feudal system in all that was of importance.

That, as can be seen by the documents of the period, was the opinion of those who wished for the abolition of feudalism. They described the decrees of 1790 as *re-establishing feudalism.*

To begin with, the distinction between the *honorary* rights, abolished without redemption, and the *profitable* rights which the peasants had to redeem, was maintained completely, and confirmed ; and, what was worse, several personal feudal rights, having been classed as *profitable* rights, were now " completely assimilated with the *simple rents and charges on the land.*" * Some rights, therefore, that were mere usurpations, mere vestiges of personal servitude and should have been condemned on account of their origin, were now put upon the same footing as obligations resulting from the location of the land.

For non-payment of these dues, the lord, even though he had lost the right of " feudal seizure " † could exercise constraint of all kinds, according to the common law. The following article confirms this : " The feudal dues and taxes (*droits féodaux et censuels*), together with all sales, rents and rights that are redeemable by their nature, shall be subject, until their redemption, to the rules that the various laws and customs of the kingdom have established."

The Constituent Assembly went still further. In their sitting of February 27, following the opinion of Merlin, they confirmed, in a great number of cases, *the right of serfdom in mortmain.* They decreed that " the landed rights of which the tenure in mortmain had been converted into tenure by annual rent, not being representative of the mortmain, should be preserved."

So much did the middle classes hold to this heritage of serfdom that Article 4 of chap. iii. of the new law declared, that " if the mortmain, *real* or *mixed*, has been converted

---

* " All honorary distinctions, superiority and power resulting from the feudal system are abolished. *As for those profitable rights which will continue to exist until they are redeemed,* they are completely assimilated to the simple rents and charges on the land " (Law of February 24, Article 1 of chap. i.). † Article 6.

since the enfranchisement into dues on the land, or into rights of mutation, these dues shall continue to be owed."

Altogether, the reading of the discussion in the Assembly on the feudal rights suggests the question—whether it was really in March 1790, after the taking of the Bastille, and on August 4 that these discussions took place, or were they still at the beginning of the reign of Louis XVI. in the year 1775.

Thus, on March 1, 1790, certain rights " of fire, . . . *chiennage* (kennels), *monéage* (coining), of watch and ward," as well as certain rights over the sales and purchases by the vassals were abolished. One would have thought, however, that these rights had been abolished, without redemption, during the night of August 4. But it was nothing of the kind. Legally, in 1790, the peasants, in many parts of France, still dared not buy a cow, nor even sell their wheat, without paying dues to the lord. They could not even sell their corn before the lord had sold his and had profited by the high prices that prevailed before much of the corn had been threshed.

However, one might think that at last these rights were abolished on March 1, as well as all the dues levied by the lords on the common oven, the mill, or the wine-press. But we must not jump to conclusions. They were abolished, true enough, but with the exception of those cases where they had formerly been the subject of a written agreement between the lord and the peasant commune, or were considered as payable in exchange for some concession or other.

Pay, peasant! always pay! and do not try to gain time, for there would be an immediate distraint, and then you could only save yourself by winning your case before a law-court.

This seems hard to believe, but so it was. Here is the text of Article 2, chap. iii., of the new feudal laws. It is rather long, but it deserves to be reproduced, because it lets us see what slavery the feudal law of February 24 to March 15, 1790, left still crushing down the peasant.

" Article 2.—And are presumed redeemable, except there is proof to the contrary (which means ' shall be paid by the peasant until he has redeemed them ') :

" (1) All the seigniorial annual dues, in money, grain,

poultry, food-stuffs of all kinds, and fruits of the earth, paid under the denomination of quit-rents, over-rents, feudal rents, manorial or emphyteutic, *champerty*, *tasque*, *terrage*, *agrier* (rights on the produce of lands and fields, or on the tenant's labour), *soète*, actual forced labour, or any other denomination whatsoever, which are payable or due only by the proprietor or holder of a piece of land, so long as he is proprietor or holder, and has the right of continuing in possession.

" (2) All the occasional fees (*casuels*) which, under the name of *quint* (fifth), *requint* (twenty-fifth), *treizains* (thirteenth), *lods* (dues on sales of inheritance), *lods et ventes*, *mi-lods*, redemptions, *venterolles*, *reliefs*, *relevoisons*, pleas, and any other denominations whatsoever, are due on account of supervening mutations in the property or the possession of a piece of land.

" (3) The rights of *acapts* (rights on succession), acapts in arrears (*arrière-acapts*) and other similar rights due on the mutation of the former lords."

On the other hand, the Assembly, on March 9, suppressed various rights of toll on the high roads, canals, &c., which were levied by the lords. But immediately afterwards they took care to add the following clause:

" It is not to be understood, however, that the National Assembly includes, as regards the present, in the suppression declared by the preceding article, the authorised toll-gates . . . &c., and the duties mentioned in the article aforesaid *which may have been acquired as compensation.*" This meant that many of the lords had sold or mortgaged certain of their rights; or else, in cases of inheritance, the eldest son having succeeded to the estate or the châteaux, the others, more especially the daughters, received *as compensation* certain rights of toll over the highways, the canals, or the bridges. In these cases, therefore, *all the rights remained, although recognised as being unjust*, because, otherwise, it would have meant a loss to some members of noble or middle-class families.

Cases like these recurred all through the new feudal law. After each suppression of feudal right some subterfuge was inserted to evade it. So that the result would have been lawsuits without end.

There was only one single point where the breath of the Revolution really made itself felt, and this was on the question of the tithes. It was decided that all tithes, ecclesiastical and enfeoffed (which means sold to the laity), should cease from January 1791. But here again the Assembly decreed that for the year 1790 they were to be paid to whom they were due, " and in full."

This is not all. They did not forget to impose penalties on those who might disobey this decree, and on opening the discussion of chap. iii. of the feudal law, the Assembly enacted: " No municipality or administration of district or department shall be able, on pain of nullity *and of being prosecuted as a guilty party and having to pay the damages, as such,* to prohibit the collection of any of the seigniorial dues, *of which payment shall be asked* under the pretext that they have been implicitly or explicitly suppressed without compensation."

There was nothing to fear from the officials of either the districts or the departments ; they were, especially the latter, body and soul with the lords and the middle-class landowners. But there were municipalities, especially in the East of France, of which the revolutionists had taken possession, and these would tell the peasants that such and such feudal dues had been suppressed, and that, if the lords claimed them, they need not be paid.

Now, under penalty of being themselves prosecuted or distrained upon, the municipal councillors of a village will not dare to say anything, and the peasant will have to pay, and they must distrain upon him. He will only be at liberty, if the payment was not due, to claim reimbursement later on from the lord, who, by that time, may have emigrated to Coblentz.

This was introducing—as M. Sagnac has well said—a terrible clause. The *proof* that the peasant no longer owed certain feudal dues, that they were personal, and not attached to the land—this proof, so difficult to make, rested with the peasant. If he did not make it, if he could not make it—as was nearly always the case—he had to pay !

CHAPTER XXVII

FEUDAL LEGISLATION IN 1790

New laws support feudal system—Sagnac's opinion of them—
Attempts to collect feudal dues resisted—Insurrection spreads
—Spurious decrees excite further risings—Peasants demand
" Maximum " and restoration of communal lands—Revolution
fixes price of bread—Middle-class suppressions—Draconian
laws against peasants (June 1790)—Tithes to be paid one
year longer—Summary of laws to protect property—Articles
of peasants' demands

THUS it was that the National Assembly, profiting by the
temporary lull in the peasant insurrections during the winter,
passed, in 1790, laws which in reality gave a new legal basis
to the feudal system.

Lest it should be believed that this is our own interpretation
of the legislation of the Assembly, it should be enough to refer
the reader to the laws themselves, or to what Dalloz says
about them. But here is what is said about them by a modern
writer, M. Ph. Sagnac, whom it is impossible to accuse of
sans-culottism, since he considers the abolition without redemption of the feudal rights, accomplished later on by the
Convention, as an "iniquitous and useless spoliation." Let
us see, then, how M. Sagnac estimates the laws of March 1790.

" The ancient law," he writes, " weighs, with all its force,
in the work of the Constituent Assembly, upon the new law
that is being worked out. It is for the peasant—if he does
not wish to pay a tribute of forced labour, or to carry part
of his harvest to the landlord's barn, or to leave his field in
order to go and work in his lord's—it is for the peasant to
bring proof that his lord's demand is illegal. But if the lord
has possessed some right for forty years—no matter what was
its origin under the old system—this right becomes legal under

the law of March 15. Possession is enough. It matters little what precisely is this possession, the legality of which the tenant denies : he will have to pay all the same. And if the peasants, by their revolt in August 1789, have compelled the lord to renounce certain of his rights, or if they have burned his title-deeds, it will suffice for him now to produce proof of possession during thirty years for these rights to be re-established." *

It is true that the new laws allowed the cultivator to purchase the lease of the land. But " all these arrangements, undoubtedly favourable to one who owed the payment of *real* dues (*droits réels*), were turned now against him," says M. Sagnac ; " because the important thing for him was, first of all, to pay only the legal dues, while now, if he could not show proof to the contrary, he had to acquit and redeem even the usurped rights." †

In other words, nothing could be redeemed unless all the dues were redeemed : the dues for the possession of the land, retained by the law, and the personal dues which the law had abolished.

Furthermore, we read what follows in the same author, otherwise so moderate in his estimations :

" The framework of the Constituent Assembly does not hold together. This Assembly of landlords and lawyers, by no means eager, despite their promises, to destroy completely the seigniorial and domanial system, after having taken care to preserve the more considerable rights [all those which had any real value], pushed their generosity so far as to permit redemption ; but immediately it decrees, in fact, the impossibility of that redemption. . . . The tiller of the soil had begged for reforms and insisted upon having them, or rather upon the registration in law of a revolution already made in his mind and inscribed—so at least he thought—in deeds ; but the men of law gave him only words. He felt that once more the lords had got the upper hand." ‡

" Never did legislation unchain a greater indignation,"

---

* Ph. Sagnac, *La législation civile de la Révolution française* (Paris, 1898), pp. 105–106.

† Sagnac, p. 120.   ‡ Sagnac, p. 120.

continues M. Sagnac. " On both sides people apparently decided to have no respect for it." *

The lords, feeling themselves supported by the National Asssembly, began, therefore, angrily to exact all the feudal dues which the peasants had believed to be dead and buried. They claimed the payment of all arrears ; writs and summonses rained in thousands on the villages.

The peasants, on their side, seeing that nothing was to be got from the Assembly, continued in certain districts to carry on the war against the lords. Many châteaux were sacked or burned, while elsewhere the title-deeds were destroyed and the offices of the fiscal officials, the bailiffs and the recorders were pillaged or burnt. The insurrection spread also west-ward, and in Brittany thirty-seven châteaux were burnt in the course of February 1790.

But when the decrees of February to March 1790 became known in the country districts, the war against the lords became still more bitter, and it spread to regions which had not dared to rise the preceding summer. Thus, at the sitting of the Assembly on June 5, mention was made of risings in Bourbon-Lancy and the Charolais, where false decrees of the Assembly had been spread, and an agrarian law was demanded. At the session of June 2, reports were read about the in-surrections in the Bourbonnais, the Nivernais and the province of Berry. Several municipalities had proclaimed martial law ; there had been some killed and wounded. The " brigands " had spread over the Campine, and at that very time they were investing the town of Decize. Great " excesses " were also reported from the Limousin, where the peasants were asking to have the maximum price of grain fixed. " *The project for recovering the lands granted to the lords for the last hundred and twenty years is one of the articles of their demand,*" says the report. The peasants evidently wanted to recover the communal lands of which the village communes had been robbed by the lords.

Spurious decrees of the National Assembly were seen everywhere. In March and April 1790, several were circulated

* Sagnac, p. 121,

in the provinces, ordering the people not to pay more than one *sou* for a pound of bread. The Revolution was thus getting ahead of the Convention, which did not pass the law of the " Maximum " until 1793.

In August, the popular risings were still going on. For instance, in the town of Saint-Etienne-en-Forez, the people killed one of the monopolists, and appointed a new municipality which was compelled to lower the price of bread; but thereupon the middle classes armed themselves, and arrested twenty-two rebels. This is a picture of what was happening more or less everywhere—not to mention the greater struggles at Lyons and in the South of France.

But what did the Assembly do? Did they do justice to the peasants' demands? Did they hasten to abolish without redemption those feudal rights, so hateful to those who cultivated the land, that they no longer paid them except under constraint?

Certainly not! The Assembly only voted new Draconian laws against the peasants. On June 2, 1790, " the Assembly, informed and greatly concerned about the excesses which have been committed by troops of brigands and robbers " [for which read " peasants "] in the departments of the Cher, the Nièvre and the Allier, and are spreading almost into the Corrèze, enact measures against these " promoters of disorder," and render the communes jointly responsible for the violences committed.

" All those," says Article 1 of this law, " who stir up the people of the towns and the country to accomplish acts of violence and outrages against the properties, possessions and enclosures, or the life and safety of the citizens, the collection of the taxes, the free sale and circulation of food-stuffs, are declared enemies of the Constitution, of the work of the National Assembly, of Nature, and of the King. Martial law will be proclaimed against them." *

A fortnight later, on June 18, the Assembly adopted a decree even still harsher. It deserves quotation.

Its first article declares that all tithes, whether ecclesiastical

* *Moniteur*, June 6.

or lay, hold good " for payment during the present year only to those to whom the right belongs and in the usual manner. . . ." Whereupon the peasants, no doubt, asked if a new decree was not going to be passed by-and-by for yet another year or two —and so they did not pay.

According to Article 2, " those who owe payments in field- and land-produce (*champart, terriers*), in cash, and in *other dues payable in kind*, which have not been suppressed without indemnity, will be held to pay them during the present year and the years following in the usual way . . . in conformity with the decrees passed on March 3 and on May 4 last."

Article 3 declares that no one can, under pretext of litiga- tion, refuse to pay either the tithes or the dues on field- produce, &c.

Above all, it was forbidden " to give any trouble during the collecting " of the tithes and dues. In the case of disorderly assemblies being formed, the municipality, by virtue of the decree of February 20–23, must proceed to take severe measures.

This decree of February 20–23, 1790, was very characteristic. It ordained that the municipality should intervene and pro- claim martial law whenever a disorderly assembly takes place. If they neglect to do this, the municipal officials were to be held responsible for all injury suffered by the owners of the property. And not only the officials, but " all the citizens being able to take part in the re-establishment of public order, the whole community shall be responsible for two-thirds of the damage done." Each citizen shall be empowered to demand the application of martial law, and then only shall he be relieved of his responsibility.

This decree would have been still worse if its supporters had not made a tactical error. Copying an English law, they wanted to introduce a clause which empowered the calling out of the soldiers or militia, and in such case " royal dicta- ture " had to be proclaimed in the locality. The middle classes took umbrage at this clause, and after long discussions the task of proclaiming martial law, in support of one another, was left to the municipalities, without any declaration in the King's name. Furthermore, the village communes were to be held responsible for any damages which might accrue to the lord, if they had not shot or hanged in good time the peasants who refused to pay the feudal dues.

The law of June 18, 1790, confirmed all this. All that had any real value in the feudal rights, all that could be represented by any kind of legal chicanery as attached to the possession of the land, was to be paid as before. And every one who refused was compelled by the musket or the gallows to accept these obligations. To *speak* against the payment of the feudal dues was held to be a crime, which called forth the death penalty, if martial law was proclaimed.*

Such was the bequest of the Constituent Assembly, of which we have been told so many fine things; for everything remained in that state until 1792. The feudal laws were only touched to make clear certain rules for the redemption of the feudal dues, or to complain that the peasants were not willing to redeem anything,† or else to reiterate the threats against the peasants who were not paying.‡

The decrees of February 1790 were all that the Constituent Assembly did for the abolition of the odious feudal system, and it was not until June 1793, after the insurrection of May 31, that the people of Paris compelled the Convention, in its "purified" form, to pronounce the actual abolition of the feudal rights.

Let us, therefore, bear these dates well in mind.

On August 4, 1789.—Abolition in principle of the feudal system; abolition of personal mortmain, the game laws, and patrimonial justice.

From August 5 to 11.—Partial reconstruction of this system by acts which imposed redemption for all the feudal dues of any value whatsoever.

End of 1789 and 1790.—Expeditions of the urban munici-

---

* During this discussion Robespierre uttered a very just saying which the revolutionists of all countries should remember: "As for me, I bear witness," he cried, "that no revolution has ever cost so little blood and cruelty." The bloodshed, indeed, came later, through the counter-revolution.

† Law of May 3 to 9, 1790.

‡ Law of June 15 to 19, 1790.

palities against the insurgent peasantry, and hangings of the same.

February 1790.—Report of the Feudal Committee, stating that the peasant revolt was spreading.

March and June 1790.—Draconian laws against the peasants who were not paying their feudal dues, or were preaching their abolition. The insurrections still spreading.

June 1791.—These laws were confirmed once more. Reaction all along the line. The peasant insurrections continuing.

Only in July 1792, as we shall see, on the very eve of the invasion of the Tuileries by the people, and in August 1792, after the downfall of royalty, did the Assembly take the first decisive steps against the feudal rights.

Lastly, it was only in August 1793, after the expulsion of the Girondins, that the definite abolition, without redemption, of the feudal rights was enacted.

This is the true picture of the Revolution.

One other question, of immense importance for the peasants, was clearly that of the communal lands.

Everywhere, in the east, north-east and south-east of France, wherever the peasants felt themselves strong enough to do it, they tried to regain possession of the communal lands, of which the greater part had been taken away from them by fraud, or under the pretext of debt, with the help of the State, chiefly since the reign of Louis XIV.* Lords, clergy, monks and the middle-class men of both towns and villages— all had had their share of them.

There remained, however, a good deal of these lands still in communal possession, and the middle classes looked on them with greedy eyes. So the Legislative Assembly hastened to make a law, on August 1, 1791, which authorised the sale of communal lands to private persons. This was to give a free hand for pilfering these lands.

The Assemblies of the village communes were at that time, in virtue of the municipal law passed by the National Assembly in December 1789, composed exclusively of the middle-class

Decree of 1669.

men of the village—of *active citizens*—that is, of the wealthier peasants, to the exclusion of the poor householders. And these village assemblies were evidently eager to put up the communal lands for sale, of which a large part could be acquired at a low price by the better-off peasants and farmers.

As to the mass of the poor peasants, they opposed with all their might the destruction of the collective possession of the land, as they are to-day opposing it in Russia.

On the other hand, the peasants, both the rich and the poor, did all they could to regain possession of the communal lands for the villages ; the wealthier ones in the hope of securing some part for themselves, and the poor in the hope of keeping these lands for the commune. All this, let it be well understood, offering an infinite variety of detail in different parts of France.

It was, however, this re-taking by the communes of the communal lands of which they had been robbed in the course of two centuries, that the Constituent and the Legislative Assemblies, and even the National Convention, opposed up to June 1793. The King had to be imprisoned and executed, and the Girondin leaders had to be driven out of the Convention before it could be accomplished.

CHAPTER XXVIII

ARREST OF THE REVOLUTION IN 1790

Insurrections necessary—Extent of reaction—Work of Constituent and Legislative Assemblies—New Constitution—Local government opposed to centralisation—Difficulties in applying new laws—*Directoires* on side of reaction—" Disorder wanted "—Active and passive citizens—The gains of insurrection—Equality and agrarian law—Disappearance of manorial courts—Workers' demands answered by bullets—Middle classes' love of order and prosperity—" Intellectuals " turn against people—Success of counter-revolution—Plutocracy—Opposition to republican form of government—Danton and Marat persecuted and exiled—Discontent and dishonesty in army—Massacres at Nancy—Bouillé's " splendid behaviour "

WE have seen what the economic conditions in the villages were during the year 1790. They were such that if the peasant insurrections had not gone on, in spite of all, the peasants, freed in their persons, would have remained economically under the yoke of the feudal system—as happened in Russia, where feudalism was abolished, in 1861, by law, and not by a revolution.

Besides, all the *political* work of the Revolution not only remained unfinished in 1790, but it actually suffered a complete set-back. As soon as the first panic, produced by the unexpected breaking-out of the people, had passed, the Court, the nobles, the rich men and the clergy promptly joined together for the reorganisation of the forces of reaction. And soon they felt themselves so well supported and so powerful that they began to see whether it would not be possible to crush the Revolution, and to re-establish the Court and the nobility in their rights.

All the historians undoubtedly mention this reaction; but still they do not show all its depth and all its extent. The reality was that for two years, from the summer of 1790 to the summer of 1792, the whole work of the Revolution was suspended. People were asking if it was the Revolution which was going to get the upper hand or the counter-revolution. The beam of the balance wavered between the two. And it was in utter despair that the revolutionist "leaders of opinion" decided at last, in June 1792, once more to appeal to popular insurrection.

Of course it must be recognised that while the Constituent Assembly, and after it the Legislative, opposed the revolutionary abolition of the feudal rights and popular revolution altogether, they nevertheless accomplished an immense work for the destruction of the powers of the King and the Court, and for the creation of the political power of the middle classes. And when the legislators in both these Assemblies undertook to express, in the form of laws, the new Constitution of the Third Estate, it must be confessed that they went to work with a certain energy and sagacity.

They knew how to undermine the power of the nobility and how to express the rights of the citizen in a middle-class Constitution. They worked out a local self-government which was capable of checking the governmental centralisation, and they modified the laws of inheritance so as to democratise property and to divide it up among a greater number of persons.

They destroyed for ever the political distinctions between the various "orders"—clergy, nobility, Third Estate, which for that time was a very great thing; we have only to remember how slowly this is being done in Germany and Russia. They abolished all the titles of the nobility and the countless privileges which then existed, and they laid the foundations of a more equal basis for taxation. They avoided also the formation of an Upper Chamber, which would have been a stronghold for the aristocracy. And by the departmental law of December 1789, they did something which helped on the Revolution enormously : they abolished every representative of the central authority in the provinces.

Lastly, they took away from the Church her rich possessions, and they made the members of the clergy simple functionaries of the State. The army was reorganised ; so were the courts of justice. The election of judges was left to the people. And in all these reforms the middle-class legislators avoided too much centralisation. In short, judged from the legislative point of view, they appear to have been clever, energetic men, and we find in their work certain elements of republican democratism, and a tendency towards local autonomy, which the advanced parties of the present day do not sufficiently appreciate.

However, in spite of all these laws, nothing was yet done. *The reality was not on the same level as the theory*, for the simple reason that *there lies always an abyss between a law which has just been promulgated and its practical carrying out in life*—a reason which is usually overlooked by those who do not thoroughly understand from their own experience the working of the machinery of State.

It is easy to say : " The property of the religious bodies shall pass into the hands of the State." But how is that to be put into effect ? Who will go, for example, to the Abbey of Saint Bernard at Clairvaux, and tell the abbot and the monks that they have to go ? Who is to drive them out if they do not go ? Who is to prevent them from coming back to-morrow, helped by all the pious folk in the neighbouring villages, and from chanting the mass in the abbey ? Who is to organise an effective sale of their vast estates ? And finally, who will turn the fine abbey buildings into a hospital for old men, as was actually done later on by the revolutionary government ? We know, indeed, that if the " sections " of Paris had not taken the sale of the Church lands into their hands, the law concerning these sales would never have begun to take effect.

In 1790, 1791, 1792, the old *régime* was still there, intact, and ready to be reconstituted in its entirety—with but slight modifications—just as the Second Empire of Napoleon III. was ready to come back to life at any moment in the days of Thiers and MacMahon. The clergy, the nobility, the old officialism, and above all the old spirit, were all ready to lift up their heads again, and to clap into gaol those who had dared to put on the tri-colour sash. They were watching for the opportunity; they were preparing for it. Moreover the new Directories (*directoires*) of the departments, established by the Revolution, but drawn from the wealthy class, were the framework, always ready for the re-establishment of the old *régime*. They were the citadels of the counter-revolution.

Both the Constituent and the Legislative Assembly had certainly drawn up a number of laws, of which people admire the lucidity and style to this day; but nevertheless, the greater majority of these laws remained a dead letter. It must not be forgotten that for more than two-thirds of the fundamental laws made between 1789 and 1793 no attempt was even made to put them into execution.

The fact is, that it is not enough to make a new law. It is necessary also, nearly always, to create the mechanism for its application; and as soon as the new law strikes at any vested interest, some sort of revolutionary organisation is usually required in order to apply this law to life, with all its consequences. We have only to think of the small results produced by the laws of the Convention concerning education, which all remained a dead letter.

To-day even, in spite of the present bureaucratic concentration and the armies of officials who converge towards their centre at Paris, we see that every new law, however trifling it may be, takes years before it passes into life. And again, how often it becomes completely mutilated in its application! But at the time of the Great Revolution this bureaucratic mechanism did not exist; it took more than fifty years for its actual development.

How then could the laws of the Assembly enter into everyday life without a *revolution by deed being accomplished* in every town, in every village, in each of the thirty-six thousand communes all over France.

Yet such was the blindness of the middle-class revolutionists that, on the one hand, they took every precaution to prevent the people—the poor people, who alone were throwing themselves with all their heart into the Revolution—from having too much share in the direction of communal affairs, and on the other hand, they opposed with all their might the breaking-out and the successful carrying-through of the Revolution in every town and village.

Before any vital work could result from the decrees of the Assembly, *disorder* was wanted. It was necessary that in every little hamlet, men of action, the patriots who hated the old *régime*, should seize upon the municipality; that a revolution should be made in that hamlet; that the whole order of life should be turned upside down; that all authority should be ignored; that the revolution should be a *social* one, if they wished to bring about the *political* revolution.

It was necessary for the peasant to take the land and begin to plough it without waiting for the orders of some authority, which orders evidently would never have been given. It was necessary for an entirely new life to begin in the village. But without disorder, without a great deal of *social* disorder, this could not be done.

Now it was precisely this disorder the legislators wanted to prevent.

Not only had they eliminated the people from the administration, by means of the municipal law of December 1789, which placed the administrative power in the hands of the *active citizens only*, and under the name of *passive citizens* excluded from it all the poor peasants and nearly all the workers in towns. And not only did they hand over all the provincial authority to the middle classes: they also armed these middle classes with the most terrifying powers to prevent the poor folk from continuing their insurrections.

And yet it was only these insurrections of the poor people which later on permitted them to deal mortal blows at the old *régime* in 1792 and 1793.*

* It is interesting to read in M. Aulard's *Histoire politique de la Révolution française* (2nd edition, Paris, 1903) the pages 55 to 60, in which he shows how the Assembly laboured to prevent the power falling into the hands of the people. The remarks of this writer, concerning the law of October 14, 1790, prohibiting the assembling of the citizens of the communes to discuss their affairs more than once a year for the elections, are very true.

Altogether the Revolution appeared at this period under the following aspect : The peasants realised that nothing was yet done. The abolition of the *personal* services had only awakened their hopes, and they claimed now the abolition of their economic servitude, for good, and without redemption. Besides, they wanted to regain possession of their communal lands.

What they had already gained, here and there, in 1789, by means of their insurrections, they wanted to keep, and to have their gains sanctioned by the National Assembly. And what they had not yet succeeded to obtain, they wanted to have without falling under the thunders of the martial law.

But these two wants of the people the middle classes opposed with all their might. They had taken advantage of the revolts against feudalism to begin their first attack on the power of the King, the nobles and the clergy. But as soon as a first outline of a middle-class Constitution had been worked out and accepted by the King—with every scope for the violation of it—the middle classes halted, terrified at the rapid conquests made by the spirit of revolution in the hearts of the people.

They knew, moreover, that the landed property of the nobility was going to pass into their hands ; and they wanted to have that property intact, with all the additional revenues that stood for the ancient feudal services transformed into payments in money. Some day, later on, they would see if it would not be advantageous to abolish the rest of these dues, and then it would be done legally, " methodically," and " in order." Because if disorder be tolerated, who knows where the people would stop ? Were they not already talking of " equality," of " agrarian law," of " equalisation of fortunes," of " farms not exceeding a hundred and twenty acres " ?

As to the towns and the artisans, and the entire working population of the cities, the same thing was going on as in the villages. The guilds and corporations of which royalty had contrived to make so many instruments of oppression had been abolished. The survivals of the feudal system which still existed, in the towns as in the country, had been sup-

pressed since the popular insurrections of the summer of
1789. The manorial courts had disappeared and the judges
were elected by the people and taken from the propertied
middle class.

But after all this did not really mean much. Work was
slack and bread was selling at famine prices. The great mass
of the workers would indeed have waited patiently if only
there was a chance of the reign of Liberty, Equality and
Fraternity being established. But as that was not being done,
they lost patience. The workers began to demand that
the Commune of Paris, like the municipalities of Rouen,
Nancy and Lyons, and elsewhere, should take charge of the
victualling so as to sell the wheat and the rye at cost price.
They demanded that maximum prices for the sale of the
bread-stuffs should be established, and that sumptuary laws
should be made, so that the rich might be taxed by a forced and
progressive tax. But then the middle classes, who had armed
themselves since 1789, while the passive citizens had been
disarmed, came forth, unfurled the red flag, and bidding the
people disperse, they shot those who did not obey at once.
This was done in Paris, as it was very nearly everywhere else
throughout France.

The progress of the Revolution was thus stopped. Royalty
began to revive. The emigrant nobles at Coblentz, Turin
and Mitau rubbed their hands. They plucked up courage
and indulged in wild speculation. From the summer of 1790
until June 1792, the counter-revolution had every reason to
believe that it would soon be victorious.

It was quite natural, after all, that such an important
revolution as that which had been accomplished between
1789 and 1793 should have its periods of check and even of
recoil. The forces at the disposal of the old *régime* were
immense, and having experienced a first defeat, they could
not but try to reconstitute themselves, in order to set up a
barrier in opposition to the new spirit. There was therefore
nothing unforeseen in the wave of reaction which appeared
in 1790. But if this reaction was so strong that it could last
until June 1792, and if, in spite of all the crimes of the Court,

it became so powerful that in 1791 the whole Revolution was set back, this was because the middle classes had joined hands with the nobility and the clergy who had rallied round the banner of royalty. The new force constituted by the Revolution itself—the middle classes—brought their business ability, their love of " order " and of property, and their hatred of popular tumult to lend support to the forces of the old *régime*. Moreover, the majority of the "intellectuals," in whom the people had put their trust, as soon as they perceived the first glimmer of a rising, turned their backs on the masses, and hurried into the ranks of the defenders of " order " to join them in keeping down the people and in opposing the popular tendencies towards equality.

Reinforced in this fashion, the counter-revolutionists succeeded so well, that if the peasants had not continued their risings in the provinces, and if the people in the towns, on seeing the foreigners invading France, had not risen again during the summer of 1792, the progress of the Revolution would have been stopped, without anything lasting having been effected.

Altogether, the situation was very gloomy in 1790. " A plutocracy is already established shamelessly," wrote Loustallot on November 28, 1789, in the *Révolution de Paris*. Who knows if it is not already a treasonable crime to say, " The nation is the sovereign." * But since then reaction had gained a good deal of ground, and it was still visibly progressing.

In his great work upon the political history of the Great Revolution, M. Aulard has described at some length the opposition that the idea of a republican form of government encountered among the middle classes and the " intellectuals " of the period—even when the abolition of monarchy was rendered unavoidable by the treacheries of the Court and the monarchists. In fact, while in 1789 the revolutionists had acted as if they wished to get rid of royalty altogether, a

---

* Aulard, *Histoire politique de la Révolution française*, p. 72. A detailed analysis of what had been done by the Assembly against the spirit of democracy will be found in Aulard.

decidedly monarchical movement began now, among these very revolutionists, in proportion as the constitutional power of the Assembly was asserted.* Even more may be said. After October 5 and 6, 1789, especially after the flight of the King in June 1791, every time that the people displayed themselves as a revolutionary force, the middle classes and the "leaders of opinion" of the Revolution became more and more monarchical.

That is a very important fact; but neither must it be forgotten that the essential thing for both middle class and intellectuals was the "preservation of property," as they used to say in those days. We see, in reality, this question of the *maintenance of property* running like a black thread all through the Revolution up to the fall of the Girondins.† It is also certain that if the idea of a Republic so greatly frightened the middle classes, and even the ardent Jacobins (while the Cordeliers accepted it willingly), it was because the popular masses linked it with that of *equality*, and this meant for them *equality of fortune and the agrarian law*—that is, the ideal of the Levellers, the Communists, the Expropriators, the "Anarchists" of the period.

It was therefore chiefly to prevent the people from attacking the sacrosanct principle of property that the middle classes were anxious to put a check on the Revolution. After October 1789, the Assembly had passed the famous martial law which permitted the shooting of the peasants in revolt, and later on, in July 1791, the massacre of the people of Paris. They put obstacles also in the way of the men of the people coming

---

* Among others, a very interesting instance of this may be found in the letters of Madame Jullien (de la Drôme): "I am cured, therefore, of my Roman fever, which did not, however, go as far as republicanism for fear of civil war. I am shut up with animals of all sorts in the sacred Ark of the Constitution. . . . One is somewhat of a Huron squaw (North American Indian) when playing the Spartan or Roman woman in Paris." Elsewhere she asks her son: "Tell me if the Jacobins have become Feuillants" (the Club of the Feuillants was the monarchist club). *Journal d'une bourgeoise pendant la Révolution*, published by Edouard Lockroy, Paris, 1881, 2nd edition, pp. 31, 32, 35.

† Marat alone had dared to put in his newspaper the following epigraph: "*Ut redeat miseris abeat fortuna superbis.*" (May fortune desert the rich and come back to the poor.)

to Paris for the *Fête* of the Federation, on July 14, 1790. And they took a series of measures against the local revolutionary societies which gave strength to the popular revolution, even at the risk of killing, in so doing, what had been the germ of their own power.

Since the first outbreaks of the Revolution some thousands of political associations had sprung into being throughout France. It was not only the primary or electoral assemblies continuing to meet; it was not only the numerous Jacobin societies, branches of the parent society at Paris—it was the sections chiefly, the Popular Societies and the Fraternal Societies, which came into existence spontaneously and often without the least formality; it was the thousands of committees and local powers—almost independent—substituting themselves for the royal authority, which all helped to spread among the people the idea of social equality by means of a revolution.

Therefore the middle classes eagerly applied themselves to the task of crushing, paralysing, or at least demoralising these thousands of local centres, and they succeeded so well that the monarchists, the clergy, and the nobles began once more to get the upper hand in the towns and boroughs of more than half of France.

Presently they resorted to judicial prosecutions, and in January 1790, Necker obtained an order of arrest against Marat, who had openly espoused the cause of the people, the poorest classes. Fearing a popular outbreak, they despatched both infantry and cavalry to arrest the people's tribune; his printing press was smashed, and Marat, at the high-tide of the Revolution, was forced to take refuge in England. When he returned, four months after, he had to remain hidden all the time, and in December 1791 he had to cross the Channel once more.

In short, the middle classes and the "intellectuals," both defenders of property, did so much to crush the popular movement that they stopped the Revolution itself. According as middle-class authority constituted itself, the authority of the King was seen to recover its youthful vigour.

"The true Revolution, an enemy to licence, grows stronger every day," wrote the monarchist, Mallet du Pan, in June 1790. And so it was. Three months later, the counter-revolution felt itself already so powerful that it strewed the streets of Nancy with corpses.

At first, the revolutionary spirit had touched the army but little, composed, as it then was, of mercenaries, partly foreign—either Germans or Swiss. But it penetrated by degrees. The *Fête* of the Federation, to which delegates from the soldiers had been invited to take part as citizens, helped in this, and in the course of the month of August, a spirit of discontent began to show itself a little everywhere, but especially in the eastern garrisons, in a series of movements among the soldiers. They wanted to compel their officers to give an account of the sums which had passed through their hands, and to make restitution of what had been withheld from the soldiers. These sums were enormous. In the regiment of Beauce they amounted to more than 240,000 livres, and from 100,000 even to two millions in other garrisons. The ferment went on growing; but, as might be expected of men brutalised by long service, part of them remained faithful to the officers, and the counter-revolutionists took advantage of this to provoke conflicts and sanguinary quarrels between the soldiers themselves. Thus, at Lille, four regiments fought among themselves—royalists against patriots—and left fifty dead and wounded on the spot.

It is highly probable that, the royalist plots having redoubled in activity since the end of 1789, especially among the officers of the Army of the East, commanded by Bouillé, it fell in with the plans of the conspirators to take advantage of the first outbreak of the soldiers by drowning it in blood, thus helping the royalist regiments to remain faithful to their commanders.

The occasion was soon found at Nancy.

The National Assembly, on hearing of the agitation among the soldiers, passed, on August 6, 1790, a law, which diminished the effectives in the army and forbade the "deliberate associations" of the soldiers in the service, but at the same time ordered also the money accounts to be rendered without delay by the officers to their respective regiments.

As soon as this decree became known at Nancy on the 9th, the soldiers, chiefly the Swiss of the Châteauvieux regiment, made up mainly of men from the cantons of Vaud and Geneva, demanded the accounts from their officers. They carried off the pay-chest of their regiment and placed it in the safe keeping of their own sentinels; they threatened their officers with violence, and sent eight delegates to Paris to plead their cause before the National Assembly. The massing of Austrian troops on the frontier helped to increase the disturbance.

The Assembly, meanwhile, acting on false reports sent up from Nancy, and incited by the Commandant of the National Guard, Lafayette, in whom the middle class had full confidence, voted on the 16th a decree condemning the soldiers for their breach of discipline, and ordering the garrisons of the National Guard of the Meurthe department to "repress the authors of the rebellion." Their delegates were arrested, and Lafayette, on his part, ssued a circular summoning the National Guards from the towns nearest Nancy to take arms against the revolted garrison in that town.

At Nancy itself, however, everything seemed as if it were going to pass off peaceably, the majority of the men who had rebelled having even signed "a deed of repentance." But apparently that was not what the royalists wanted.*

Bouillé set out from Metz on the 28th, at the head of three thousand faithful soldiers, with the firm intention of dealing the rebels the crushing blow desired by the Court.

The double-dealing of the Directory of the department helped Bouillé, and while everything could yet be arranged peacefully, Bouillé offered the garrison quite impossible conditions, and immediately attacked it. His soldiers com-

---

* Vide *Grands détails par pièces authentiques de l'affaire de Nancy* (Paris, 1790); *Détail très exact des ravages commis . . . à Nancy* (Paris, 1790); *Relation exacte de ce qui s'est passé à Nancy le 31 août 1790*; *Le sens commun du bonhomme Richard sur l'affaire de Nancy* (Philadelphie (?)), *l'an second de la liberté française*, and other pamphlet in the rich collection at the British Museum, vol. vii. pp. 326, 327, 328 962.

mitted the most frightful carnage, they killed the citizens as well as the rebellious soldiers, and plundered the houses.

Three thousand corpses strewed the streets of Nancy as the outcome of the fight, and after that came the "legal" reprisals. Thirty-two rebels were executed by being broken on the wheel, and forty-one were sent to penal servitude.

The King at once expressed his approval by letter of "the splendid behaviour of M. Bouillé"; the National Assembly thanked the assassins; and the municipality of Paris held a funeral service in honour of the *conquerors* who had fallen in the battle. No one dared to protest, Robespierre no more than the others. Thus ended the year 1790. Armed reaction was uppermost.

CHAPTER XXIX

THE FLIGHT OF THE KING—REACTION—END OF THE CONSTITUENT ASSEMBLY

June 21, 1791—Royalist plot—Flight to Varennes—Drouet pursues King—Decision of people—Effect of this decision—France without a King—Middle classes recant—Causes of their reaction—King declared re-established—Massacre of republicans—Danton escapes to England—Robert, Marat and Féron go into hiding—Electoral rights of people further restricted—King takes oath to Constitution—Constituent Assembly dissolved—Legislative Assembly obtains power—Views of Marat and Desmoulins—Reaction continues—Treason in the air

THE Great Revolution is full of events, tragic in the highest degree. The taking of the Bastille, the march of the women on Versailles, the attack on the Tuileries, the execution of the King, have resounded all over the world—we were taught the dates of them in our childhood. However, there are also other dates, which are often forgotten, but have an equally great significance, as they sum up the meaning of the Revolution at a given moment, and its further progress.

Thus, as regards the downfall of monarchy, the most significant moment of the Revolution—the moment that most clearly sums up its first part and gives, moreover, to all its further progress a certain popular character—is June 21, 1791 : that memorable night when some obscure men of the people arrested the fugitive King and his family at Varennes, just as they were about to cross the frontier and to throw themselves into the arms of the foreigner. On that night royalty was wrecked in France. And from that night the people entered upon the scene, thrusting the politicians into the background.

The episode is well known. A plot had been formed in Paris to enable the King to escape, and to get him across the frontier, where he was to put himself at the head of the *émigrés* and the German armies. The Court had been concocting this plot since September 1789, and it appears that Lafayette was aware of it.*

That the royalists should have seen in this escape the means of placing the King in safety, and of crushing the Revolution at the same time, was but natural. But many of the revolutionists among the middle classes also favoured the plan : once the Bourbons were out of France, they thought, Philippe, Duke of Orléans, would be put on the throne and he could be made to grant a middle-class Constitution, without having any need of assistance from the always dangerous popular risings.

The people frustrated this plot.

An unknown man, Drouet, ex-postmaster, recognised the King as he passed through a village. But the royal carriage was already off at full speed. Losing no time, Drouet and one of his friends, Guillaume, set off at once, in the dark, in hot pursuit after the carriage. The forests along the road were, they knew, scoured by hussars who had come to meet the royal fugitives at Pont-de-Somme-Vesle, but not seeing the carriage and fearing the hostility of the people had retreated into the woods. Drouet and Guillaume managed, however, to avoid these patrols by following paths known to themselves, but did not overtake the royal carriage until Varennes, where an unexpected delay had detained it—the relay of horses and the hussars not having been met at the exact place which had been appointed. There, Drouet, getting a little ahead, had just time to run to the house of a friendly innkeeper. " You are a good patriot, are you ? " " I should think so ! " " Very well then, let us arrest the King."

Then, without making any noise, they blocked, first of all, the road for the heavy royal carriage, by placing across the bridge over the Aire a cart laden with furniture, which they found there by chance. After that, followed by four or five

* In the letter of the Count d'Estaing to the Queen, of which the rough draft, found afterwards, was published in the *Histoire de la Révolution*, by the *Deux amis de la liberté*, 1792, vol. iii. pp. 101-104. Also Louis Blanc, 1832, vol. iii. pp. 175-176.

citizens armed with muskets, they stopped the fugitives, just as their carriage, coming down from the upper town towards the bridge, was passing under the archway of the church of Saint Gencoult.*

Drouet and his friends made the travellers alight despite their protestations and, while waiting for the municipality to verify their passports, made them go into the back-parlour of Sauce, the grocer.   There, the King, being openly recognised by a judge residing at Varennes, was compelled to abandon his character of servant to "Madame Korff" (the passport obtained for the Queen from the Russian ambassador bore that name) and with his usual duplicity began to plead the dangers to which his family was exposed in Paris from the Duke of Orléans, to excuse his flight.

But the people of Varennes were in no wise deceived. They understood at once the King's stratagems. The tocsin was rung, and the alarm rapidly spread in the night from Varennes, all round to the country villages, whence there came flocking on every side peasants armed with hay-forks and sticks. They guarded the King until day broke, two peasants, hay-fork in hand, acting as sentinels.

Thousands upon thousands of peasants from the neighbouring villages flocked now on the road leading from Varennes to Paris, and these crowds entirely paralysed the hussars and

---

* It seems most probable, according to authentic documents collected and analysed by M. G. Lenôtre (*Le Drame de Varennes, Juin 1791*, Paris, 1905, pp. 151 *et seq.*), and a pamphlet, *Rapport sommaire et exact de l'arrestation du roi à Varennes, près Clermont*, by Bayon (Collection of the British Museum, F. 893, 13), that Drouet had at first only suspicions concerning the travellers, that he had hesitated and only dashed through the woods in pursuit after his suspicions had been confirmed by Jean de Lagny. This boy of thirteen, who was the son of the postmaster at Chantrix, J. B. Lagny, arrived at Sainte-Menehould, having ridden full speed, bringing the order for the arrest of the royal carriage, signed by Bayon, one of the volunteers who were sent from Paris in pursuit of the King. Bayon having covered thirty-five leagues in six hours, by changing horses ten times, was probably quite exhausted, and halting for a moment at Chantrix, he hurried off a courier before him. It is also highly probable that Louis XVI. had been already recognised at Chantrix by Gabriel Vallet, who had just married one of J. B. Lagny's daughters, and who had been in Paris during the *Fête* of the Federation. This Vallet drove the royal carriage as far as Châlons, where he certainly did not keep the secret.

dragoons of Bouillé, in whom the King had put his trust for escape. At Sainte-Menehould the tocsin was rung immediately after the departure of the royal carriage ; and it was the same at Clermont-en-Argonne. At Sainte-Menehould the people even disarmed the dragoons, who had come to form an escort for the King, and then fraternised with them. At Varennes the sixty German hussars, under the command of sub-lieutenant Rohrig, who had come to escort the King until he would be met by Bouillé, and who had posted themselves in the lower town on the other side of the Aire, scarcely showed themselves. Their officer disappeared without any one ever knowing what had become of him, and the men, after drinking all day with the inhabitants, who did not abuse them, but won them over to their cause in a brotherly way, took no further interest in the King. They were soon shouting " *Vive la Nation !* " as they drank, while the whole town, roused by the tocsin, was crowding into the neighbourhood of Sauce's shop.

The approaches to Varennes were barricaded to prevent Bouillé's uhlans' from entering the town. And as soon as day dawned, the cry of the crowd was " To Paris ! To Paris ! "

These cries became even more menacing, when, about ten o'clock in the morning, the two commissioners—despatched on the morning of the 21st, one by Lafayette and the other by the Assembly, to stop the King and his family—arrived at Varennes. " Let them set out. They must set out. We shall drag them into the carriage by force ! " shouted the peasants, growing furious when they saw Louis XVI. trying to gain time in expectation of the arrival of Bouillé and his uhlans. The King and his family had to obey, and after having destroyed the compromising papers which they carried with them in the carriage, they saw that there was nothing left to do but begin their return to Paris.

The people took them back to Paris as prisoners. All was over with royalty. It was covered with opprobrium.

On July 14, 1789, royalty had lost its fortress, but it had retained its moral force, its prestige. Three months later, on October 6, the King became the hostage of the Revolution, but the monarchical principle was still firm. Louis XVI., around whom the propertied classes had rallied, was still powerful. The Jacobins themselves dared not attack him.

But on that night, when the King, disguised as a servant, passed the night in the back-parlour of a village grocer, elbowed by " patriots " and lighted by a candle stuck in a lantern—that night when the tocsin was rung to prevent the King from betraying the nation, and the peasant crowds brought him back as prisoner to the people of Paris—that night royalty was wrecked for ever. The King, who had been in olden times the symbol of national unity, lost now his right to be so regarded by becoming the symbol of an international union of tyrants against the peoples. All the thrones of Europe felt the shock.

Moreover, on that same night, the people entered the political arena, to force the hand of the political leaders. The ex-postmaster Drouet, who, on his own initiative, stopped the King and thus frustrated the deep-laid plots of politicians; this villager, who, obeying his own impulse at dead of night, urged his horse and made him gallop over hills and dales in pursuit of the secular traitor—the King—is a symbol of the people who from that day, at every critical juncture of the Revolution, took the lead and dominated the politician.

The invasion of the Tuileries by the people on June 20, 1792, the march of the faubourgs of Paris against the Tuileries on August 10, 1792, the dethronement of Louis XVI. with all its consequences—all these great events were to follow each other now, as a historic necessity.

The King's intention, when he tried to escape, was to put himself at the head of the army commanded by Bouillé, and supported by a German army, to march on Paris. Once the capital should be reconquered, we know exactly what the royalists intended to do. They were going to arrest all the " patriots ": the proscription lists were already drawn up. Some of them would have been executed, and the others deported or imprisoned. All the decrees voted by the Assembly for the establishment of the Constitution or against the clergy were going to be abolished; the ancient *régime*, with its orders and its classes, was to be re-established; the mailed fist would have been re-introduced, and, by means of summary executions, the tithes, the feudal laws, the game laws, and all the feudal rights of the old *régime* would have been reinstituted.

Such was the plan of the royalists; they did not trouble to conceal it. " Just wait, you gentlemen patriots," said they, to whoever would listen to them, "soon you will pay for your crimes."

The people, as we have said, frustrated this plan. The King, arrested at Varennes, was brought back to Paris and placed under the guardianship of the patriots of the faubourgs.

One might think that now was the time for the Revolution to pursue its logical development with giant strides. The King's treachery having been proved, were they not going to proclaim his dethronement, overthrow the old feudal institutions and inaugurate the democratic republic?

But nothing of the sort happened. On the contrary, it was reaction that triumphed definitely a few weeks after the King's flight to Varennes, and the middle classes handed over to royalty a new patent of immunity.

The people had grasped at once the situation. It was evident that the King could not be left on the throne. Re-instated in his palace, would he not resume all the more actively the web of his conspiracies and plots with Austria and Prussia? Since he had been prevented from leaving France, he would doubtless the more zealously hasten the foreign invasion. This was obvious, the more so as he had learned nothing by his Varennes adventure. He continued to refuse his signature to the decrees directed against the clergy, and the prerogatives of the nobles. Evidently the only possible solution was to declare his dethronement without further delay.

This is how the people of Paris and a large part of the provinces understood the situation. At Paris they began, the day after June 21, to demolish the busts of Louis XVI. and to efface the royal inscriptions. The crowd rushed into the Tuileries, openly inveighing against royalty and demanding the dethronement. When the Duke of Orléans took his drive through the streets of Paris, with a smile on his lips, believing as he did that he would pick up a crown there, people turned their backs on him: they did not want any King. The Cordeliers openly demanded the republic and signed an address in which they declared themselves to be all against the King —all "tyrannicides." The municipal body of Paris issued a similar declaration. The sections of Paris proclaimed their permanénce; the woollen caps and the men with pikes reappeared in the streets; every one felt that it was the eve of another July 14. The people of Paris were, in fact, ready to rise for the definite overthrow of royalty.

The National Assembly, under the pressure of the popular movement, went ahead: they acted as if there was no longer a King. Had he noi, in effect, abdicated by his flight? They seized the executive power, gave orders to the ministers and took over the diplomatic correspondence. For about a fortnight France existed without any King.

But then the middle classes suddenly changed their mind; they recanted, and set themselves in open opposition to the republican movement. The attitude of the Assembly changed in the same way. While all the popular and fraternal societies declared themselves in favour of dethronement, the Jacobin Club, composed of the middle-class statists, repudiated the idea of a republic, and declared for the maintenance of a constitutional monarchy. "The word republic frightened the haughty Jacobins," said Réal from the platform of their club. The most advanced among them, including Robespierre, were afraid of compromising themselves: they did not dare to declare for dethronement, they said it was calumny when they were called republicans.

The Assembly which were so decidedly anti-royalist on June 22, now suddenly reversed their decisions, and on July 15 they published in great haste a decree which declared the King to be blameless and pronounced against his dethronement; and therefore against the republic. Thenceforth, to demand a republic became a crime.

What had happened during those twenty days that the leaders should have tacked so suddenly and formed the resolution of keeping Louis XVI. on the throne? Had he shown any signs of repentance ? Had he given any pledges of submission to the Constitution ? No, nothing of the kind ! The explanation lies in the fact that the middle-class leaders had again seen the spectre which had haunted them since July 14 and October 6, 1789 : *the rising of the people !* The men with the pikes were out in the streets and the provinces seemed ready to rise, as in the month of August 1789. Thousands of peasants were hastening from their villages, at the sound of the tocsin, on the road to Paris, and bringing the King back to the capital ; the mere sight of this had given them a shock. And now they saw the people of Paris ready to rise, arming themselves and demanding that the Revolution should go on : asking for the republic, for the abolition of the feudal laws, for equality pure and simple. The agrarian law, the bread tax, the tax upon the rich, were they not going to become realities ?

No, rather the traitor King, the invasion of the foreigner, than the success of the popular Revolution !

This is why the Assembly hastened to make an end of all republican agitation, in hurrying through, on July 15, the decree which exculpated the King, re-established him on the throne, and declared all those who wished to push forward the Revolution to be criminals.

Whereupon the Jacobins, those pretended leaders of the Revolution, after one day of hesitation, abandoned the republicans, who were proposing to get up a huge popular demonstration against royalty, on July 17, in the Champ-de-Mars. And then, the middle-class counter-revolutionists, sure of their position, assembled their National Guard commanded by Lafayette, and brought them up against the masses as they assembled, unarmed, in the Champ-de-Mars, round the " altar of the fatherland," to sign a republican petition. The red flag was unfurled, martial law proclaimed, and the people, the republicans, were massacred.

From that time began a period of open reaction, which went on increasing until the spring of 1792.

The republicans, authors of the Champ-de-Mars petition which demanded the dethronement of the King, were fiercely persecuted. Danton had to cross over to England (August 1791), Robert, a declared republican and editor of the *Révolutions de Paris*, Fréron, and above all Marat, had to go into hiding.

Profiting by this period of terror, the middle classes took care to limit further the electoral rights of the people. Henceforth, to be an elector, besides paying in direct contributions ten days' labour, a man had to possess, either as owner, or in usufruct, property valued at 150 to 200 days' work, or to hold as a farmer property valued at 400 days' labour. The peasants, as we see, were deprived absolutely of all political rights.

After July 17, 1791, it became dangerous to call oneself or to be called a republican, and soon some of the revolutionists, who had "nothing to lose and everything to gain from disorder and anarchy," themselves began to treat as "depraved men" those who asked for a republic instead of a king.

By degrees the middle classes became still bolder, and it was in the middle of a pronounced royalist movement, to the accompaniment of enthusiastic cheers for the King and Queen from the Paris middle classes, that the King came on September 14, 1791, before the Assembly to accept and solemnly swear fealty to the Constitution which he betrayed the same day.

Fifteen days later, the Constituent Assembly dissolved, and this was made another occasion for the constitutionalists to renew their manifestations of loyalty in honour of Louis XVI. The Government then passed into the hands of the Legislative Assembly, elected on a restricted suffrage, and clearly even more middle class than the Constituent Assembly had been.

And still the reaction grew. Towards the end of 1791 the best revolutionists completely despaired of the Revolution. Marat believed all was lost. "The Revolution," he wrote in his *Ami du peuple*, "has failed. . . ." He demanded that in appeal should be made to the people, but the politicians did not listen to him. "It was a handful of poor folk," he said in his journal, on July 21, "who knocked down the walls of the Bastille. Only set them to work, and they will prove themselves as they did that first day ; they ask nothing better than to fight against their tyrants ; *but then they were free to act, now they are chained.*" Chained by the leaders, be it understood. " The patriots dare not show themselves," says Marat again on October 15, 1791, " and the enemies of liberty fill the galleries of the Senate-house, and are seen everywhere."

Similar words of despair were uttered by Camille Desmoulins at the Jacobin Club, on October 24, 1791. The " reactionaries have turned," he said, " the popular movement of July and August 1789, to their advantage. The Court favourites talk to-day about the sovereignty of the people and the rights of man, of equality among the citizens, to deceive the people, and they parade in the uniform of the National Guard to seize or even buy the posts of leaders. Around them gather the tools of the throne. The aristocratic devils have displayed an infernal cleverness."

Prudhomme said openly that the nation was betrayed by its representatives ; the army by its chiefs.

But Prudhomme and Desmoulins could at least show themselves, while a popular revolutionist, such as Marat, had to hide himself for several months, not knowing sometimes where to find a shelter for the night. It has been well said of him that he pleaded the cause of the people with his head upon the block. Danton, on the point of being arrested, had gone to London.

The Queen herself, in her correspondence with Fersen, by whose intermediary she arranged for invasion and prepared for the entry of the German armies into the capital, bore witness to " a marked change in Paris." " The people," she said, " no longer read the papers." " They are only interested in the dearness of bread and the decrees," she wrote on October 31, 1791.

The dearness of bread—and the decrees ! Bread, so that they might live and carry on the Revolution, for bread was scarce already in October ! And the decrees against the priests and the *émigrés*, which the King refused to sanction !

Treason was everywhere, and we know now that at that

very time—at the close of 1791, Dumouriez, the Girondist General who commanded the armies in the East of France, was already plotting with the King. He was drawing up for Louis a secret memorandum on the means for checking the Revolution. This memorandum was found after the taking of the Tuileries in the iron safe of Louis XVI.

CHAPTER XXX

THE LEGISLATIVE ASSEMBLY—
REACTION IN 1791-1792

King and Assembly—Fear of foreign invasion—Feuillants and Girondins—Count d'Artois and Count de Provence—Emigration of nobles—Assembly summon Count de Provence and *émigrés* to return—Declaration of war against Austria—Fall of royalist Ministry—Girondins in power—Was war necessary?—Equalisation of wealth—Socialistic ideas of people—Mayor of Étampes killed by peasants—Robespierre and agrarian law—Middle classes rally round royalty—Royalist *coup d'état* imminent—Lafayette's letter to Assembly

THE new National Assembly, elected by *active* citizens only, which took the name of National Legislative Assembly, met on October 1, 1791, and from the first moment, the King, encouraged by the manifestations of the temper of the middle classes who thronged round him, assumed an arrogant attitude towards it. Now began, just as in the early days of the States-General, a series of malicious petty annoyances on the side of the Court, with feeble attempts at resistance on the part of the representatives. In spite of this, as soon as the King entered the Assembly, he was received with the most servile marks of respect and the liveliest marks of enthusiasm. On such occasions Louis XVI. spoke of an enduring harmony and an inalienable confidence between the legislative body and the King. "May the love of country unite us, and public interest render us inseparable," he would say—and at that very time he would be arranging the foreign invasion which was to overawe the constitutionalists and re-establish representation by Three Orders and the privileges of the nobility and clergy.

Generally speaking, since October 1791—in reality, since the flight of the King and his arrest at Varennes in June, the fear of a foreign invasion obsessed all minds and had become the chief object of consideration. There were, it is true, in the Legislative Assembly two parties: the royalist Right, represented by the *Feuillants*, and the Left, represented by the *Girondins*, serving as a half-way house between those of the middle classes who were partly constitutional and those who were partly republican. But neither one nor the other of them took any interest in the great problems bequeathed to them by the Constituent Assembly. Neither the establishing of a republic nor the abolition of the feudal privileges excited the Legislative Assembly. The Jacobins themselves and even the Cordeliers seemed to have agreed not to mention the republic, and it was about questions of secondary importance, such as who should be mayor of Paris, that the passions of the revolutionists and anti-revolutionists came into collision.

The two great questions of the moment concerned the priests and the emigrated nobles. They dominated everything else on account of the attempts at anti-revolutionary risings organised by the priests and the *émigrés*, and because they were intimately connected with the foreign war, which, every one felt, was close at hand.

The youngest brother of the King, the Count d'Artois, had emigrated, as we know, immediately after July 14, 1789. The other brother, the Count de Provence, had escaped at the same time as Louis XVI., in June 1791, and had succeeded in getting to Brussels. Both of them had protested against the King's acceptance of the Constitution. They declared that the King could not alienate the rights of the ancient monarchy, and that, consequently, his act was null. Their protestation was published by the royalist agents all over France and produced a great effect.

The nobles left their regiments or their châteaux and emigrated *en masse*, and the royalists threatened those who did not do the same that they would be relegated to the middle class when the nobility returned victorious. The *émigrés*

assembled at Coblentz, Worms and Brussels were openly
preparing a counter-revolution which was to be supported by
the foreign invasion; and it became more and more evident
that the King was playing a double game, for it was impossible
not to see that everything done by the emigrant nobles had
his assent.

On October 30, 1791, the Legislative Assembly decided to
proceed against the King's younger brother, Louis-Stanislas-
Xavier, who had received from Louis XVI., at the time of
his flight, a decree conferring upon him the title of regent,
in case the King should be arrested. The Assembly, therefore,
summoned the Count de Provence to return to France within
two months; if not, he was to lose his right of regency.
A few days later, on November 9, the Assembly ordered
also all *émigrés* to return before the end of the year; if
not, they should be treated as conspirators, condemned,
sentenced in default, and their revenues should be seized
for the profit of the nation—" without prejudice, however,
to the rights of their wives, their children and their lawful
creditors."

The King sanctioned the decree concerning his brother,
but opposed his " veto " to the second, concerning the *émigrés*.
He vetoed also a decree which ordered the priests to take the
oath to the Constitution, under pain of arrest as suspects,
in case of religious disturbances in the communes to which
they ministered.

The most important act of the Legislative Assembly was
the declaration of war against Austria, which was openly
preparing for an invasion, in order to re-establish Louis XVI.
in those rights he had held before 1789. The King and Marie-
Antoinette urged it upon the Emperor of Austria, and their
entreaties became still more urgent after their flight had been
stopped. But it is extremely probable that the warlike preparations of Austria would have been prolonged, perhaps
until the following spring, if the Girondins had not pressed
for war.

Lack of cohesion in the royalist Ministry, one of its members,

Bertrand de Moleville, being strongly opposed to the constitutional *régime*, whilst Narbonne wanted to make it one of the props to the throne, had led to its fall; whereupon, in March 1792, Louis XVI. called into power a Girondist Ministry, with Dumouriez for foreign affairs, Roland, that is to say, Madame Roland, for the Interior, Grave, soon to be replaced by Servan, at the War Office, Clavière for Finance, Duranthon for Justice, and Lacoste for the Marine.

It need not be said, as Robespierre quickly made it appear, that far from hastening the Revolution, the coming of the Girondins into power was on the contrary a weight in the scales for reaction. Henceforth all was for moderation, since the King had accepted what the Court called the "*Ministère sans-culotte.*" It was only in the affair of the war that this Ministry showed any ardour, against the advice of Marat and Robespierre, and on April 20, 1792, the Girondins triumphed. War was declared against Austria, or as they said then, "against the King of Bohemia and Hungary."

Was the war necessary? Jaurès * has put the question, and in the answering of it has placed before the reader's eyes many documents of that time. And the conclusion that must be drawn from these documents, and is deduced from them by Jaurès himself, is the same as that which was defended by Marat and Robespierre. The war was *not* necessary. The foreign sovereigns no doubt feared the development of republican ideas in France; but from that to their rushing to the help of Louis XVI. was far enough; they were very far from eager about entering upon a war of that kind. It was the Girondins who wanted the war, because they saw in it the means of combating the royal power.

Marat told the plain truth concerning the matter. "You want the war," he said, "because you do not want to appeal to the people for the giving of a decisive blow to royalty." The Girondins and a mass of the Jacobins preferred indeed a foreign invasion, which, by arousing patriotism and laying bare the treachery of the King, would lead to the downfall of

* *Histoire socialiste, La Législative,* p. 815 *et seq.*

royalty without any popular rising. "We want some great treachery," said Brissot, who hated the people, their disorderly risings, and their attacks upon property.

Thus the Court on one side, and the Girondists on the other, found themselves in agreement in encouraging the invasion of France. Under such conditions war was inevitable. It blazed out, and it raged for twenty-three years with all its fatal consequences, fatal to the Revolution and to European progress. "You do not want to appeal to the people; you do not want the popular revolution—very well, you shall have war, and perhaps the general break-up!" How many times has this truth been verified since.

The spectre of the people, armed and insurgent, demanding from the middle classes their share of the national wealth, never ceased to haunt those members of the Third Estate who had attained power, or who had, through the clubs and newspapers, acquired an influence upon the course of events. It must be said also that, by degrees, the revolutionary education of the people was being accomplished by the Revolution itself, and that the masses were by degrees emboldened to demand measures imbued with a communist spirit, which to some extent would have contributed to efface the economic inequalities.

"Equalisation of wealth" was very much spoken of among the people. The peasants who possessed only miserable little plots, and the town-workers, thrown out of work, began to affirm their right to the land. In the villages, the peasants demanded that no one should possess a farm of more than a hundred and twenty acres, and in the towns it was said that any one who wished to cultivate the land should have a right to a certain quantity.*

A tax upon food-stuffs, to prevent speculation in objects of prime necessity, laws against monopolists, municipal purchasing

* After the decrees of March 15, the objections raised against these decrees had been numerous. They have been pointed out by Doniol (*La Révolution*, &c., pp. 104 *et seq.*), and by Professor N. Karéiev (*Les paysans et la question paysanne en France dans le dernier quart du XVIIIᵉ Siècle* (Paris: Giard, 1899), pp. 489 *et seq.*, and Appendix No. 33.

of food-stuffs which should be delivered to the inhabitants at cost price, a progressive tax on the rich, a forced loan and heavy taxes on all inheritances, these ideas were discussed by the people and found their way into the press. The very instantaneousness with which they manifested themselves each time the people gained a victory, either in Paris or in the provinces, proved that these ideas were widely circulating among the disinherited, even though the revolutionary writers did not dare to express them too openly. " You do not then perceive," said Robert in his *Révolutions de Paris*, in May 1791, " that the French Revolution, for which you are fighting, as you say, *as a citizen*, is a veritable agrarian law put in execution by the people. They are re-entering on their rights. One step more, and they will re-enter upon their possessions . . ." *

It is easy to guess the horror with which these ideas inspired the middle classes, who were eager to enjoy now, and at their ease, their acquired wealth, as well as their new, privileged position in the State. We can imagine the fury which was kindled among them in March 1792, when the news came to Paris that the Mayor of Etampes, Simonneau, had just been killed by the peasants. He, as well as so many other middle-class mayors, had shot down the peasants who had revolted without any legal formalities and no one had said a word. But when the hungry peasants, who asked only that the price of bread should be fixed, killed this mayor with their pikes, a chorus of indignation was raised among the Parisian middle classes.

" The day has come when the landowners of *all classes* must feel at length that they are falling under the scythe of anarchy," groaned Mallet du Pan in his *Mercure de France ;* and he demanded a " coalition of the landowners " against the people, against the " brigands," the preachers of agrarian law. Every one began to perorate against the people, Robespierre as well as the others. The priest Dolivier was alone in raising his voice in favour of the masses and to declare that " the nation is really the owner of its land." " There is no law," he said, " which could justly prevent the peasant from eating when

* Quoted by Aulard, p. 91.

he is hungry, so long as the servants and even the beasts of the rich have all they need."

As for Robespierre, he declared that " the agrarian law was only an absurd bogey displayed to stupid men by wicked ones." And he rejected beforehand every attempt that was made in the direction of the " equalisation of wealth." Always careful never to go beyond the opinion of those who represented the dominant power at a given moment, he took care not to side with those who marched with the people but knew that it was the ideas of equalisation and communism which alone could give the Revolution the force that was necessary for the final demolition of the feudal system.

This fear of popular risings and of their economic consequences impelled the middle classes also to rally closer and closer round royalty and to accept whatever kind of Constitution came from the hands of the Constituent Assembly, with all its defects and its compliance with the King's wishes. Instead of progressing in the way of republican ideas, the middle classes and the " intellectuals " developed in a contrary direction. If in 1789, in all the actions of the Third Estate, a decidedly republican and democratic spirit was to be seen, now, according as the people manifested communistic and equalising tendencies, these same men became the defenders of royalty ; while the sincere republicans, such as Thomas Paine and Condorcet, represented an infinitesimal minority among the educated members of the middle classes. As the people became republican, the " intellectuals " retrograded towards constitutional royalty.

On June 13, 1792, scarcely eight days before the invasion of the Tuileries by the people, Robespierre was still inveighing against the republic. " It is in vain," he cried on that date, " for any one to wish to seduce ardent and uninstructed minds by the lure of a freer government under the name of a republic : the overthrow of the Constitution at this moment can only kindle civil war, which will lead to anarchy and to despotism."

Did he fear the establishing of a sort of aristocratic republic, as in the Netherlands ? Such is, at least, the supposition of Louis Blanc, and it is possible, after all ; but to us it seems more probable that having remained up till then a fierce defender of property, Robespierre feared at that moment, as nearly all the Jacobins did, the fury of the people, their attempts at levelling down fortunes, " expropriation," as we say to-day. He feared to see the Revolution wrecked in its attempts at Communism. The fact is, that even up to the eve of August 10, at a time when the whole Revolution, unfinished as it was, checked in its onrush, and assailed by a thousand conspiracies, was almost on the point of being defeated, and nothing could save it except the overthrow of royalty by a popular rising, Robespierre, like all the Jacobins, preferred to maintain the King and his Court rather than risk a fresh appeal to the revolutionary fire of the people. Just as the Italian and Spanish republicans of our own times prefer to retain monarchy rather than risk a popular revolution which they foresee would surely be inspired with communistic tendencies.

History thus repeats itself, and how many times it may again repeat itself, when Russia, Germany and Austria begin their great revolution !

The most striking thing in the condition of mind of the politicians of the period is shown by the fact that exactly at this moment, July 1792, the Revolution found itself menaced by a formidable royalist *coup d'état*, long preparing, which was to be supported by widespread insurrections in the south and west, and also by a German, English, Sardinian and Spanish invasion.

Thus in June 1792, after the King had dismissed Roland, Clavière and Servan, the three Girondist ministers, Lafayette, chief of the Feuillants and royalist at heart, at once wrote his famous letter to the Legislative Assembly, dated June 18, in which he offered to make a *coup d'état* against the revolutionists. He openly demanded that France should be purged of the " Jacobins," and he added that in the army " the principles of liberty and equality are cherished, the laws respected, and property sacred "—not as in Paris, for example, where attacks were openly made upon it in the Commune and at the Club of the Cordeliers.

Lafayette demanded—and this already gives the measure of the progress of reaction—that the royal power should remain "intact and independent." He desired "a revered King"—and this after the flight to Varennes; this, at the very moment when the King was keeping up an active correspondence with Austria and Prussia, expecting from them his "liberation," and treating the Assembly with more or less contempt, according to the tenor of the news he received concerning the progress of the German invasion.

And to think that the Assembly was upon the point of sending out this letter of Lafayette's to the eighty-three departments, and that only a stratagem of the Girondins prevented it—Gaudet pretending that the letter was a forgery, that it could not have come from Lafayette! All this within two months of August 10.

Paris was inundated at this time by royalist conspirators. The *émigrés* came and went freely between Coblentz and the Tuileries, whence they returned after receiving the caresses of the Court and plenty of money. "A thousand houses of ill-fame were open to the conspirators," wrote Chaumette, then Public Prosecutor of the Commune of Paris, in his Notes.* The departmental administration of Paris which had Talleyrand and La Rochefoucauld in its midst, belonged entirely to the Court. The municipality, a great many of the Justices of the Peace, "the majority of the National Guard, and all its General Staff, were for the Court, serving it as an escort and as watch-dogs in the frequent excursions that royalty were making in the streets and in the theatres." June 21 was then apparently forgotten.

"The semi-military household of the King, composed very largely of old body-guards, returned *émigrés*, and some of

---

* *Mémoires sur la Révolution du 10 août, 1792,* with preface by F. A. Aulard (Paris, 1893). Chaumette accused even the Directory of the department of having gathered together sixty thousand counter-revolutionists and lodged them. If there seems to be any exaggeration in the number of sixty thousand, the fact that a great number of counter-revolutionists were assembled in Paris is certain.

those heroes of February 28, 1791, known under the name of "knights of the dagger" (*chevaliers du poignard*), irritated the people by their insolence, insulted the National Representatives and loudly declared their liberticide intentions," continues Chaumette.

The monks, the nuns and an immense majority of the priests stood on the counter-revolutionary side.*

As to the Assembly, this is how Chaumette characterised it : " A National Assembly, without force, without respect, divided against itself, lowering itself in the eyes of Europe by petty and vexatious debates, humiliated by an insolent Court, and replying to insult only by redoubling its servility ; without power, without any stability of purpose." In fact, this Assembly, which used to discuss for hours in succession how many members should compose such and such a deputation to the King, and whether one or two wings of the folding-doors should be open for them—which really spent its time, as Chaumette wrote, " in listening to declamatory speeches, all ending in . . . *addressing some new message to the King* "— such an Assembly could inspire nothing but contempt in the Court itself.

Meanwhile, all through the west and the south-east of France, up to the very gates of the revolutionary towns, such as Marseilles, secret royalist committees were at work, collecting arms in the châteaux, enrolling officers and men, and preparing for the levy of a powerful army, which was to march upon Paris, under the command of chiefs who would be sent from Coblentz.

These movements in the south are so characteristic that it is necessary to give at least a general view of them.

* Here is a piece of news of which all Paris was talking at the time, as related by Madame Jullien : " The Superior of the Grey Sisters of Rueil lost her portfolio, which was found and opened by the municipality of the place. It is estimated that they have sent 48,000 livres to the *émigrés* since January 1." (*Journal d'une bourgeoise*, p. 203.)

· CHAPTER XXXI

THE COUNTER-REVOLUTION IN THE
SOUTH OF FRANCE

Condition of provinces—Coblentz centre of royalist plots
— Counter - revolutionary federation — Loyalist activity—
Royalists receive money from Pitt, and help from other
Powers—Risings and counter-risings in provinces

WHEN studying the Great Revolution, one is so much attracted
by the magnitude of the struggles which unfolded themselves
in Paris, that one is tempted to neglect the condition of the
provinces, and to overlook the power which the counter-
revolution possessed there all the time. This power, however,
was enormous. The counter-revolution had for it the support
of the past centuries, and the interests of the present ; and
it is necessary to study it in order to understand how small
is the power of a representative assembly during a revolution
—even if its members could all be inspired with the very
best intentions only. When it comes to a struggle, in every
town and in every little village, against the forces of the old
régime, which, after a moment of stupor, reorganise themselves
to stop the revolution—it is only the impulse of the revolutionists on the spot which can overcome that powerful resistance.

It would take years and years of study in the local archives
to trace out all the doings of the royalists during the Great
Revolution. A few episodes will, however, allow us to gain
some idea of them.

The insurrection in the Vendée is more or less known. But
we are only too much inclined to believe that there, in the
midst of a half-savage population, inspired by religious fanaticism, is to be found the only real hotbed of the counter-

revolution. Southern France represented a similar hotbed, all the more dangerous as there the country districts and cities had furnished some of the best contingents to the Revolution.

The direction of these various movements emanated from Coblentz, the little German town situated in the Electorate of Trèves, which had become the chief centre of the royalist emigration. Since the summer of 1791, when the Count d'Artois, followed by the ex-minister Calonne, and, later, by his brother, the Count de Provence, had settled in this town, it had become the head centre of the royalist plots. Thence came the emissaries who were organising throughout the whole of France anti-revolutionary risings. Everywhere soldiers were being recruited for Coblentz, even in Paris, where the Editor of the *Gazette de Paris* publicly offered sixty livres for each recruit. For some time these men were almost openly sent to Metz and afterwards to Coblentz.

"Society followed them," says Ernest Daudet, in his monograph, *Les Conspirations royalistes dans le Midi ;* "the nobility imitated the princes, and many of the middle class and common people imitated the nobility. They emigrated for fashion, for poverty or for fear. A young woman who was met in a *diligence* by a secret agent of the Government, and questioned by him, replied : "I am a dressmaker ; my customers are all gone off to Germany ; so I have turned *émigrette* in order to go and find them."

A complete Court, with its ministers, its chamberlains and its official receptions, and also its intrigues and its infamies, was evolved round the King's brothers, and the European sovereigns recognised this Court, and treated and plotted with it. Meanwhile, they were expecting to see Louis XVI. arrive and set himself at the head of the troops formed by the *émigrés.* He was expected in June 1791, when he fled to Varennes, and later, in November 1791, and in January 1792. Finally it was decided to prepare for a great stroke in July 1792, when the royalist armies of western and southern France, supported by English, German, Sardinian and Spanish invasions, were to march on Paris, rousing Lyons and other large towns on the way, whilst the royalists of Paris would strike their great blow, disperse the Assembly and punish the hot-headed Jacobins.

"To replace the King on the throne," which really meant making him again an absolute monarch, and reintroducing the old *régime* as it had existed at the time of the Convocation of the States-General—that was their intention. And when the King of Prussia, more intelligent than those phantoms of Versailles, asked them : "Would it not be justice, as well as prudence, to make the nation the sacrifice of certain abuses of the old government ?" "Sire," they replied, "not a single change, not a single favour ! " *

It is needless to add that all the cabals, all the tale-bearings, all the jealousies, which characterised Versailles were repro-duced at Coblentz. The two brothers had each his Court, his acknowledged mistress, his receptions, his circle, while the nobles indulged in Court gossip which grew more and more malicious according as they grew poorer and poorer.

Around this centre gravitated, quite openly now, those fanatical priests who preferred civil war to the constitutional submission proposed by the new decrees, as well as those noble adventurers who chose to risk a conspiracy rather than resign themselves to the loss of their privileged position. They went to Coblentz, obtained the prince's sanction for their plots, and returned to the mountainous regions of the Cévennes or to the shores of the Vendée, to kindle the religious fanaticism of the peasants and to organise royalist risings.

The historians who sympathise with the Revolution pass, as a rule, too rapidly over these counter-revolutionary resist-ances, so that many readers may consider them as unimportant events, or as the work of but a few fanatics who could have been easily subdued by the Revolution. But in reality, the royalist plots extended over whole regions, and as they found support among the big men of the middle classes, in the great commercial cities—and, in certain regions, in the religious hatred between Protestants and Catholics as in the south— the revolutionists had to carry on a terrible struggle for life

---

* Document in the *Archives des affaires étrangères,* quoted by E. Daudet.

in every town and in every little commune to save the Revolution from defeat.

Thus, while the people of Paris were preparing for July 14, 1790, the great *Fête* of the Federation, in which all France took part, and which was to give to the Revolution a firm communal basis—the royalists were preparing the federation of the counter-revolutionists in the south-east. On August 18 of the same year, nearly 20,000 representatives of 185 communes of the Vivarais assembled on the plain of Jalès, all wearing the white cross on their hats. Led by the nobles, they formed that day the nucleus of the royalist federation of the south, which was solemnly constituted in the month of February following.

This federation prepared, first, a series of insurrections for the summer of 1791, and afterwards the great insurrection which was to break out in July 1792, simultaneously with the foreign invasion, and which was expected to give the finishing blow to the Revolution. The Jalès confederation existed in this way for two years, keeping up regular correspondence with both the Tuileries and Coblentz. Its oath was " to reinstate the King in all his glory, the clergy in their possessions, and the nobility in their honours." And when their first attempts failed, they organised, with the help of Claude Allier, the prior of Chambonnaz, a widely spread conspiracy, which was to bring out more than fifty thousand men. Led by a large number of priests, marching under the folds of the white flag, and supported by Sardinia, Spain and Austria, this army would have gone to Paris " to free " the King, to dissolve the Assembly, and to chastise the patriots.

In the Lozère, Charrier, notary and ex-deputy to the National Assembly, whose wife belonged to the nobility, was invested with the supreme command by the Count d'Artois. He openly organised a counter-revolutionary militia, and even got together some artillery.

Chambéry, at that time a town in the kingdom of Sardinia, was another centre of the *émigrés*. Bussy had even formed there a royalist legion which exercised in open day. In this way the counter-revolution was being organised in the south, while in the west the priests and nobles were preparing for the rising of the Vendée, with the help of England.

It may perhaps be said that, even all taken together, the conspirators and the confederations of south-eastern France were not very numerous. But the revolutionists, too, those at least who were determined to act, were not numerous either. Everywhere and in all times, the men of action have been an insignificant minority. But thanks to inertia, to prejudice, to acquired interests, to money and to religion, the counter-revolution held entire provinces ; and it was this terrible power of reaction which explains the fury of the Revolution in 1793 and 1794, when it had to make a supreme effort to escape from the clutches that were strangling it.

Whether the adherents of Claude Allier, ready to take arms, really amounted to sixty thousand men, as he stated when he visited Coblentz in January 1792, may be doubted. But this much is certain, that in every town in the south, the struggle between the revolutionists and the counter-revolutionists continued without intermission, making the balance sway sometimes to one side and sometimes to the other.

At Perpignan, the military royalists were ready to open the frontier to the Spanish army. At Arles, in the local struggle between the *monnetiers* and the *chiffonistes*, that is, between the patriots and the counter-revolutionists, the latter were victorious. " Warned," says one writer, " that the Marseillais were organising an expedition against them, that they had even pillaged the arsenal of Marseilles the better to be able to make the campaign, they prepared for resistance. They fortified themselves, built up the gates of their town, deepened the fosses along the enclosure, made safe their communications with the sea, and reorganised the National Guard in such a way as to reduce the patriots to impotence."

These few lines borrowed from Ernest Daudet * are characteristic. They give a picture of what was taking place

---

* *Histoire des Conspirations royalistes du Midi sous la Révolution* (Paris, 1881). Daudet is a moderate, or rather a reactionary, but his history is documentary, and he has consulted the local archives.

more or less all through France. Four years of revolution, that is, the absence of a strong government for four years, and incessant fighting on the part of the revolutionists were necessary to paralyse to some extent the reaction.

At Montpellier, the patriots had founded a league of defence against the royalists, in order to protect the priests who had taken the oath to the Constitution, as well as those parishioners who attended mass when the constitutional priests officiated. There was frequent fighting in the streets. At Lunel in the Hérault, at Yssingeaux in the Haute-Loire, at Mende in the Lozère, it was the same. People remained in arms. It might be truly said that in every town in that region similar struggles took place between the royalists, or the " Feuillants " of the place, and the " patriots," and later on between the Girondins and the " anarchists." We may even add that in the vast majority of the towns of the centre and of the west, the reactionaries got the upper hand, and that the Revolution was seriously supported only in thirty out of the eighty-three departments. More than that ; the revolutionists themselves, for the most part, began to defy the royalists only by degrees and in proportion as their own revolutionary education was effected by events.

In all these towns the anti-revolutionists joined hands. The rich people had a thousand means, which the generality of the patriots did not possess, of moving about, of corresponding by means of special messengers, of hiding in their châteaux, and of accumulating arms in them. The patriots corresponded undoubtedly with the Popular Societies and the Paris Fraternities, with the Society of the Indigent, as well as with the mother society of the Jacobins ; but they were very poor ! Arms and means of moving about both failed them.

Besides, those who were against the Revolution were supported from without. England has always followed the policy she pursues to this day : that of weakening her rivals and creating partisans among them. " Pitt's money " was no phantom. Very far from that. With the help of this money the royalists passed quite freely from their centre and depôt of arms, Jersey, to St. Malo and Nantes, and in all the great seaports of France, especially those of St. Malo, Nantes, Bordeaux, the English money gained adherents and supported the "commercialists" (*les commerçantistes*) who took sides against the Revolution. Catherine II. of Russia did as Pitt did. In reality, all the European monarchs took part in this. If in Brittany, in the Vendée, at Bordeaux, and at Toulon the royalists counted upon England, in Alsace and Lorraine they counted on Germany, and in the south upon the armed help promised by Sardinia, as well as on the Spanish army which was to land at Aigues-Mortes. Even the Knights of Malta were going to help with two frigates in this expedition.

In the beginning of 1792, the department of the Lozère and that of the Ardèche, both rendezvous of the refractory priests, were covered with a network of royalist conspiracies, of which the centre was Mende, a little town hidden away in the mountains of the Vivarais, where the population was very backward, and where the rich and the nobles held the municipality in their hands. Their emissaries went through the villages of the province, enjoining on the peasants to arm themselves with guns, scythes and pitch-forks, and to be ready to turn out at the first call. In this way they were preparing for the insurrection which, they hoped, would raise the Gévaudan and the Velay, and compel the Vivarais to follow suit.

It is true that none of the royalist insurrections which took place in 1791 and 1792, at Perpignan, Arles, Mende, Yssingeaux and in the Vivarais, were successful. It was not enough to shout "Down with the patriots!" to rally a sufficient number of insurgents, and the patriots promptly dispersed the royalist bands. But during those two years the struggle was incessant. There were moments when the whole country was a prey to civil war, and the tocsin rang without intermission in the villages.

There was even a moment when it was necessary that armed bands of the Marseillais should come to hunt out the counter-revolutionists in that region, to take possession of Arles and Aigues-Mortes, and to inaugurate the reign of terror which, later on, attained such vast proportions in the South of Lyons, and in the Ardèche.   As to the rising organised by the Count de Saillans, which broke out in July 1792, at the same time as that of the Vendée, and at the moment when the German armies were marching on Paris, it would certainly have had a fatal influence on the progress of the Revolution if the people had not promptly suppressed it.   Fortunately, the people took this upon themselves, while Paris, on her side, made preparations to seize, at last, the centre of all royalist conspiracies —the Tuileries.

CHAPTER XXXII

THE TWENTIETH OF JUNE 1792

State of Revolution at beginning of 1792 — Constitution lacks power—Legislative Assembly—Preparations of counter-revolutionists—People recognise dangers of Revolution—Jacobin fears—Great republican demonstration—Effect of demonstration — Republican leaders imprisoned — Assembly and Revolution—"The Lamourette kiss"—People decide to do away with royalty—Critical point of Revolution—Girondins warn King—Their fears of popular revolution—Despair of Marat and patriots—Royalist hopes—Petty disputes of revolutionists

WE see, by what has just been said, in what a deplorable condition the Revolution was in the early months of 1792. If the middle-class revolutionists could feel satisfied with having conquered a share in the government and laid the foundations of the fortunes they were going soon to acquire with the help of the State, the people saw that nothing had yet been done for them. Feudalism still stood erect, and in the towns the great mass of the proletarians had gained nothing to speak of. The merchants and monopolists were making huge fortunes as Government contractors and stock-jobbers, and by means of speculating in the bonds upon the sale of the Church property and buying up the communal lands, but the price of bread and of all things of prime necessity went up steadily, and hunger became permanent in the poorer quarters of the great cities.

The aristocracy meanwhile became bolder and bolder. The nobility, the rich, lifted up their heads and boasted that they would soon bring the *sans-culottes* to reason. Every day they expected the news of a German invasion, advancing triumphantly on Paris to restore the old *régime* in all its splendour. In the provinces, as we have seen, reaction was openly organising its partisans for a general rising.

As to the Constitution, which the middle classes and even the intellectual revolutionaries spoke of preserving at every cost, it existed only for passing measures of minor importance, while all serious reforms remained suspended. The King's authority had been limited, but in a very modest way. With the powers left him by the Constitution—the civil list, the military command, the choice of ministers and the rest—but above all the interior organisation of the local government, which placed everything in the hands of the rich, the people could do nothing.

No one certainly would suspect the Legislative Assembly of radicalism, and it is evident that its decrees concerning the feudal dues and the priests were sufficiently imbued with middle-class moderation; and yet even these decrees the King refused to sign. Every one felt that the nation was living simply from day to day, under a system which offered no stability and could be overthrown at any moment in favour of the old *régime*.

Meanwhile the plot which was concocting in the Tuileries spread further into France itself, and drew in the Courts of Berlin, Vienna, Stockholm, Turin, Madrid and Petersburg. The hour was near when the counter-revolutionists were to strike the great blow they had prepared for the summer of 1792. The King and Queen urged the German armies to march upon Paris; they even named the day when they should enter the capital, and when the royalists, armed and organised, would receive them with open arms.

The people, and those of the revolutionists who, like Marat and the Cordeliers, held by the people—those who brought the Commune of August 10 into existence—understood perfectly well the dangers by which the Revolution was surrounded. The people had always had a true inkling of the situation, even though they could not express it exactly, nor support their premonitions by learned arguments; and the mass of the French people guessed, infinitely better than the politicians, the plots which were being hatched in the

Tuileries and in the châteaux of the nobility. But they were disarmed, while the middle classes had organised their National Guard battalions ; and what was worse, those of the " intellectuals " whom the Revolution had pushed to the front, those who were held as the spokesmen of the Revolution— among them honest men like Robespierre—had not the necessary confidence in the Revolution, and still less in the people. Just like the parliamentary Radicals of our own times, who dread to see the people come out into the streets, lest they should become masters of the situation, they did not dare to avow their dread of revolutionary equality. They explained their attitude as one of care to preserve, at least, the few liberties acquired by the Constitution. To the indeterminate chances of a new insurrection, they preferred, they said, a constitutional monarchy.

Events of such an importance as the declaration of war (on April 21, 1792) and the German invasion were necessary to change the situation. Then only, seeing themselves betrayed on all sides, even by the leaders in whom they had put their trust, the people began to act for themselves, and to exercise pressure on the " leaders of opinion." Paris began to prepare for a great insurrection which was to allow the people to dethrone the King. The sections, the Popular Societies, and the Fraternal Societies—that is, the " unknown ones," the crowd, seconded by the Club of the Cordeliers, set themselves this task. The keenest and most enlightened patriots, says Chaumette,* assembled at the Club of the Cordeliers and there they used to pass the night, preparing the popular insurrection. There was, among others, one committee which got up a red flag, bearing the inscription : " Martial Law of the People against the Rebellion of the Court." Under this flag were to rally all free men—the true republicans, those who had to avenge a friend, a son or some relative assassinated in the Champ-de-Mars on July 17, 1791.

Most historians, paying a tribute to their authoritarian training, represent the Jacobin Club as the initiator and the head of all the revolutionary movements in Paris and the

* *Mémoires*, p. 13.

provinces, and for two generations every one believed this.
But now we know that such was not the case. The initiative
of June 20 and August 10 did not come from the Jacobins.
On the contrary, for a whole year they were opposed, even
the most revolutionary of them, to appealing again to the
people. Only when they saw themselves outflanked by the
popular movement, they decided, and again only a section
of them, to follow it.

But with what timidity ! They wished to see the people
out in the street, combating the royalists ; but they dared
not wish for the consequences. What if the people were not
satisfied with overthrowing the royal power ? If popular
wrath should turn against the rich, the powerful, the cunning
ones, who saw in the Revolution nothing but a means of
enriching themselves ? If the people should sweep away the
Legislative Assembly, after the Tuileries ? If the Commune
of Paris, the extremists, the "anarchists"—those whom
Robespierre himself freely loaded with his invectives—those
republicans who preached "the equality of conditions"—
what if they should get the upper hand ?

This is why, in all the conferences which took place before
June 20, we see so much hesitation on the part of the prominent
revolutionists. This is why the Jacobins were so reluctant
to approve the necessity of another popular rising. It was
only in July, when the people, setting aside the constitutional
laws, proclaimed the "permanence" of the sections, ordered
the general armament, and forced the Assembly to declare
"the country in danger"—it was only then that the Robespierres, the Dantons and, at the very last moment, the Girondins
decided to follow the people's lead and declare themselves
more or less at one with the insurrection.

It was quite natural that under these circumstances the
movement of June 20 could not have either the spirit or the
unity that was necessary to make of it a successful insurrection
against the Tuileries. The people came out into the streets,
but, uncertain as to the attitude of the middle classes, the
masses did not dare to compromise themselves too much.
They acted as if they wanted to find out first how far they

could go in their attack of the palace—leaving the rest to the chances of all great popular demonstrations. If anything comes of this one—all the better; if not, they will at least have seen the Tuileries at close quarters and estimated its strength.

This is, in fact, what happened. The demonstration was perfectly peaceful. Under the pretence of petitioning the Assembly to celebrate the anniversary of the Oath in the Tennis Court, and to plant a tree of Liberty at the door of the National Assembly, an immense multitude of people came out on this day. It soon filled all the streets leading from the Bastille to the Assembly, while the Court filled with its adherents the Place du Carrousel, the great courtyard of the Tuileries and the outskirts of the palace. All the gates of the Tuileries were closed, cannon were trained on the people; cartridges were distributed to the soldiers, and a conflict between the two bodies seemed inevitable.

However, the sight of the ever-increasing multitudes paralysed the defenders of the Court. The outer gates were soon either opened or forced, and the Place du Carrousel as also the courtyards were inundated with people. Many were armed with pikes and sabres, or with sticks at the end of which a knife, a hatchet, or a saw was fixed, but the section had carefully selected the men who were to take part in the demonstration.

The crowd were beginning to break in one of the doors of the palace with the blows of an axe, when Louis XVI. himself ordered it to be opened. Immediately thousands of men burst into the inner courtyards and the palace itself. The Queen, with her son, had been hurried away by her friends into a hall, part of which was barricaded with a large table. The King being discovered in another room, it was filled in a few minutes by the crowd. They demanded that he should sanction the decrees which he had vetoed; that the "patriot ministers"—that is, the Girondist Ministry—whom he had dismissed on June 13, should be recalled; that the rebel priests should be driven out of France; and his choice be made between Coblentz and Paris. The King took off his hat, and allowed a woollen cap to be put on his head; the crowd also made him drink a glass of wine to the health of the nation. But for two hours he withstood the crowd, repeating that he should abide by the Constitution.

As an attack on royalty, the movement had failed. Nothing came of it.

But the rage of the well-to-do classes against the people was only the greater on that account. Since the masses had not dared to attack the palace, and had, by that, shown their weakness, they fell upon them with all the hatred that can be inspired only by fear.

When a letter from Louis XVI., complaining of the invasion of his palace, was read at the sitting of the Assembly, the members broke out into applause, as servile as the plaudits of the courtiers before 1789. Jacobins and Girondins were unanimous in thus disowning any share in the demonstration.

Encouraged undoubtedly by this manifestation of support, the Court had a tribunal set up in the palace of the Tuileries itself, for the punishing of those guilty of the movement. They were thus resuscitating, says Chaumette in his *Mémoires*, the odious methods of procedure which had been resorted to after October 5 and 6, 1789, and after July 17, 1791. This tribunal was composed of justices of the peace in the pay of royalty. The Court sent them their food, and the Wardrobe-Keeper of the Crown had orders to provide for all their wants.* The most vigorous of the writers were prosecuted and sent to prison. Several presidents and secretaries of the sections shared the same fate. Again it became dangerous to call oneself a republican.

The Directories of the departments and a large number of municipalities joined in the servile protestations of the Assembly and sent letters of indignation against the " faction." In reality, thirty-three out of the eighty-three Directories of departments—that is, the whole west of France—were openly royalist and counter-revolutionary.

Revolutions, we must remember, are always made by minorities, and even when a revolution has begun, and a part

---

* *Journal de Perlet* of June 27, quoted by Aulard in a note added to the *Mémoires* of Chaumette.

of the nation accepts its consequences, there is always only a very small minority who understands what still remains to be done to assure the triumph of what has been obtained, and who have the courage of action. This is why an Assembly, always representing the average of the country, or rather something below the average, has always been, and will always be, a check upon revolution ; it can never be an instrument of revolution.

The Legislative Assembly gives us a striking case in point. On July 7—that is, four days before the country had to be declared in danger in consequence of the German invasion, and one month only before the downfall of royalty—the following occurrence took place in the Assembly. They had been discussing for several days what measures should be taken for the general safety, when, at the instigation of the Court, Lamourette, Bishop of Lyons, proposed, on a motion of order, a general reconciliation of the parties, and to bring it about, he suggested a very simple means : " One party in the Assembly attributes to the other the seditious design of wishing to destroy the monarchy. The others attribute to their colleagues the design of wishing the destruction of constitutional equality and the aristocratic government known under the name of the Two Chambers. Well, gentlemen, let us annihilate by a common execration, and by an irrevocable oath, let us annihilate both the Republic and the Two Chambers." Hats were thrown into the air, members embraced each other, the Right fraternised with the Left, and a deputation was sent at once to the King, who came to join in the general gaiety. This scene is known in history as " the Lamourette kiss." Fortunately public opinion was not captured by such scenes. The same evening Billaud-Varennes protested at the Jacobin Club against this hypocritical attempt at reconciliation, and it was decided to send his speech out to the affiliated societies. The Court on its side had no intention of disarming. Pétion, Mayor of Paris, had been suspended from his office that very day by the royalist Directory of the Seine department, for his negligence on June 20. But then, the people of Paris took up the cause of their mayor passionately, so that six days later, on July 13, the Assembly thought fit to rescind the suspension.

The people had made up their minds. They understood that the moment had come when they must get rid of royalty, and that, if June 20 were not quickly followed by a popular rising, all would be over with the Revolution. But the politicians in the Assembly judged otherwise. " Who could tell what would be the result of a rising ? " they asked themselves, and the result was that with but a few exceptions the legislators of the Assembly were already arranging for a way out, in case the counter-revolution should be victorious.

The fears of those who intend to become " statesmen," and their desire of securing for themselves pardon in case of defeat —there lies the danger for every revolution.

For all those who seek instruction from history, the seven weeks which elapsed between the demonstration of June 20 and the taking of the Tuileries on August 10, 1792, are of the highest importance.

Although the demonstration on June 20 had had no immediate result, it produced nevertheless a great awakening all over France. " The revolt ran from town to town," as Louis Blanc says. The foreigner was at the gates of Paris, and on July 11 the country was proclaimed in danger. On the 14th, the Federation was celebrated, and on this occasion the people made a formidable demonstration against royalty. From every side the revolutionary municipalities sent addresses to the Assembly calling on it to take action. Since the King had betrayed his country they demanded his dethronement or, at least, his suspension. The word Republic, however, was not yet mentioned ; there was rather an inclination towards a regency. Marseilles was an exception, as it had demanded the abolition of royalty since June 27, and had sent five hundred volunteers who arrived in Paris singing the " Marseillaise Hymn." Brest and other towns also sent some volunteers, and the sections of Paris, sitting in permanence, armed themselves and organised their popular battalions.

It was felt on all sides that the Revolution was approaching a decisive moment.

What, then, did the Assembly do ? And what those middle-class republicans—the Girondins ?

When the strongly worded address from Marseilles was read in the Assembly, demanding that measures in consonance with the seriousness of events should be taken, nearly the whole of the Assembly protested. And when Duhem, on July 27, demanded that the dethronement should be discussed, his proposition was received with howls.

Marie-Antoinette certainly was not mistaken when she wrote, on July 7, to her intimate correspondents abroad, that the patriots were frightened and wanted to negotiate—which is what really came to pass a few days later.

Those who were with the people, in the sections, no doubt felt that they were on the eve of some great event. The sections of Paris had declared themselves permanent, as well as several of the municipalities. Taking no notice of the law concerning the *passive* citizens, they admitted them to their deliberations, and armed them with pikes. It was evident that a great insurrection was on the way.

But the Girondins, the party of "the statesmen," were just then sending to the King, through his *valet de chambre*, Thierry, a letter telling him that a formidable insurrection was preparing, that the dethronement and something yet more terrible might result from it, and that only one way remained to prevent this catastrophe, and that was to recall the Ministry of Roland, Servan and Clavière within eight days at latest.

Certainly it was not "the twelve millions promised to Brissot" which impelled the Girondins to take this step. Neither was it, as Louis Blanc wrote, their ambition to re-grasp the power. The cause was much deeper than that, and Brissot's pamphlet *A ses commettants* discloses clearly what the Girondins thought at this moment. It was their fear of a popular revolution—a revolution which would touch upon property—their fear and their contempt for the people —the mob of ragged wretches, who guided them : their fear of a system in which property and more than that, authoritarian training and the " managing capacity," would lose the privileges they had conferred until then—the fear of seeing themselves reduced to the level of " the Great Unwashed."

This fear paralysed the Girondins as to-day it paralyses all the parties who occupy in Parliaments the same position, more or less Governmental, which the Girondins occupied at that time.

We can comprehend, therefore, the despair which seized upon the true patriots and expressed by Marat in these words :

" For three years," he wrote, " we have striven to regain our liberty, and we are now as far off from it as ever. The Revolution has turned against the people. For the Court and its supporters it is an eternal motive for intrigue and corruption ; for the legislators, an occasion for prevarication and trickery. . . . Already it is for the rich and the avaricious nothing but an opportunity for illicit gains, monopolies, frauds and spoliations, while the people are ruined, and the numberless poor are placed between the fear of perishing from hunger and the necessity of selling themselves. . . . Let us not be afraid to repeat : we are further from liberty than ever ; for, not only are we slaves, but we are so legally."

" On the stage of the State, the scenery only has been changed," he writes further on. " The same actors, the same intrigues, the same motives have remained." " It was fatal," continues Marat, " for the lower classes of the nation to be left alone to struggle against the highest class. At the moment of an insurrection the people will break down all before them by their weight ; but whatever advantage they may gain at first, they will end by succumbing to the machinations of the superior classes, who are full of cunning, craft and artifice. Educated men, those who are well off, and the crafty ones of the superior classes, had at first taken sides against the despot ; but that was only to turn against the people, after they had wormed themselves into the people's confidence and had made use of the people's forces to set themselves up in the place of the privileged orders whom they have proscribed."

" Thus," continues Marat—and his words are of gold, since one might say they were written to-day, in the twentieth century—"thus it is that the revolution has been made and maintained only by the lowest classes of society—by the workers, the artisans, the little tradesmen, the agriculturists, by the plebs, by those luckless ones whom the shameless rich call *canaille*, and whom Roman insolence called *proletarians*. But who would ever have imagined that it would be made only in favour of the small landowners, the men of law, the supporters of fraud."

The day after the taking of the Bastille, it would have been easy for the representatives of the people " to have suspended from their offices the despot and his agents," wrote Marat further on. " But for doing that, they ought to have had perspicacity and virtue." As to the *people, instead of arming themselves universally, they permitted one part only of the citizens to arm* (meaning the National Guard composed of *active* citizens). And instead of attacking the enemies of the Revolution without further delay, the people gave up the advantages of their victory by remaining merely in a state of defence.

" To-day," says Marat, " after three years of everlasting speeches from patriotic societies and a deluge of writings . . . the people are further from feeling what they ought to do in order to be able to resist their oppressors, than they were on the very first day of the Revolution. At that time they followed their natural instincts, their simple good sense which made them find the true way for subduing their implacable foes. . . . Now, behold them—chained in the name of the law, tyrannised over in the name of justice ; they are constitutional slaves ! "

This might have been written yesterday, yet it is taken from No. 657 of the *Ami du peuple*.

A profound discouragement took hold of Marat, and he could see only one exit : " some fit of civic fury " on the part of the people, as on July 13 and 14 and on October 5 and 6, 1789. Despair was devouring him, until the federates came from the departments to Paris. This filled him with new hope.

The chances of the counter-revolution were so great at the end of July 1792, that Louis XVI. curtly refused the

proposition of the Girondins.   Were not the Prussians already
marching upon Paris ?   And Lafayette and Luckner too, were
they not ready to turn their armies against the Jacobins, against
Paris ? Lafayette, who enjoyed great power in the North, and
was the idol of the middle-class National Guards in Paris !

In fact, the King had many reasons to expect a victory.
The Jacobins dared not act.   And when Marat, on July 18,
after the treachery of Lafayette and Luckner became known
—they had wanted to carry off the King on July 16, and to
set him in the midst of their armies—when Marat proposed
to take the King as a hostage for the nation against the foreign
invasion, every one turned his back on him, and treated him
as a madman : he had none but the *sans-culottes* in the hovels
to approve him.   Because he had dared to say at that moment
what to-day we know to be *the truth*, because he had dared
to denounce the plottings of the King with the foreigner,
Marat was abandoned by every one, even by those few patriotic
Jacobins upon whom he, who is represented as so suspicious,
had, however, depended.   They refused even to give him an
asylum when he was hunted down for arrest and knocked
for shelter at their doors.

As to the Girondins, after the King had refused their
proposal, they again parleyed with him, through the intermediary of the painter, Boze.   They sent him another message
on July 25.

Fifteen days only separated Paris from August 10.   Revolutionary France was chafing the bit.   It knew that the
supreme moment had come.   Either the finishing blow must
be struck at royalty, or else the Revolution would remain
unaccomplished.   How could they allow royalty to surround
itself with troops, and to organise the great plot which was
to deliver Paris to the Germans ?   Who knows how many
years longer royalty, slightly rejuvenated, but still very nearly
absolute, would have continued to rule France ?

And yet, at this supreme moment, the whole care of the
politicians was to dispute among themselves as to whose hands
the power should fall into if it should drop from the hands
of the King !

The Girondins wanted it to go to their Committee of Twelve, which should then become the Executive Power. Robespierre, for his part, demanded fresh elections—a renovated Assembly—a Convention, which should give France a new Republican Constitution.

As to acting, as to preparing the dethronement, nobody thought of that except the people : the Jacobins thought of it as little as all other politicians. It was once more " the unknown men," the favourites of the people—Santerre, Fournier, the American, the Pole, Lazowski, Carra, Simon,* Westermann, at that time a simple law-clerk—who came together at the Soleil d'Or to plan the siege of the palace and the general rising, with the red flag at its head. It was the sections—the majority of the Paris sections, and a few here and there in the north of France—in the department of Maine-et-Loire, and in Marseilles ; and finally, the volunteers from Marseilles and Brest, whom the people of Paris had enlisted in the cause of the insurrection.

The people : always the people !

" There (in the National Assembly) they were like lawyers crazily disputing, without cessation, over trifling matters, under the whip of their masters. . . ."

" Here (in the Assembly of the Sections) the very foundations of the Republic were being laid," as Chaumette expressed it in his notes on August 10.

* J. F. Simon was a German tutor, an old collaborator of Basedow in the Philantropium at Dessau.

CHAPTER XXXIII

THE TENTH OF AUGUST : ITS IMMEDIATE CONSEQUENCES

Peasants ignore feudal system—Change in state of France—
Royalist plans—Administration—Army—Lafayette—Feudal
laws—King and Germans—Revolutionists fear popular risings
—Robespierre—Revolutionary leaders at length join hands—
People prepare to strike—New " Commune " springs up—
August 10—Royalists anticipate victory—Indecision of
Assembly—Abolition of royalty—Triumph of popular revolu-
tion—Decrees passed under compulsion by Assembly—Feudal
laws—Lands of *émigrés*—Proposal of Mailhe—Legislative
Assembly dissolves—Commune of Paris

WE have seen what was the condition of France during the
summer of 1792. For three years the country had been in
open revolution and a return to the old state of affairs had
been made absolutely impossible. For, if the feudal system
still existed according to law, in actuality it was no longer
acknowledged by the peasants. They paid the feudal dues
no more ; they got hold of the lands of the clergy and the
emigrant nobles ; and in certain places they, themselves,
retook from the landlord the lands which formerly belonged
to the village communities. In their village municipalities,
they considered themselves the masters of their own
affairs.

The State institutions were equally upset. The whole of
the administrative structure, which seemed so formidable
under the old *régime*, was crumbling away under the breath
of the popular revolution. Who had any respect now for the
ex-governor of the province, or for the Marshals' Courts
and the judges of the old *parlement* ? The new municipality,
closely watched over by the local *sans-culottes*, the Popular

Society of the place, the Primary Assembly, the men with the pikes—these represented the new powers of France.

The whole aspect of the country, the whole spirit of the people, its language, its manners, its ideas, had been changed by the Revolution. *A new nation was born*, and in its political and social conceptions it completely differed from what had been scarce twelve months before.

But still the old *régime* was left standing. Royalty continued to exist and represented an enormous force, round which the counter-revolutionists were ready to rally. The nation was living under provisional conditions. To give back to royalty its former power was clearly a dream in which no one but some Court fanatics believed any longer. But the powers of royalty for evil were still immense. If it could not restore the feudal system, what evil might it not do, all the same, to the liberated peasants, if, after having got the upper hand, its supporters should dispute in every village the land and the liberties the peasants had won. This was, in fact, what the King and a good many of the Constitutional Monarchists, the "Feuillants," proposed to do as soon as the Court party should have crushed those whom they called the "Jacobins."

As to the Administration in two-thirds of the departments, and even in Paris, the departmental administration and that of the districts were against the people, against the Revolution, they were ready to adapt themselves to any simulacrum of a constitution that would have permitted the middle classes to share the power of governing with the King and the Court.

The army, commanded by men like Lafayette and Luckner, could be used at any moment against the nation. In fact, we have seen how, after June 20, Lafayette left his camp and came to Paris to offer the King the support of "his" army against the people, to break up the patriotic societies and to make a *coup d'état* in favour of the Court.

And to crown all, the feudal laws still remained in force. If the peasants had ceased to pay the feudal dues this was a breach of the law; and the moment the King recovered his authority the peasants would have been compelled to pay everything, so long as they had not freed themselves from

the clutches of the feudal past by redeeming their servitude
—they would have had to restore all the land they had taken
from the landlord and even what they had bought from the
State.

It was clear that this provisional state of things could not
last long. A nation cannot go on living with a sword suspended
over its head. And, moreover, the people, guided by their
unfailing instincts, knew perfectly well that the King was
conniving with the Germans, and inviting them to march on
Paris. At that time, it is true, no written proof of his treachery
was yet known. The correspondence of the King and Marie-
Antoinette had not been discovered, and it was not known
how these two traitors were urging the Austrians and the
Prussians to hasten their march on Paris ; that they were
keeping them informed as to all the movements of the French
troops ; transmitting to them all the military secrets, thus
delivering up France to the invaders. All this was only learned
later, and even then, rather vaguely, after the taking of the
Tuileries, when certain papers of the King's were seized in a
secret cupboard made for him by locksmith Gamain. But
treason is not easily hidden, and by a thousand indications,
upon which the men and women of the people were quick to
seize, they were convinced that the Court had made an agreement with the Germans and that France was going to be
delivered up to them.

The idea gradually spread then, through Paris and the
provinces, that it was necessary to strike a great blow against
the Tuileries : that the old *régime* would remain a perpetual
menace to France so long as Louis XVI. remained on the
throne.

And in order to strike that blow, an appeal had to be made
for a rising of the people of Paris—to the men with the pikes
—as had been done in 1789 before July 14. And this was
what the middle classes refused to do—what they dreaded
most. We find, indeed, in the writings of the period a kind
of terror of " the men with the pikes." Were they going
to reappear, these men so terrible to the rich ?

The worst was that this fear was felt not only by the propertied classes, but also by the advanced politicians. Robespierre up to June 1792 also opposed the appeal for a popular rising. "The overthrow of the Constitution at this moment," he said, "can only kindle civil war, which will lead to anarchy and despotism." He did not believe in the possibility of a republic. "What," he exclaimed, "is it in the midst of so many fatal dissensions that they want to leave us suddenly without a Constitution!" The republic, in his opinion, would be "the arbitrary will of the few." He meant of the Girondins. "This is the aim of all the intrigues which have agitated us this long while." And to baffle these intrigues he preferred to retain the King and the intrigues of the Court! This was how he spoke as late as June, two months before August 10.

To convince the revolutionary "leaders of opinion" of the necessity of striking a blow at the Tuileries and of making an appeal, therefore, for a popular rising, nothing less was required than that they should have visible testimony of the reaction which began after June 20—the coming of Lafayette to Paris to offer "his" army for a royalist *coup d'état*, the Germans making ready to march on Paris "to deliver the King" and "to punish the Jacobins," and finally, the active military preparations made by the Court for attacking Paris. Only then did they make up their minds, and understand the necessity of the rising. But once this was decided upon, the people undertook to do the rest.

It is certain that Danton, Robespierre, Marat, Robert and a few others came to a preliminary understanding. Robespierre detested everything about Marat; his military fervour, which he called exaggeration, his hatred of the rich, his absolute distrust of politicians—everything even to the poor and dirty clothing of the man, who since the Revolution had broken out had eaten nothing but the food of the people, bread and water, and had entirely devoted himself to the people's cause. And yet the elegant and punctilious Robespierre, as well as Danton, approached Marat and his followers, approached the men of the Paris sections of the Commune, to come to an understanding with them as to the means of rousing the people again, as on July 14. They at last understood that if the provisional state of things lasted much longer the Revolution would die out without having accomplished anything durable.

Either an appeal should be made to the people, and then full liberty would have to be left to the poor to strike their enemies as it seemed best to them, and to levy what they could upon the property of the rich, or else the royal power would win in the struggle and this would mean the triumph of the counter-revolution, the destruction of the little that had been obtained in the direction of equality—the White Terror of 1794 would have begun in 1792.

An understanding was, therefore, arrived at between a small number of the more advanced Jacobins, and those of the people who wanted to strike a decisive blow at the Tuileries. But the moment they had come to this understanding, from the moment when " the leaders of opinion "—the Robespierres, the Dantons, and their followers—promised to oppose no longer a popular insurrection, and declared their readiness to support it, the rest was left to the people, who understood, much better than the leaders of the parties, the necessity for common action when the Revolution was on the point of striking such a decisive blow.

The people, the Great Unknown, now began to prepare for the rising and they created, spontaneously, for the needs of the moment, the kind of sectional organisation which was judged the fittest to give the necessary cohesion to the movement. As to the details, they were left to the organising spirit of the people of the faubourgs, and when the sun rose over Paris no one could have predicted how that great day would end. The two battalions of federals from Marseilles and Brest, well organised and armed, numbered only about a thousand men, no one except those who had been working the preceding days and nights in the red-hot furnace of the faubourgs could say whether the faubourgs would rise in a body or not.

" And the ordinary leaders, where were they and what were they doing ? " asks Louis Blanc. " There is nothing to indicate," he replies, "what action Robespierre took on this supreme night, or whether he did anything at all." Nor does Danton seem to have taken any active part in the preparations for the rising or in the fight itself on August 10.

It is quite clear that, from the moment that the movement was decided, the people had no need of the politicians. What was necessary was to arm the people, to distribute weapons among those who knew how to use them, to organise the nucleus of each battalion, to form a column in each street of the faubourgs. For this work, the politicians would only have been in the way, and the men of the people told them to go to bed while the movement was being definitely organised on the night of August 9 and 10. That is what Danton did, and he slept peacefully, as we know from Lucile Desmoulin's journal.

New men, "unknown ones," came to the front in those days, when a new General Council, the Revolutionary Commune of August 10, was appointed by the sections. Taking the law into their own hands, each section nominated three commissioners, "to save the country," and the people's choice fell, so the historians tell us, upon obscure men. The "extremist," Hébert, was one of them, that was a matter of course; but we find neither Marat nor Danton among them at first.*

Thus it was that a new "Commune"—the insurrectionary Commune—sprang up in the midst of the people and took upon itself the direction of the rising. And we shall see this Commune exercising a powerful influence over the progress of subsequent events; dominating the Convention and urging "the Mountain" to revolutionary action so as to secure, at least, the conquests already won by the Revolution.

It would be useless to narrate here the whole day's doings on August 10. The dramatic side of the Revolution is what

---

* "How great that Assembly was!" says Chaumette in his *Mémoires*, p. 44. "What sublime outbursts I witnessed during the discussion on the King's dethronement! What was the National Assembly, with its paltry passions, its petty measures, its decrees stifled at birth, then crushed by the veto, what was that Assembly, I say, in comparison with the Assembly of the Commissioners from the Paris sections?"

has been told best by the historians, and excellent descriptions of its events will be found in Michelet and Louis Blanc. We shall, therefore, confine ourselves to recalling the chief features of that day.

Ever since Marseilles had declared for the dethronement of the King, petitions and addresses for the dethronement had come in great numbers to the Assembly. In Paris forty-two sections had pronounced in favour of it. Pétion had even gone on August 4 to bring forward this resolution of the sections at the bar of the Assembly.

As to the politicians they did not realise in the least the gravity of the situation ; and though we find in letters written from Paris by Madame Jullien on August 7 and 8, such passages as these : " A terrible storm is coming up on the horizon. . . . At this moment the horizon is heavy with vapours which must produce a terrible explosion "—the Assembly in its sitting of the 8th calmly voted the absolution of Lafayette for his letter as if no such thing as a movement of hatred against royalty existed.

All the while the people of Paris were preparing for a decisive battle. The insurrectionary committee had, however, the good sense not to fix any date for the rising beforehand. They merely sounded the varying moods of the population of Paris, did their best to brace up their minds, and kept watch for the moment when the appeal to arms could be made. Thus, they tried, apparently, to provoke a rising on June 26, after a popular banquet among the ruins of the Bastille, in which the whole faubourg had taken part—people bringing to it their tables and provisions.* And they tried another rising on July 30, but again the attempt did not succeed.

Altogether the preparations for the rising, badly seconded by " the leaders of opinion," would, perhaps, have dragged out to some length, if the plots of the Court had not helped to precipitate matters. With the aid of the courtiers, who had sworn to die for the King, along with some battalions of the National Guard that had remained faithful to the Court

* Mortimer Ternaux, *La Terreur*, vol. ii. p. 130.

and the Swiss, the royalists felt sure of victory. They had fixed August 10 for their *coup d'état*. "That was the day fixed for the counter-revolution," we read in one of the letters of the period ; "the following day was to see all the Jacobins of the kingdom drowned in their own blood."

The insurrection, therefore, could not be postponed any longer. On the night of the 9th and 10th, just about midnight, the tocsin rang in Paris. At first, however, its call seemed not to be well attended, and it was asked at the Commune whether the rising should not be countermanded. At seven o'clock in the morning certain quarters were still tranquil. In reality, however, it appears that the people of Paris, with their admirable instinct for revolution, did not want to enter into conflict with the royal troops in the dark, because such a fight might easily have ended in their being routed.

In the meantime the Insurrectionary Commune had taken possession of the Hôtel de Ville during the night, and the legal council of the Commune had abdicated in the presence of this new revolutionary power, which immediately gave an impetus to the insurrection.

About seven o'clock in the morning only some men with pikes, led by the Federates from Marseilles, debouched upon the Place du Carrousel ; but an hour later large masses of the people began to move, and the King was informed that "all Paris" was marching on the Tuileries.

It was indeed all Paris, that is, all the Paris of the poor, supported by the National Guards from the workers' and artisans' quarters.

About half-past eight, as these masses were already approaching the palace, the King, haunted by the recent memory of what had happened on June 20, and fearing to be killed this time by the people, quitted the Tuileries, and went to take refuge with the Assembly, leaving his faithful servitors to defend the palace and to massacre its assailants. But as soon as the King had gone, entire battalions of National Guards from the rich middle-class quarters dispersed, so as not to have to face the people in revolt.

Compact masses of the people then thronged into the

approaches to the Tuileries, and their vanguard, encouraged
by the Swiss Guards, who flung their cartridges out of the
palace windows, penetrated into one of the courtyards of the
Tuileries. But here, others of the Swiss, commanded by the
officers of the Court and posted on the great staircase of the
chief entrance, fired upon the crowd, and in a few minutes
four hundred of the assailants lay dead in heaps at the foot
of the stairs.

This shooting decided the issue of the day. The cries of
" Treachery! Death to the King! Death to the Austrian
woman! " rapidly spread all over the town, and the people
of Paris ran towards the Tuileries from all sides—the Faubourgs
Saint-Antoine and Saint-Marceau rushed there in a body—
and soon the Swiss, under the furious assault of the people,
were either disarmed or massacred.

Need we recall the fact that even at the supreme moment
the Assembly remained undecided, not knowing what to do ?
They acted only when the armed people burst into the hall
where they were sitting threatening to kill the King and his
family, as well as the deputies who did not dare to pronounce
the dethronement. Even after the Tuileries had been taken
and when royalty no longer existed in fact, the Girondins,
who formerly had loved to orate about the Republic, still
hesitated to face any decisive action. All that Vergniaud
dared demand was " a provisional suspension of the head of
the executive power "—who, henceforth, should be installed
int he Palace of the Luxembourg.

It was only two or three days later that the Revolutionary
Commune transferred Louis XVI. and his family from the
Luxembourg, whence they might easily have escaped, to the
tower of the Temple, and undertook to hold them there as
the people's prisoners.

Royalty was thus abolished *de facto*. Henceforth the
Revolution was able to develop for awhile without fear of
being suddenly checked in its progress by a royalist *coup
d'état* or by a massacre of the revolutionists by the " White
Terror."

For the politicians the chief interests of the revolution of

August 10 lay in the blow it had struck at royalty. For the people it lay especially in the abolition of that force, which was opposing the carrying out of the decrees against the feudal rights, against the emigrant nobles and against the priests, and which at the same time had appealed to a German invasion to re-establish the feudal monarchy. It lay in the triumph of a popular revolution, in a triumph of the masses, who could now push on the Revolution towards Equality—that dream and aim of the poor. Consequently, on the very day after August 10, the Legislative Assembly, reactionary as it was, had to pass, under pressure from without, some decrees which were to send the Revolution a step forward.

Every priest who had not yet taken the oath (so ran these decrees), and who, within the next fortnight, did not swear to obey the Constitution, and yet was found after that time upon French territory, should be transported to Cayenne.

All the lands of the emigrant nobles, in France and in the colonies, were to be sequestrated, and put up for sale in small lots.

All distinctions between *passive* citizens (the poor) and *active* citizens (the propertied classes) were abolished. Every one became an elector on attaining his twenty-first year, and was eligible for election at twenty-five.

As to the feudal laws, we have seen how the Constituent Assembly, on March 15, 1790, had made a decree, according to which the feudal dues were supposed to represent the price of a certain concession of land, made once upon a time by the landowner to the tenant—which was, of course, false—and, as such, all the feudal dues had to be paid so long as they were not redeemed by the tenant. This decree, by thus confounding the *personal* dues, the outcome of rent, wiped out, *de facto*, the decree of August 4, 1789, which had declared the former to be abolished. By the decree of March 15, 1790, these decrees came up again under the fiction which represented them as payment for the possession of the land. This is what Couthon had made quite evident in his report, read before the Assembly on February 29, 1792.

But on June 14, 1792, that is to say, when June 20 was

close at hand, and it was necessary to conciliate the people, the Left, taking advantage of the accidental absence of certain members of the Right, abolished *without indemnity* some of the personal feudal dues, the most noteworthy being the *casuel*, that is, the right of the lord to levy dues in cases of legacies left by his tenants, on marriages, on sales and on the wine-press, the mill and other communal necessaries.

After three years of revolution a parliamentary trick was thus necessary to obtain from the Assembly the abolition of these odious dues. In reality even this decree did not finally abolish them : in certain cases they still had to be redeemed ; but let us pass over that.

As to the annual feudal levies, such as the quit-rents, the field-tax and so on, which were paid in addition to the rent and represented relics of the ancient servitude, they remained in full force.

But now came August 10. The people had taken possession of the Tuileries, and the King was dethroned and imprisoned. And as soon as this news spread to the villages, petitions from the peasants flooded the Assembly, demanding the total abolition of the feudal rights.

These were the days before September 2, when the attitude of the people of Paris was not altogether reassuring for the Legislative Assembly, which was accused of plotting with royalty, and the Assembly, seeing itself compelled to take some steps forward, issued the decrees of August 16 to 25, 1792.

In virtue of these decrees all prosecution for non-payment of feudal dues was suspended. The feudal and seigniorial rights of all kinds, which were not the price of an original concession of land, were suppressed without indemnity.

And by the decree of August 20, it was permitted to redeem separately, either the *casuel* rights, or the annual rights, the legitimacy of which could be proved by presenting the original title of the concession of land. All this, however, only in case of a *new* purchase by a new owner.

The abolition of the prosecutions represented, undoubtedly, a great step in advance. But the feudal rights still remained.

They had still to be redeemed. The new law only added to the confusion—the result being that, henceforth, the peasants could pay nothing and redeem nothing. And this was what the peasants did while waiting for some new victory for the people and some new concession on the part of the ruling classes.

At the same time all tithes and prestations, or obligatory unpaid labour for the clergy, which had been retained from the days of serfdom or mortmain, were suppressed without indemnity. This was a substantial gain. If the Assembly protected the lands and the middle-class monopolists, they, at least, delivered up the priests, since the King was no longer there to defend them.

But at the same time the Assembly took a measure which, if it had been applied, would have stirred up the whole of the French peasantry against the Republic. It abolished the joint responsibility for payments which existed in the peasant communes,* and accepting the motion of François de Neuf-château, the Assembly ordered the communal lands to be divided among the citizens. It appears, however, that this decree, expressed in a few lines and in very vague terms, was never taken seriously. Its application, besides, would have involved such difficulties that it remained a dead letter; and when the question came up again, the Legislative Assembly, having finished its term of office, dissolved without coming to any decision.

Concerning the lands of the emigrant nobles it was decided to put them up for sale in small lots of two, three, or not more than four acres. And this sale was to be made, "on lease, at a money rent," always redeemable. That is to say, he who had not the money could purchase all the same, on condition of paying a perpetual rent, which he might, some day, be able to redeem. This was, of course, to the advantage of the poor peasant, but all sorts of difficulties were evidently put in the way of small purchasers. Well-to-do middle-class people preferred to buy the estates of the emigrant nobles

---

* It was the same thing evidently as that which exists in Russia under the name of *krougovaia porouka*, "responsibility all round."

in bulk and to speculate in the sale of them broken up into lots later on.

Finally—and this, too, was typical—one of the members, Mailhe, took advantage of the condition of men's minds at this moment to propose a measure which was really revolutionary and was accepted later on, in 1793, after the fall of the Girondins. He demanded that the effects of the royal ordinance of 1669 might be broken, and that the lords should be compelled to restore to the village communes the land which they had taken away from them in virtue of that ordinance. His proposal, however, was not accepted; a new revolution was required for that.

These then were the results of August 10: Royalty was overthrown, and now it was possible for the Revolution to turn over a new page in the direction of equality, provided the Assembly and the governing classes in general did not oppose it.

The King and his family were in prison. A new Assembly, a National Convention, was convoked. The elections were to be made by universal suffrage, but still in two degrees.

Some measures were taken against the priests who refused to recognise the Constitution, and against the emigrant nobles. Orders were given to put up for sale the lands of the *émigrés* which had been sequestrated in accordance with the decree of March 30, 1792.

The war against the invaders was to be pushed on vigorously by the *sans-culotte* volunteers.

But the great question—"what was to be done with the traitor King"—and that other great question, which was so vital for fifteen million peasants—the question of the feudal rights—remained in suspense. It was still necessary to redeem those rights in order to do away with them. And the new law concerning the partition of the communal lands threw the villages into alarm.

It was over this that the Legislative Assembly dissolved, after doing all they could to prevent the Revolution from developing normally, and from putting an end to those two heritages of the past : the absolute authority of the King and the feudal laws.

But by the side of the Legislative Assembly there had grown up, since August 10, a new power, the Commune of Paris, which took into its hands the revolutionary initiative and, as we shall see presently, managed to retain it for nearly two years.

Antonio Tellez

SABATE

*Guerilla
Extraordinary*

Anarchist
Pocketbooks

1

Elephant Editions

Anarchist Pocketbooks

1 — **Sabate, Guerrilla Extraordinary**—Antonio Tellez
    208 pages—2.95p
2 — **Strange Victories—The Anti-Nuclear Movement in the US
    and Europe**—Midnight Notes
    88 pages—1.95p
3 — **The Angry Brigade—Documents and Chronology**
    74 pages—1.20p
4 — **The Conquest of Bread**—Peter Kropotkin
    214 pages—3.60p
5 — **Anarchism and Violence—Severino Di Giovanni in
    Argentina 1923-1931**—Osvaldo Bayer
    250 pages—3.95p

Elephant Editions,
B.M. Elephant,
London WCIN 3XX.